Clinical Interpretation of the Woodcock-Johnson Tests of Cognitive Ability— Revised

CLINICAL INTERPRETATION OF THE WOODCOCK-JOHNSON TESTS OF COGNITIVE ABILITY— REVISED

Kevin S. McGrew
St. Cloud State University

Allyn and Bacon
Boston • London • Toronto • Sydney • Tokyo • Singapore

Copyright © 1994, 1986 by Allyn and Bacon
A Division of Paramount Publishing
160 Gould Street
Needham Heights, Massachusetts 02194

Portions of this book were previously printed in *Clinical Interpretation of the
Woodcock-Johnson Tests of Cognitive Ability* by Kevin S. McGrew, published by
Grune & Stratton, Inc. Copyright © 1986.

Library of Congress Cataloging-in-Publication Data

McGrew, Kevin S.
    Clinical interpretation of the Woodcock-Johnson Tests of Cognitive
Ability—Revised / Kevin S. McGrew.
        p.   cm.
    Includes bibliographical references and index.
    ISBN 0-205-14801-8
    1. Woodcock-Johnson Tests of Cognitive Ability.   I. Title.
BF432.5.W66M34   1994
153.9′323—dc20   93-31670
                                                        CIP

Printed in the United States of America
10 9 8 7 6 5 4 3 2   98 97 96

To Julie, Beth, and Chris—
Thanks for your love and support

ABOUT THE AUTHOR

Dr. Kevin McGrew is an Associate Professor in Applied Psychology at St. Cloud State University and a researcher with the National Center on Educational Outcomes (NCEO) and the Institute on Community Integration at the University of Minnesota. He has 14 years of experience as a school psychologist. Dr. McGrew publishes and conducts research in the areas of psychoeducational assessment, personal competence, community adjustment of individuals with disabilities, family-focused assessment, and the use of educational indicators for policy research in special education. Dr. McGrew has authored or coauthored a number of WJ/WJ-R–related articles and books including *Subtest Norms for the WJ/SIB Assessment System,* the *WJ-R Technical Manual,* and *Clinical Interpretation of the Woodcock-Johnson Tests of Cognitive Ability.* He is a coauthor of the forthcoming *Woodcock-McGrew-Werden Mini-Battery of Achievement (MBA).*

CONTENTS

PREFACE

This book is a revision of my original text (McGrew, 1986) on clinical interpretation of the 1977 Woodcock-Johnson Tests of Cognitive Ability (WJTCA-R). The revision and significant expansion of the WJTCA-R in 1989 necessitated a revised book. In addition, my training, consultation, and research experience with both the WJTCA and WJTCA-R have resulted in a revision and evolution of my own thinking regarding the interpretation of tests of intelligence. This text reflects the revision and evolution of the WJTCA-R and my thinking related to its use.

GOALS OF THIS BOOK

Four primary goals guided the preparation of this book: (1) to demonstrate the clinical potential of the WJTCA-R, (2) to describe recent innovations in intelligence testing, (3) to provide a "bridge" between research and practice, and (4) to facilitate change in intelligence testing schemas.

The Clinical Potential of the WJTCA-R

The three Wechsler scales and the Stanford-Binet have until recently dominated the field of intelligence testing. Since the publication of my 1986 WJTCA text, the landscape of intelligence testing has changed. Two of the Wechslers (i.e., WPPSI-R, WISC-III) and the Stanford-Binet (SB-IV) have been revised. Allan Kaufman, the author of the Kaufman Assessment Battery for Children (K-ABC), has recently published the Kaufman Adolescent and Adult Intelligence Test (KAIT). In addition, in 1990 the Differential Ability Scales (DAS) was added to the pool of instruments.

The large array of instruments from which to choose has increased discussion, controversy, and debate among practitioners and scholars regarding the relative merits of each intelligence battery. Each battery has developed its own following, as well as a variety of prominent advocates. Because of the historical monopoly enjoyed by the Stanford-Binet and Wechsler scales, the newer intelligence tests have often been greeted with initial resistance. Some of this resistance is understandable, as clinicians will not readily abandon "tried and true" instruments that have a wealth of interpretive material amassed through extensive research and clinical experience.

As in my first WJTCA text, a goal of this book is to provide clinicians with the necessary information to engage in clinical interpretation of the WJTCA-R in the way they have become accustomed to with other instruments. A clinical interpretation process based on the generation of hypotheses derived from shared abilities among groups of WJTCA-R tests is presented. The reader should detect obvious similarities between the interpretive process and philosophy described in this book and the classic interpretive philosophy first articulated in Kaufman's (1979) *Intelligent Testing With the WISC-R*.

Recent Innovations in Intelligence Testing

The WJTCA-R is the first individually administered intelligence battery to incorporate a number of innovations in intelligence testing. Foremost is the organization of the WJTCA-R according to modern *Gf-Gc* theory, the most comprehensive empirically based theoretical conceptualization of intelligence available today. Clinicians need to become familiar with the *Gf-Gc* theoretical framework, as it will no doubt be found with increasing frequency in the intelligence testing literature. This book not only helps clinicians interpret the WJTCA-R from the *Gf-Gc* framework; it informs others who seek to become familiar with this theoretical model.

Additional innovations introduced in the WJTCA-R or maintained from the WJTCA are: (a) the use of differential aptitude clusters (i.e., Scholastic Aptitude clusters) for making statements about a person's predicted achievement, (b) the use of actual aptitude-achievement discrepancy norms that account for regression to the mean, and (c) the use of norm-based intra-cognitive discrepancy scores. The discussion of these topics in this book should result in increased understanding of these features by clinicians who use the WJTCA-R. It is also hoped that this material will stimulate the development of new or improved intelligence batteries.

Bridge Between Research and Practice

As I have consulted with clinicians and trainers regarding the WJTCA-R and other intelligence tests, I have been repeatedly dismayed to find that important technical information (e.g., test reliability, test specificity, results of factor analysis studies) is often ignored during interpretation. I have frequently been asked interpretive questions that could be answered if an individual was familiar with information presented in research reports or technical manuals. I have concluded that the presentation of tables upon tables of statistical information in a test's technical manual or a research article is often overwhelming to clinicians who deal with the day-to-day pressures of high case loads and referral rates. I now believe that researchers and developers of intelligence tests need to develop newer, more "user friendly" methods of presenting technical information that can easily be accessed during interpretation.

To facilitate the use of basic empirical information in the interpretation of the WJTCA-R, I have made frequent use of visual or graphic methods to summarize statistical information in a usable format. These visual aids provide a bridge between the clinician and the original statistical information. For example, in Chapter 3, unique graphic summaries for each of the 21 WJTCA-R tests are presented that convey important information regarding each test's reliability, uniqueness (i.e., specificity), and factor characteristics. All of this information for each test is presented without the use of numbers or statistics. Although the exact precision of the original technical information is missing, the critical aspects of these empirical characteristics as they relate to clinicial interpretation are preserved. The use of visual diagrams and figures to demonstrate other abstract concepts or empirical results can be found in other chapters. It is hoped that this method of presenting technical information will facilitate its incorporation into the everyday practice of clinicians. "Quantoids" who need exact statistics can turn to the WJTCA-R technical manual or referenced research reports.

The Need for Change in Intelligence Testing Schemas

According to Piaget's theory of cognitive development, whenever individuals encounter a new experience that does not fit their current mental organization of the world, they are placed in a state of disequilibrium. To return to a state of equilibrium, individuals must either accommodate the new experience within their existing mental schemas or reorganize their mental schemas through adaptation. A goal of this book is to encourage the reorganization of the intelligence testing schemas held by many assessment personnel by presenting information that will place clinicians into a state of disequilibrium regarding current intelligence testing practice.

Much of current psychological and psychoeducational assessment practice is based on assessment technology that is over 50 years old. For example, the dominant Wechslers have their roots in the 1939 Wechsler-Bellevue. Although they have been renormed and revised, the Wechsler scales are still based on a model of intelligence first presented over 50 years ago. Research in cognitive science, particularly that focusing on the factor analysis of a wide variety of cognitive variables, has suggested that our conceptualization of intelligence has improved and changed significantly since the publication of the original Stanford-Binet and Wechsler scales.

Unfortunately, assessment technology has lagged behind these developments. The inertia of tradition often keeps outdated beliefs alive, even in the face of large amounts of evidence that may question their validity (Horn, 1985). The incorporation of a number of innovations in the WJTCA-R, and the use of *Gf-Gc* theory in particular, is bound to meet up with the inertia of tradition in psychological and psychoeducational assessment practice.

I have dealt head on with the questions that are asked about the new features of the WJTCA-R. Most often these questions are the result of certain WJTCA-R innovations not fitting a clinician's intelligence "schema." By directly challenging long-held beliefs, primarily by presenting empirical data, I hope to disturb many assessment professionals. It is only when clinicians, trainers, and the developers of intelligence tests enter a state of disequilibrium regarding current intelligence testing practice that progressive change can occur.

INTENDED AUDIENCE AND ASSUMPTIONS

This book is intended for students, educators, psychologists, and scholars who engage in the practice of intelligence testing, train others to administer and interpret intelligence tests, or conduct research regarding the applied science of psychological and psychoeducational assessment. Clinicians who use the WJTCA-R in their daily practice will benefit from an increased understanding and appreciation of the strengths and limitations of the WJTCA-R. This text should help clinicians become more skilled in the art and science of WJTCA-R interpretation.

This book is also useful for professionals who do not use the WJTCA-R in clinical practice. The material presented here should assist professionals who are considering the merits of the WJTCA-R in comparison to other intelligence batteries. Professionals who teach courses on psychological or psychoeducational assessment that include the WJTCA-R will find the material particularly useful in their training of others. Also, trainers, researchers, test developers, and/or scholars in the field of intelligence testing who seek to become better informed regarding the innovations in intelligence testing that are incorporated in the WJTCA-R will find this book useful. Finally, any professional interested in becoming familiar with the *Gf-Gc* theoretical model of intelligence and the operationalization of this model in an applied assessment instrument should find this text useful.

In order to keep the length of this book manageable, certain basic introductory material is not included. Detailed discussion of the basics of intelligence testing practice and research, such as that presented by Kamphaus (1993) and Sattler (1990), is not included. It is assumed that the reader has a basic working knowledge of such information or will acquire this basic information prior to using the WJTCA-R. In addition, clinicians who use the information in this book for clinical interpretation of the WJTCA-R are assumed to have a working knowledge of the test. Basic administration and scoring information is not covered. Introductory information related to the administration, scoring, and basic interpretation of the WJTCA-R can be found in the WJTCA-R's examiners manual (Woodcock & Mather, 1989), as well as in the works of Hessler (1993) and Mather (1991). In addition, this book is similar to other books devoted to the interpretation of other intelligence batteries (e.g., see Kaufman's 1979 and 1990 texts regarding the Wechsler series) and does not deal with the translation of test-based findings into detailed intervention recommendations. Such information can be found in the WJTCA-R-related works of Hessler (1993), Mather (1991), and Mather and Jaffe (1992).

This book will have succeeded if the reader comes away from it agreeing with my conclusion that the WJTCA-R is a major measure of intellectual functioning that should enjoy a status similar to that accorded other major intelligence batteries and if the WJTCA-R users become more "intelligent" in their use of the instrument.

Kevin S. McGrew

ACKNOWLEDGMENTS

I wish to thank a number of individuals who contributed either directly or indirectly to this book.

The preparation of the text was aided by the competent help of two individuals. Suzanne Murphy put in countless hours preparing most of the tables and figures in the book. In addition, her assistance in the completion of research studies whose results are incorporated in this book is appreciated. The diligent editing work of Laurie Schroeder on the final versions of the manuscript was extremely helpful.

A number of colleagues provided valuable assistance during this lengthy project. The feedback and case study material provided by Mark St. Martin during the early stages of my writing was valuable. I especially appreciate the critical reviews of all chapters by Barbara Reid and Dr. Richard Woodcock. Their comments and feedback substantially improved the overall quality of the text. I am also grateful for the formal critiques provided by three individuals; Dr. Nancy Mather (University of Arizona), Dr. Randy Kamphaus (University of Georgia), and Dr. R. Steve McCallum (University of Tennessee–Knoxville). Their detailed comments resulted in a number of important revisions and additions.

Many individuals indirectly affected the final product. I am grateful for the support I have received for pursuing my scholarly activities by my dean, Dr. Owen Hagen, and my department chair, Dr. Robert Murphy. I also owe a great deal of debt to Dr. Jim Henning, Dr. Robert Bruininks, and Dr. Richard Woodcock for their mentoring during different stages of my professional and academic career.

Finally, the contributions of Mylan Jaixen and Susan Hutchinson and the rest of the staff of Allyn and Bacon, as well as the production editorial assistance provided by Michael Bass and Associates, are gratefully acknowledged. Their expertise and cooperative working relationship made this a pleasant and productive experience.

1

THE WOODCOCK-JOHNSON TESTS OF COGNITIVE ABILITY—REVISED

The *Woodcock-Johnson Tests of Cognitive Ability—Revised* (WJTCA-R) is an expanded revision of the 1977 *Woodcock-Johnson Tests of Cognitive Ability* (WJTCA) (Woodcock & Johnson, 1977) and is one of two components of the *Woodcock-Johnson Psycho-Educational Battery-Revised* (WJ-R) (Woodcock & Johnson, 1989). The original WJTCA consisted of 12 individually administered tests designed to assess the broad and complex domain of cognitive ability (Woodcock, 1978).

The WJTCA-R consists of 21 individual tests that provide for comprehensive assessment of simple to complex abilities in seven (eight when including the achievement section of the battery) areas of intellectual functioning as described by the *Gf-Gc* theory of intelligence, a "fluid"/crystallized" model that will be discussed in more detail in Chapter 2. Similar to the original WJTCA, the WJTCA-R covers the continuum of lower- to higher-level mental processing and contains traditional as well as original, innovative, and creative measures of cognitive ability (Cummings, 1985; Kaufman, 1985, 1990). Although the act of assembling 21 tests into a measure of intellectual ability invites instant comparisons with other intelligence batteries (e.g., Wechsler scales) (Wechsler, 1981, 1989, 1991), the WJTCA-R has many unique characteristics that distinguish it from other instruments.

Much of the WJTCA-R's uniqueness stems from its position in a larger assessment battery (i.e., WJ-R) (Woodcock & Johnson, 1989), a statistical link to the *Scales of Independent Behavior—Revised* (Bruininks, Woodcock, Weatherman, Hill, in press), and the ability to interpret performance from

1

both a theoretical structure-of-intellect and pragmatic decision-making perspective. Before embarking on a detailed analysis of the various nuances of the WJTCA-R, one must obtain the proper perspective from which the view the instrument. However, for users of the original WJTCA, a brief comparison to the WJTCA-R is presented first.

COMPARISON TO THE 1977 WJTCA

The WJTCA revision was guided by a number of objectives that focused on: (a) revising and expanding the cognitive battery to reflect state-of-the-art concepts of intellectual processing, (b) updating and extending the age range of the norms, (c) subjecting all 1977 items to thorough reviews and item analyses, (d) simplifying the reporting and analyzing of certain scores for interpretation, (e) providing new interpretative options, and (f) addressing a number of issues that had been raised about the original instrument. In keeping with these revision objectives, the following major changes were made in the WJTCA-R (McGrew, Werder, & Woodcock, 1991).

Interpretation was enhanced by organizing the cognitive tests according to the *Gf-Gc* theory of intellectual processing. This resulted in the WJTCA-R measuring seven different cognitive factors (an eighth factor is in the achievement section) versus the four measured by the WJTCA.

Exploratory and confirmatory factor analysis procedures were used extensively to develop and empirically confirm the cognitive factor structure.

Ten new tests were added, and one (Quantitative Concepts) was moved to the achievement section of the WJ-R battery.

For some tests the number of sample items was increased and the examinee training procedures were clarified and extended.

The Spatial Relations test was changed to function as a power rather than speed test.

The scoring of Memory for Sentences was changed from a two-point (0 or 1) to three-point (0, 1, or 2) procedure.

The norms were extended to allow for the measurement of individuals from the very young (2 years of age) to the very old (90+), and separate college and university norms were included.

Unique standard score–based discrepancy norms were developed that allow for the evaluation of aptitude/achievement and intra-cognitive discrepancies. The area of Oral Language was added to the aptitude/achievement discrepancies.

New scoring and interpretive features were added, such as simplified grade and age equivalent scoring, developmental profiles, and combined standard score and percentile rank profiles for all test and cluster scores.

More color was used in the stimulus pictures and materials.

Detailed descriptions of these changes can be found in the WJTCA-R manuals (McGrew et al., 1991; Woodcock & Mather, 1989). Tables 1-1 to 1-3 compare selected content, interpretive, and technical features of the WJTCA and WJTCA-R.

THE MULTIFACETED BATTERY/SYSTEM

The Woodcock-Johnson Psycho-Educational Battery—Revised

The WJTCA was originally published in 1977 as Part 1 of the three-part *Woodcock-Johnson Psycho-Educational Battery* (WJ) (Woodcock & Johnson, 1977). The WJ battery represented the first significant attempt to develop an individually administered, multifaceted, wide–age range battery of tests of more than one major domain of functioning. In 1977 it also represented the first major broad–age range measure of intelligence to be developed in almost 40 years. Parts 2 and 3 of the WJ consisted of measures of achievement (Tests of Achievement) and scholastic and nonscholastic interests (Tests of Interest Level), respectively. These three WJ sections and their subcomponents formed the assessment structure presented in Figure 1-1.

The WJ-R battery structure is illustrated in Figure 1-2. Similar to the WJ assessment structure, the WJ-R battery includes both Tests of Cognitive Ability and Tests of Achievement sections. Missing from the WJ-R battery, but present in the WJ battery, are the Tests of Interest Level.

A significant difference between the original and revised batteries is the organization of the WJ-R into Standard and Supplemental batteries. Depending on the purpose of the assessment, the Standard cognitive and achievement batteries can be used alone or in conjunction with the Supplemental cognitive and achievement batteries. The listing of the various components in the Supplemental batteries section of Figure 1-2 indicates that in order to obtain their scores, tests from the Supplemental batteries must be administered together with tests from the Standard batteries. However, not all Supplemental tests must be administered to obtain specific cognitive or achievement scores listed in Figure 1-2. Selective testing tables in the test books and manuals provide the specific information needed to determine which tests must be administered to obtain each cluster.

Four major interpretive components—Broad Cognitive Ability, Cognitive Factors, Scholastic Aptitudes, and Psycho-Educational Discrepancies—are available for the Tests of Cognitive Ability. Each of these components, as

TABLE 1-1   Content Features of 1977 WJTCA and 1989 WJTCA-R

Content Feature	WJTCA	WJTCA-R
Age range of battery	Age 3-0 to 80+	Age 2-0 to 90+
Number of cognitive subtests	12 total Ages 3-0 to 5 =6 Kdg to Age 80+ = 12	21 total Age 2-0 to 90+ = 5 Age 4 to 90+ = 21
Content organized according to theoretical model of intelligence	No	Yes *Gf-Gc* Theory
Includes a broad measure of intelligence	Yes 1. Full Scale 2. Preschool Scale 3. Brief Scale	Yes 1. Extended Scale 2. Standard Scale 3. Early Development Scale
Includes measures of multiple intelligence	Yes 1. Verbal Ability 2. Reasoning 3. Perceptual Speed 4. Memory (short-term)	Yes 1. Long-Term Retrieval 2. Short-Term Memory 3. Processing Speed 4. Auditory Processing 5. Visual Processing 6. Comprehension-Knowledge 7. Fluid Reasoning 8. Quantitative Ability (in WJ-R-ACH)
Includes differential scholastic aptitude measures	Yes 1. Reading Aptitude 2. Mathematics Aptitude 3. Written Language Aptitude 4. Knowledge Aptitude	Yes 1. Oral Language Aptitude 2. Reading Aptitude 3. Mathematics Aptitude 4. Written Aptitude 5. Knowledge Aptitude
Includes a measure of oral language ability	Yes	Yes
Includes controlled-learning tests (with corrective feedback)	Yes 1. Visual-Auditory Learning 2. Analysis-Synthesis 3. Concept Formation	Yes 1. Memory for Names 2. Analysis-Synthesis 3. Visual-Auditory Learning 4. Concept Formation
Use of colorful pictures and material	Some	Yes
Spanish language version	Yes, Bateria, 1982	In preparation
Source of Spanish norms	1. Costa Rica 2. Mexico 3. Puerto Rico 4. Peru 5. Spain	1. Costa Rica 2. Mexico 3. Puerto Rico 4. Peru 5. Spain 6. United States

Adapted from *ASB No. 13: Comparative features of major cognitive batteries*, 1990, Chicago: The Riverside Publishing Company. Copyright 1990 by the Riverside Publishing Company. Adapted by permission.

TABLE 1-2 Interpretation Features of 1977 WJTCA and 1989 WJTCA-R

Interpretation Features	WJTCA	WJTCA-R
Uses a psychoeducational discrepancy model	Yes	Yes
Common norms provided with tests of achievement	Yes	Yes
	1. Reading	1. Oral Language
	2. Mathematics	2. Reading
	3. Written Language	3. Mathematics
	4. Knowledge	4. Written Language
		5. Knowledge
Aptitude/Achievement analysis based on discrepancy norms	Yes	Yes
	Relative Performance Index based	Standard score based
Intra-cognitive analysis based on discrepancy norms	No	Yes
		Standard score based
University/College norms	No	Yes
Norms provided for each cognitive subtest	Yes	Yes
	McGrew & Woodcock (1980)	
Peer comparison scores	Yes	Yes
	1. Percentile Rank	1. Percentile Rank
	2. Standard Score	2. Standard Score
	3. T-Score	3. T-Score
	4. Normal Curve Equivalent	4. Normal Curve Equivalent
	5. Stanine	5. Stanine
Error of measurement confidence bands available	Yes	Yes
Confidence bands plotted on profile	Yes	Yes
Types of derived scores:		
Developmental level scores	Yes	Yes
	1. Age Equivalent	1. Age Equivalent
	2. Grade Equivalent	2. Grade Equivalent
Mastery level scores	Yes	Yes
(quality of performance)	1. Relative Performance Index (RPI)	1. Relative Mastery Index (RMI)
	2. Instructional Range	2. Development Level Band
		3. Instructional Range
Computer scoring	Yes	Yes
	Apple, IBM	Apple, IBM

Adapted from *ASB No. 13: Comparative features of major cognitive batteries,* 1990, Chicago: The Riverside Publishing Company. Copyright 1990 by the Riverside Publishing Company. Adapted by permission.

TABLE 1-3 Technical Features of 1977 WJTCA and 1989 WJTCA-R

Technical Features	WJTCA	WJTCA-R
Extensive technical manual	Yes Woodcock (1978)	Yes McGrew, Werder, & Woodcock (1991)
Item analysis and scaling based on Rasch procedure (provides an equal-interval scale of growth across entire range of test)	Yes	Yes
Size of norming sample	4732	6359
Community variables in norming plan	1. Location 2. Size 3. 13 community socio-economic variables	1. Location 2. Size 3. 13 community socio-economic variables
Person variables in norming plan	1. Sex 2. Race (White, Black, Indian, other, Hispanic) (Note: Hispanic origin confounded with race) 3. Occupation of adults 4. Education of adults	1. Sex 2. Race (White, Black, Indian, Asian/Pacific) 3. Hispanic origin 4. Occupation of adults 5. Education of adults
Comparative concurrent validity studies report a matrix of results among major competitive tests	Yes WISC-R WAIS	Yes K-ABC MSCA SB IV WISC-R WAIS-R
Evidence provided to support factor structure organization	Some Exploratory factor analysis and cluster analysis	Yes Exploratory and confirmatory factor analysis
Precision of age norm tables	By 1-month blocks (age 3-0 to 18-11) By 1-year blocks (Age 19-80+)	By 1-month blocks (age 2-0 to 18-11) By 1-year blocks (Age 19-90+)
Precision of grade norm tables	By month (K.0 to 12.9)	By month (K.0 to 16.9)
Precision of norm tables increased by use of difference scores (rather than absolute scores)	Yes	Yes

Adapted from *ASB No. 13: Comparative features of major cognitive batteries*, 1990, Chicago: The Riverside Publishing Company. Copyright 1990 by the Riverside Publishing Company. Adapted by permission.

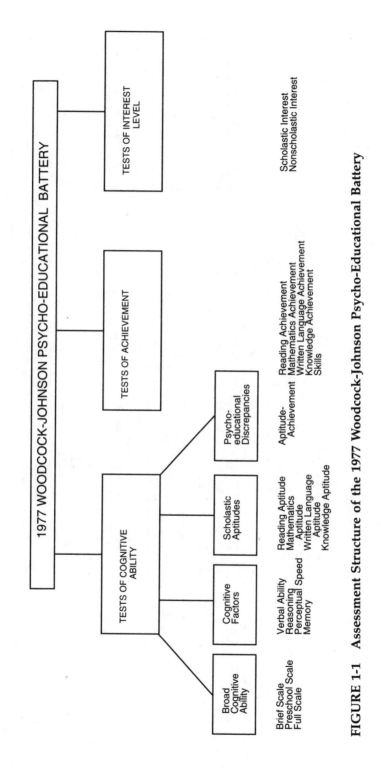

FIGURE 1-1 Assessment Structure of the 1977 Woodcock-Johnson Psycho-Educational Battery

7

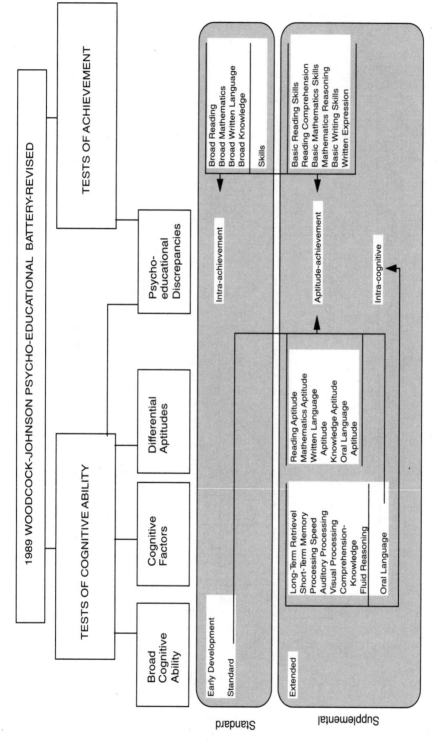

FIGURE 1-2 Assessment structure of Woodcock-Johnson Psycho-Educational Battery—Revised

well as the subcomponents displayed in Figure 1-2, is based on various combinations of the 21 individual tests. Each component listed under Broad Cognitive Ability, Cognitive Factors, and Differential Aptitudes is referred to as a *cluster*, which is intended to be the primary level of interpretation. Since these broad clusters are based on various combinations of the WJTCA-R tests, they minimize the danger of overgeneralizing from a single, narrow sample of behavior (i.e., individual test) to a broad, multidimensional ability (Woodcock, 1978; McGrew et al., 1991). The use of clusters in interpretation provides for higher validity. In contrast to the WJTCA, all WJTCA-R clusters are based on equally weighted combinations of individual tests.

Broad Cognitive Ability Clusters

The three WJCTA-R Broad Cognitive Ability clusters provide broad-based estimates of intellectual functioning. The Broad Cognitive Ability—Extended Scale is the broadest of the WJTCA-R clusters and represents an individual's performance on the first 14 cognitive tests. Two tests from each of the seven *Gf-Gc* cognitive factors are included in this broad ability score. The Broad Cognitive Ability—Standard Scale consists of the first 7 cognitive tests, each representing one of the *Gf-Gc* factors. These two broad measures are analogous to the Wechsler Full Scale (Wechsler, 1981, 1989, 1991), Kaufman Assessment Battery for Children (K-ABC) Mental Processing Composite (Kaufman & Kaufman, 1983), and the Stanford-Binet IV Composite (Thorndike, Hagen, & Sattler, 1986).

The Broad Cognitive Ability—Early Development Scale consists of five standard cognitive tests. This scale is intended for use with preschool children, although it can be used with low-functioning individuals of any age. The Early Development Scale is analogous to the WJTCA Preschool Scale. In the WJTCA a two-test Brief cluster was provided. The WJTCA-R does not provide a brief screening index of general ability.

Cognitive Factor Clusters

The WJTCA-R Cognitive Factor component consists of seven factors that were derived from the *Gf-Gc* theory of intellectual processing. The eighth *Gf-Gc* factor (Quantitative Abilities) is measured in the achievement section of the battery. In addition, a special five-test Oral Language cluster is also provided. Each of the *Gf-Gc* factor clusters consists of an equally weighted combination of two tests of each factor as determined through extensive exploratory and confirmatory factor analyses (McGrew et al., 1991). Although consisting of fewer tests than the Wechsler Verbal and Performance scales or the K-ABC Successive and Simultaneous scales, the WJTCA-R cognitive factors are analogous to this level of intelligence test interpretation, as they lie between the level of the individual tests and the broad-based full scale scores.

Differential Aptitude Clusters

The Differential aptitude component distinguishes the WJTCA-R from all other major individual tests of intelligence. Four of these clusters (viz., Reading,

Mathematics, Written Language, and Knowledge Aptitude) were also present in the WJTCA. They are labeled Scholastic Aptitudes. Each of these clusters is based on an equally weighted combination of the four cognitive tests that when combined best predicted achievement in each domain across the age range assessed by the WJTCA-R. The four Scholastic Aptitude clusters are designed to provide differentiated estimates of predicted achievement in reading, mathematics, written language, and knowledge (McGrew et al., 1991; Woodcock, 1984c). In simple terms, the four Scholastic Aptitude clusters are specialized intelligence tests for predicting achievement in reading, mathematics, written language, and knowledge. When combined with the appropriate WJ-R achievement clusters, these aptitude clusters help determine the presence or severity of aptitude/achievement discrepancies. A new addition to the WJTCA-R is the Oral Language Aptitude cluster, a combination of four tests that best predicted oral language performance.

Psychoeducational Discrepancies

Three types of psychoeducational discrepancy scores are available in the WJ-R battery. As with the original WJ battery, comparisons can be made between predicted achievement (based on aptitude) and actual achievement as measured by the various WJ-R achievement clusters. This comparison provides information regarding an examinee's *aptitude/achievement discrepancies*. A difference from the original WJ battery is the option to use either the Broad Cognitive Ability—Standard Scale *or* the Scholastic Aptitude clusters when determining the predicted achievement levels used in these discrepancy calculations. In contrast to the WJ battery, actual scores are now available for quantifying the presence and degree of *intra-cognitive* or *intra-achievement* discrepancies.

The WJ-R battery provides for comprehensive assessment across the domains of intelligence and achievement. The WJTCA-R, the component of interest in this current text, represents the cognitive aspect of this multi-faceted assessment battery. The WJ-R achievement tests and the WJ interest tests are not discussed here. The reader is referred to Hessler (1982) and Woodcock (1978) for comprehensive discussions of all components of the original WJ battery and to Mather (1991), Mather and Woodcock (1989), and McGrew et al. (1991) for detailed discussions of the complete WJ-R battery. Also, for those engaged in assessment of Hispanic subjects, the parallel *Batería Woodcock psico-educativa en Español* is available (Woodcock, 1982), while a parallel Hispanic version (Woodcock & Muñoz-Sandoval, in preparation) will also complement the WJ-R battery.

THE WJ-R/SIB-R ASSESSMENT SYSTEM

The original WJ battery was eventually expanded to a "system" with the addition of a fourth component. This addition was the *Scales of Independent*

Behavior (SIB) (Bruininks, Woodcock, Weatherman, & Hill, 1984), a comprehensive measure of problem behaviors and functional independence and adaptive behavior. This measure of adaptive behavior is administered through a structured interview. Like the WJ battery, the SIB covers a wide age range, in this case from infants to mature adults. The SIB has also been recently revised (SIB-R) (Bruininks et al., in press) and is statistically linked to the WJ-R.

Although not developed at the same time nor sharing the same standardization sample as the WJ-R battery, the SIB-R has been statistically and interpretively linked to the WJ-R through equating studies. Although the SIB-R is also intended to stand alone, when it is used in combination with the WJ-R battery, the result is a comprehensive assessment system. Thus, the WJTCA-R can be considered as one-third (one-fourth with the 1977 Tests of Interest Level) of a comprehensive diagnostic assessment system.

The comprehensiveness of this system is supported by a series of studies and reviews of the literature on the major domains of personal competence (Ittenbach, Spiegel, McGrew, & Bruininks, 1992; McGrew & Bruininks, 1990; McGrew, Bruininks, and Johnson, 1993). Using parts of either the WJ or WJ-R batteries and the SIB or related *Inventory for Client and Agency Planning* (ICAP) (Bruininks, Hill, Weatherman, & Woodcock, 1986) for a variety of samples of persons with or without disabilities, support was found for this assessment system as providing reliable and valid indicators of portions of four of the five major domains included in a comprehensive model of personal competence (McGrew et al., 1993). The relationship between the tests and domains of personal competence is summarized in Figure 1-3. With the exception of Social Competence, the complete WJ-R/SIB-R assessment system provides for assessment of the major domains of personal competence.

DEVELOPMENT AND NORMING OF THE WJTCA-R

The test construction and norming of the WJTCA-R, as well as the entire battery, were extensive and thorough (Kamphaus, 1993; McGrew et al., 1991). During all phases of development, steps were taken to meet the major criteria established for the development of educational and psychological tests (American Psychological Association, 1985). The concepts of latent-trait theory and the analysis of data by the Rasch model (Crocker & Algina, 1986; Wright & Stone, 1979) were employed extensively in the development of the entire battery.

The normative data for the WJTCA-R, as well as the entire battery, were gathered from 6,359 subjects in over 100 communities selected during a three-stage stratified sample based on the 1980 U.S. Census. Representativeness of the norming sample was achieved by controlling for 5 person variables

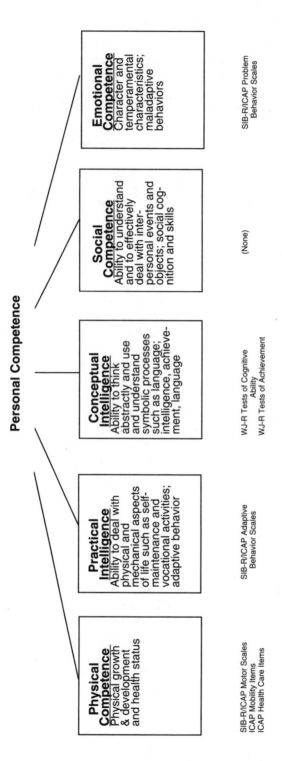

Personal Competence

Physical Competence	Practical Intelligence	Conceptual Intelligence	Social Competence	Emotional Competence
Physical growth & development and health status	Ability to deal with physical and mechanical aspects of life such as self-maintenance and vocational activities; adaptive behavior	Ability to think abstractly and use and understand symbolic processes such as language; intelligence, achievement, language	Ability to understand and to effectively deal with inter-personal events and objects; social cognition and skills	Character and temperamental characteristics; maladaptive behaviors
SIB-R/ICAP Motor Scales ICAP Mobility Items ICAP Health Care Items	SIB-R/ICAP Adaptive Behavior Scales	WJ-R Tests of Cognitive Ability WJ-R Tests of Achievement	(None)	SIB-R/ICAP Problem Behavior Scales

FIGURE 1-3 Correspondence Between WJ-R/SIB-R Assessment System Measures and Major Domains of Adapted Greenspan Model of Personal Competence

12

(sex, race, Hispanic origin, and occupation and education of adults) and 15 community variables (location, size, and 13 community socioeconomic variables) in the norming plan. The preschool sample (2 to 5 years of age and not enrolled in kindergarten) consisted of 705 subjects, the kindergarten to 12th-grade sample consisted of 3,245 subjects, the college and university sample consisted of 916 subjects, and the adult nonschool sample (14 to over 90 years of age and not enrolled in secondary school or college) consisted of 1,493 subjects. The size of the WJTCA-R school-age sample (3,245) was very similar to that for the WJTCA (3,935). The major differences were increases of approximately 27% and 300% in the WJTCA-R preschool and adult sample sizes, respectively, over those for the WJTCA.

An evaluation of the reliability and validity characteristics of the WJTCA-R components is presented in later chapters. Independent reviews of the WJTCA-R have been positive. After reviewing the original WJ battery, Kaufman (1985) concluded that "great care went into the development of the W-J. Tasks were developed over a period of years, with considerable pilot testing, item-analysis studies, and item editing. The Rasch latent-trait model was applied with considerable sophistication to calibrate the items in each subtest" (p. 1762).

Similar procedures and care were used in the development and revision of the WJ-R battery, and independent reviews were again positive. Kaufman (1990) and Kamphaus (1993) both spoke positively about the WJ-R battery when they concluded:

> The new battery is incredibly comprehensive. Woodcock's tests invariably possess excellent psychometric properties, the data are treated with statistical sophistication, and the subtests include a huge dose of originality. The WJ-R is no exception. The standardization sample is large and adequate. The factor loadings . . . indicate strong factor analytic support for the construct validity of the battery. . . . In addition, reliability coefficients are excellent. (Kaufman, 1990, pp. 602–603)

> The W-J is clearly the product of a thorough test development process. The result is a test with substantial psychometric support. . . . This edition of the W-J deserves serious research attention and a clinical trial. (Kamphaus, 1993, p. 302)

Other independent reviews have reached similar positive conclusions about the psychometric properties of the WJTCA-R. Although still voicing concerns about the treatment relevance of the WJTCA-R and all traditional intelligence tests, Reschly (1990) evaluated the WJTCA-R positively when he stated:

> The Woodcock-Johnson Revised Cognitive Battery appears to be an impressive advance in the identification and measurement of multiple abilities. (p. 259)

The WJ-R COG appears to be a psychometrically sound, well-standardized measure of cognitive functioning. (p. 260)

The WJ-R measures a broader variety of abilities than traditional measures. (p. 262)

The psychometrically sound, relatively clean measures of eight factors are a major accomplishment. (p. 265)

Finally, although voicing a similar concern about treatment relevance, Ysseldyke (1990) reached a number of positive conclusions when he stated:

The WJ-R Tests of Cognitive Ability is probably the most comprehensive measure of cognitive functioning available. (p. 269)

The Horn-Cattell *Gf-Gc* theory provides the most salient and promising model of intelligence and the one around which cognitive measures ought to be developed. (p. 272)

Given the evidence that the WJ-R subtests provide relatively clean measures of specific factors, there is now an opportunity to use this test in ATI investigations. (p. 273)

The WJ-R represents a significant milestone in the applied measurement of intellectual abilities. The manner in which theory and prior research were used in the development of the WJ-R and in the analysis of other major measures of intelligence should serve as a model for future research and development in the fields of applied psychometrics and psychoeducational assessment. (p. 272)

In conclusion, although the WJTCA-R has many positive features (most of which will be highlighted in the remaining chapters), the attention paid to test construction and standardization can be considered a key strength.

THE UNDERLYING ASSESSMENT MODELS

The final contextual perspectives from which to view the WJTCA-R are the two assessment models that served as the blueprint for the development of the tests.

The original WJTCA was criticized for not being organized according to a theoretical model of intelligence (Kaufman, 1985). According to Woodcock (1984a, 1984c), the WJTCA was based on an underlying assessment model—namely, a *pragmatic decision-making model*. This approach to the development of a major intelligence test was unfamiliar to many clinicians who were more familiar with instruments (e.g., Wechsler's) based on a theoretical *structure-of-intellect model*. The WJCTA-R maintains its underlying pragmatic decision-making foundation. In addition, the WJTCA-R is now based on a major theoretical model of intelligence.

The **Gf-Gc** *Model of Intellectual Processing*

The most significant change from the WJTCA to the WJTCA-R is the organization of the latter around a comprehensive theoretical model of intelligence. According to Woodcock (1990), the WJTCA-R is an operational representation of the *Gf-Gc* theory of intellectual processing. Although reference is frequently made in the WJTCA-R manuals to the Horn-Cattell version of *Gf-Gc* theory, support for this theory is also found in the work of others (Carroll, 1983, 1985, 1993). As noted by Kamphaus (1993), "The greater dependence of the W-J revision on an explicitly stated theoretical orientation is a major improvement over the original W-J" (p. 297).

The impact of the *Gf-Gc* theory on the organization of the WJTCA-R runs throughout the Standard and Supplemental batteries. Of the nine broad *Gf-Gc* intellectual abilities that have been consistently identified by Cattell, Horn, and others, the WJTCA-R contains tests that measure seven (Woodcock, 1990). (An eighth Quantitative Abilities or *Gq* factor is present in the achievement section of the *WJ-R*.) The Broad Cognitive Ability Standard and Extended scales include one and two tests, respectively, of the *Gf-Gc* factors of *Glr* (long-term retrieval), *Gsm* (short-term memory), *Gs* (processing speed), *Gc* (comprehension-knowledge or crystallized intelligence), and *Gf* (fluid reasoning or fluid intelligence).

A detailed discussion of the *Gf-Gc* theory, how it guided the development of the WJTCA-R, as well as evidence that supports the WJTCA-R *Gf-Gc* factor structure, is presented in Chapters 2 and 4. This evidence indicates that the WJTCA-R provides for reliable and valid measurement of seven major factors of the *Gf-Gc* theory (Kaufman, 1990; Reschly, 1990; Ysseldyke, 1991).

The Psychoeducational Discrepancy Model

In contrast to a theory-driven approach to test design, a decision-based design strategy (Woodcock, 1984a, 1984c) starts by first identifying the important decisions that need to be addressed by practitioners. Tests are then developed that provide the necessary information to make these decisions. The major difference from the structure-of-intellect approach is that the decision-based approach *begins* with the decisions that need to be made and then proceeds to develop measures that will provide the necessary decision-making information.

To operationalize the pragmatic decision-making model, portions of the WJ-R battery were designed to provide information regarding three types of discrepancies (McGrew, et al., 1991; Woodcock, 1984a, 1984c). These three discrepancies are identified in the WJ-R discrepancy model presented in Figure 1-4.

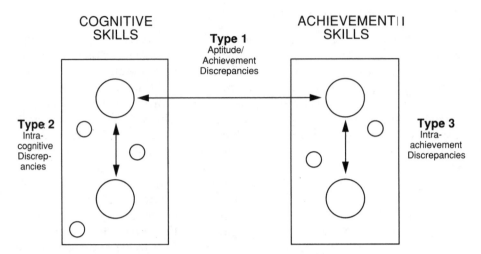

FIGURE 1-4   The Underlying WJ-R Decision-Making Discrepancy Model

Adapted from the *WJ-R Technical Manual* (p. 7) by K. McGrew, J. Werder, and R. Woodcock, 1991, Chicago, IL: Riverside Publishing. Copyright 1991 by the Riverside Publishing Company. Adapted by permission.

Type I Discrepancies: Aptitude / Achievement

A *Type I discrepancy* provides information about differences between an individual's aptitude and achievement. This type of discrepancy is most frequently employed in the field of learning disabilities (LD) to demonstrate the existence of ability-achievement gaps. Type I discrepancies are derived by comparing certain WJTCA-R aptitude cluster scores with scores from the relevant clusters from the WJ-R Tests of Achievement. The specific WJTCA-R measures used for the Type I discrepancy are either the Broad Cognitive Ability—Standard Scale or the Reading, Mathematics, Written Language, and Knowledge Scholastic Aptitude clusters. An examinee's performances on these cognitive measures are used to establish predicted levels of achievement that are then contrasted with the appropriate achievement clusters.

The WJ-R aptitude/achievement discrepancy scores are based on three design characteristics that result in these discrepancy scores being some of the most psychometrically sound Type I discrepancy scores available (McGrew, 1986; Ysseldyke, 1990). First, the WJ-R discrepancy scores are based on aptitude and achievement measures that were standardized in the same norming sample. The WJ was the first major assessment battery to address the now widely accepted recommendation that discrepancy scores should be calculated from measures normed on the same sample (Cone & Wilson, 1981; Reynolds, 1985; Reynolds et al., 1984–1985; Salvia & Ysseldyke, 1981; Wilson & Cone, 1984).

The second advantage of the WJ-R aptitude/achievement discrepancy scores is that the predicted achievement score from which an examinee's actual achievement is subtracted is based on the average achievement score obtained by other subjects in the standardization sample of the same age (age norms) or grade (grade norms) with the same measured aptitude (McGrew et al., 1991). The use of norm-based predicted values in the discrepancy calculation accounts for the regression-to-the-mean phenomenon, a procedural issue that must be addressed in any discrepancy calculation (Cone & Wilson, 1981; McLeod, 1979; Reynolds, 1985; Reynolds et al., 1984–1985; Salvia & Ysseldyke, 1981; Wilson & Cone, 1984). Finally, an examinee's aptitude/achievement discrepancy score can be evaluated against actual distributions of aptitude/achievement discrepancies observed in the norming sample. Thus, the WJTCA and WJTCA-R are part of the only individually administered psychoeducational batteries to provide actual *discrepancy norms* (McGrew et al., 1991).

Type II Discrepancies: Intra-Cognitive
A *Type II discrepancy* is present when an individual demonstrates significant variability within his or her profile of cognitive abilities. This form of discrepancy analysis has a long history in the field of psychoeducational assessment; it usually takes the form of an examination of an individual's cognitive strengths and weaknesses.

Although procedures were described for completing intra-cognitive analysis with the 12 individual tests in the original WJTCA (McGrew, 1986; Woodcock & Johnson, 1977), norm-based comparisons were not possible. In the WJTCA-R, norm-based intra-cognitive discrepancy scores are provided. The procedures used to develop the intra-cognitive discrepancy scores parallel those used in the development of the WJ-R aptitude/achievement scores (McGrew et al., 1991). Each of the seven WJTCA-R cognitive clusters is compared to a predicted or expected score, which is based on the average of the other six cognitive clusters. Informal intra-cognitive analysis at the individual test level is possible through an "intelligent testing" approach to interpretation (Kaufman, 1979) that is described later in Chapter 6.

Type III Discrepancies: Intra-Achievement
Type III discrepancies are the achievement analog of intra-cognitive discrepancies, where the intent is to analyze an individual's pattern of achievement strengths and weaknesses. Since Type III discrepancies deal only with the domain of achievement and not with cognitive ability, they will not be discussed in this text. The reader is referred to the work of Mather (1991) for detailed information on the use and interpretation of WJ-R intra-achievement discrepancies.

CONCLUDING COMMENTS

The WJTCA-R is a collection of 21 individual tests embedded within a larger psychoeducational assessment battery that is also linked to other measures (i.e., adaptive and maladaptive behavior) within a larger diagnostic system. The WJTCA-R is a psychometrically sound collection of tests that were standardized on a large, nationally representative sample of individuals from early childhood to late adulthood. The pragmatic decision-making model that served as the primary foundation of the original WJTCA is maintained in the revision, joined now by the grounding of the WJTCA-R in the comprehensive *Gf-Gc* theory of intelligence. The results of independent reviews, as well as material to be presented in this text, indicate that the WJTCA-R is an instrument that should command the attention of practitioners who routinely use intelligence tests in their assessment activities.

2

THE WJTCA-R AND
Gf-Gc THEORY

*Useful technology is based on scientific understanding;
the better the science, the more effective and efficient the
technology can be. So it is with psychological tests.
They should be based on the most dependable evidence of
science.* J. L. Horn (1991, p. 197)

Until recently, most intelligence tests have not been based on the most dependable evidence from cognitive science (Horn, 1991). This point is particularly noteworthy given the dominance of the Wechsler intelligence tests
in psychoeducational assessment. The venerable Wechsler series of intelligence
tests is still based largely upon Wechsler's conception of intelligence first
operationalized in the form of the 1939 Wechsler-Bellevue (Wechsler, 1939).
Despite over 50 years of research, the most frequently used intelligence tests
(i.e., WPPSI-R, WISC-III, WAIS-R) (Kaufman, 1990) are still based on David
Wechsler's original verbal/performance dichotomy. Does research during the
past half century substantiate the continued use and development of intelligence tests based an a verbal/nonverbal dichotomy, or does the evidence from
cognitive science suggest an alternative conceptualization?

FACTOR ANALYSIS OF HUMAN ABILITIES

Factor analysis is a set of statistical procedures that analyze the
intercorrelations or covariances among a set of variables (tests). Factor analy-
isis helps to identify a smaller number of dimensions or *factors* that explain

the various patterns of correlations among the variables or tests. These methods have been used extensively during the past 50 to 60 years to analyze the factor structure of different intelligence batteries and collections of other cognitive measures Although the application of factor-analytic methods to the analysis of intelligence tests has not been without problems (Carroll, 1983, 1989), when "given its due and used 'correctly' and appropriately, researchers can arrive at a reasonable and confirmable picture of the structure of mental abilities" (Carroll, 1983, p. 9).

Recent reviews of the extant factor-analytic research on human intelligence indicate that significant progress has been made in identifying the major domains of intelligence (Carroll, 1983, 1989, 1993; Gustaffson, 1984, 1988; Horn, 1988, 1991; Lohman, 1989; Snow, 1986). These scholars have concluded that the scientific evidence does not support a single general intelligence model of human cognitive abilities and that our conceptualization of intelligence has changed significantly since the publication of the original Binet and Wechsler scales.

Snow (1986) concluded that recent studies and reanalysis of old data sets with contemporary research methods have produced a largely coherent picture consistent with the multiple intelligence conceptualization often called modern *Gf-Gc* theory. Lohman (1989) reached a similar conclusion regarding *Gf-Gc* theory when he stated that the *Gf-Gc* theoretical model "summarizes much of what is known about the organization of human abilities, and it is, in the main, consistent with the abilities Carroll . . . has thus far identified in his massive review and reanalyses of 60 years of factor-analytic studies of human abilities" (p. 340). Unfortunately, until recently there has been a significant intelligence theory-technology gap as most intelligence tests have not been grounded in this established base of scientific knowledge. Much of the current intelligence testing practice and technology lags behind established cognitive science by 20 to 40 years (Woodcock, 1993).

Although many researchers have written about *Gf-Gc* theory and have produced slightly different models, most conceptualizations have been largely consistent with the comprehensive research syntheses of Carroll (1983, 1989, 1992, 1993) and Horn (1991). Carrol's (1993) work is particularly impressive. He completed a review and reanalysis of over 460 different data sets that meet specific criteria. Carroll's review covers the factor-analytic research over the past 50 years and includes nearly all of the more important and classic factor-analytic investigations. Carroll applied a consistent methodology to the reanalysis of nearly all of the data sets. He used exploratory factor analysis since these methods "are designed to 'let the data speak for themselves', that is, to let the structure of the data suggest the most probable factor-analytic model" (Carroll, 1993, p. 82).

Figure 2-1 presents an adapted version of Carroll's (1993) model of the major domains of human intelligence that have been consistently identified and replicated in the factor-analytic research literature. Carroll's *Three-*

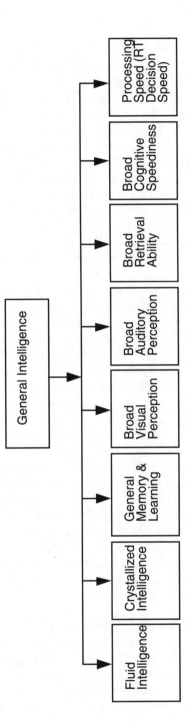

FIGURE 2-1 Broad Intellectual Abilities Identified in Carroll's Review of the Extant Factor Analytic Research Literature

Adapted from J. B. Carroll, 1993, Human cognitive abilities: A survey of factor-analytic studies (p. 626). Copyright 1993 by Cambridge University Press. Adapted by permission.

Stratum Theory includes narrow (Stratum I), broad (Stratum II), and general (Stratum III) abilities. The *broad* abilities are represented by the eight smaller rectangles in Figure 2-1. The large "general intelligence" rectangle is the *general* level in Carroll's model. Not included in the figure are the listing of 69 *narrow* abilities below the broad abilities. A review of Figure 2-1 indicates that Carroll has identified eight broad domains of human intelligence—Fluid Intelligence, Crystallized Intelligence, General Memory and Learning, Broad Visual Perception, Broad Auditory Perception, Broad Retrieval Ability, Broad Cognitive Speediness, and Processing Speed. These eight broad abilities represent "basic constitutional and long-standing characteristics of individuals that can govern or influence a great variety of behaviors in a given domain" (Carroll, 1993, p. 634).

Building on the work of Cattell (1941, 1943), Horn's (1991) *Gf-Gc* research and reviews of the extant factor-analytic literature have suggested that a single general factor (i.e., *g*) conceptualization of human intelligence is inadequate to account for the interrelations observed in data sets that have included indicators of different cognitive abilities. Horn (1991) notes that "as scientific evidence on the relationships among abilities accumulated in the 20th century, it became clear that the idea of a single general intelligence was inadequate. The evidence indicated reliable independence among human abilities and theory needed to accommodate this evidence" (p. 203). According to Horn, evidence in support of independent abilities and the inadequacy of general intelligence theories has resulted in the development of theories of multiple abilities or intelligences.

A variety of factor- and non–factor-analytic evidence supports the identification of at least nine broad *Gf-Gc* abilities (Horn, 1991). Horn's nine-factor model has become known as Horn-Cattell *Gf-Gc* theory. The nine broad Horn-Cattell *Gf-Gc* abilities are listed together with the eight broad abilities identified by Carroll (1993) in Table 2-1. Although using slightly different terms, Carroll and Horn both identify eight broad abilities that appear similar. Carroll and Horn differ primarily in the inclusion or exclusion of a quantitative ability factor and in the acceptance of a higher-order general intelligence factor. Despite these differences, Carroll concludes that the Horn-Cattell *Gf-Gc* model "appears to offer the most well-founded and reasonable approach to an acceptable theory of the structure of cognitive abilities" (Carroll, 1993, p. 62).

Also included in Table 2-1 are the names of the eight WJ-R clusters and the WJ-R *Gf-Gc* factor notation system and their correspondence to the Carroll and Horn factors. Given that the WJTCA-R was designed to measure almost all of the factors identified by the extant factor-analytic research summarized by Carroll and Horn (McGrew et al., 1991), the close correspondence is expected. To reduce confusion that may arise when changing between the different terms used by Carroll, Horn, and the WJ-R, the WJ-R *Gf-Gc* cluster labels will be used throughout the remainder of this text to refer to the similar abilities identified by Carroll and Horn.

TABLE 2-1 Correspondence Between WJ-R Cognitive Factors and Carroll's and Horn's Review of the Extant Factor-Analytic Research

Carroll (1993)	Horn (1991)	WJ-R (1989)	*Gf-Gc* Label
Fluid Intelligence	Broad Reasoning or Fluid Intelligence	Fluid Reasoning	*Gf*
Crystallized Intelligence	Knowledge or Crystallized Intelligence	Comprehension-Knowledge	*Gc*
General Memory & Learning	Short-Term Acquisition & Retrieval	Short-Term Memory	*Gsm*
Broad Visual Perception	Broad Visual Intelligence	Visual Processing	*Gv*
Broad Auditory Perception	Broad Auditory Processing or Auditory Intelligence	Auditory Processing	*Ga*
Broad Retrieval Ability	Long-Term Storage & Retrieval	Long-Term Retrieval	*Glr*
Broad Cognitive Speediness	Cognitive Processing Speed	Processing Speed	*Gs*
Processing Speed	Correct Decision Speed	—	CDS
—	Quantitative Knowledge	Quantitative Ability	*Gq*

It is clear that scholars (Carroll, 1983, 1989, 1993; Gustaffson, 1984, 1988; Horn, 1988, 1991; Lohman, 1989; Snow, 1986) who cast a broad net in their review of the extant factor-analytic research literature have converged on modern *Gf-Gc* theory as being the most comprehensive conceptualization of intelligence currently available. An important feature of *Gf-Gc* theory is that it is not based on a single battery of tests, but instead is derived from the analyses of hundreds of data sets that have included many of the major intelligence test batteries as well as unpublished tests and tasks (Carroll, 1993; Woodcock, 1993).

A common misconception about *Gf-Gc* theory is that it is a two-factor theory consisting only of fluid *(Gf)* and crystallized *(Gc)* intelligence. The dichotomous *Gf-Gc* model has not been the view of Horn or Cattell for over 25 years (Woodcock, 1993) and is inconsistent with the most recent writings of Carroll (1993) and Horn (1991). Gradually this misconception will be eliminated as *Gf-Gc*–related writings enter the mainstream psychological and educational literature. Although much of the information outlining the multidimensional nature of modern *Gf-Gc* theory was reported as early as the 1980s (Carroll, 1983, 1985, 1986a, 1986b, 1987; Horn, 1985), it has only recently begun to appear in professional textbooks or test manuals (Hammill & Bryant, 1991; Kamphaus, 1993; Kaufman, 1990; McGrew et al., 1991; Sattler, 1988; Thorndike et al., 1986; Woodcock & Johnson, 1989).

THE *Gf-Gc* FACTORS

Up to nine broad *Gf-Gc* abilities have been identified in the factor-analytic research literature (See Table 2-1). The following section provides definitions of these abilities. These definitions draw from the works of Carroll (1993), Horn (1991), McGrew et al. (1991), and Woodcock (1993). Example tests of these abilities are presented in Chapter 4.

Long-Term Storage and Retrieval (Glr)

Long-Term Storage and Retrieval refers to the ability to store information in long-term memory and to fluently retrieve it later through association. This ability is called Broad Retrieval Ability and Long-Term Storage and Retrieval by Carroll (1993) and Horn (1991), respectively. Although the word *storage* was not included in the original WJTCA-R factor description for this ability, in more recent writings Woodcock (1993) has placed equal emphasis on both the storage and retrieval aspects of this ability. Long-Term Storage and Retrieval abilities have been prominent in research on creativity, where they have been referred to as *idea production, ideational fluency,* or *associative fluency.*

It is important not to confuse Long-Term Storage and Retrieval with a person's store of acquired knowledge. In the *Gf-Gc* framework, acquired stores of knowledge or information are labeled Comprehension-Knowledge *(Gc)* and Quantitative Ability *(Gq)*. Comprehension-Knowledge and Quantitative Ability represent what is stored in long-term memory. Long-Term Storage and Retrieval represents the ease or fluency by which information is stored and subsequently retrieved from long-term memory.

The acquired stores of knowledge (i.e., *Gc* and *Gq*) represent a network of linked information that conceptually could be represented by a fishing net. The points where different strings of the net meet (i.e., nodes) represent pieces of information, with the fibers between nodes each representing an information link. The fish net represents a person's Comprehension-Knowledge and Quantitative Ability. Long-Term Storage and Retrieval refers to the ease and fluency by which information is stored and retrieved from the network, a person's ability to move around rapidly in his or her "fishing net" of stored knowledge.

Different processes are involved in Long-Term Storage and Retrieval and Short-Term Memory *(Gsm)*. Although the term *long-term* frequently carries with it the connotation of days, weeks, months, and years in the clinical literature, long-term storage processes can begin within a few minutes or hours of performing a task. The amount of time intervening between a task and recall is not critically important in defining Long-Term Storage and Retrieval. More important is the occurrence of an intervening task that engages short-term memory during the interim before recall of the stored information (i.e., *Gc* or *Gq*) is attempted (Woodcock, 1993).

Short-Term Memory (Gsm)

Short-Term Memory is the ability to apprehend and hold information in immediate awareness and then use it within a few seconds. Short-Term Memory abilities are subsumed under the General Memory and Learning and Short-Term Acquisition and Retrieval labels of Carroll (1993) and Horn (1991), respectively. Carroll (1993) considers this to be a broader ability than Horn does, and suggests that there may be several different types of memory and learning.

Short-Term Memory is a limited-capacity system, as most individuals can only retain five "chunks" of information (plus or minus two chunks) in this system at one time. A classic example of Short-Term Memory is the ability to remember a telephone number long enough to dial the phone. The limited amount of information that can be held in short-term memory typically is retained for only a few seconds before it is lost.

As most individuals have experienced, it is difficult to remember an unfamiliar telephone number for more than a few seconds unless they consciously use a cognitive learning strategy (e.g., constantly repeating the numbers). Once a new task requires individuals to use their Short-Term Memory abilities, the previous information is lost or begins to be stored through the use of Long-Term Storage and Retrieval *(Glr)* abilities.

Processing Speed (Gs)

Processing Speed is the ability to perform automatic cognitive tasks quickly, especially when under pressure to maintain focused attention and concentration. Historically it has been referred to as *clerical* or *perceptual speed*, and is labeled Broad Cognitive Speediness and Cognitive Processing Speed by Carroll (1993) and Horn (1991), respectively. Processing Speed is typically measured by timed tasks that require little in terms of thinking abilities. Processing Speed is implicated whenever a task or multiple tasks must be completed within a fixed interval of time.

Recent interest in information processing models of cognitive functioning has resulted in a renewed interest in Processing Speed (Kail, 1991; Lohman, 1989). A central construct in information processing models is the idea of limited processing resources (e.g., the limited capacities of short-term or working memory). Processing Speed refers to the fact "that many cognitive activities require a person's deliberate efforts and that people are limited in the amount of effort they can allocate. In the face of limited processing resources, the speed of processing is critical because it determines in part how rapidly limited resources can be reallocated to other cognitive tasks" (Kail, 1991, p. 152). Woodcock (1993) likens Processing Speed to a valve in a water pipe. The rate of flow of the water in the pipe (i.e., Processing Speed) is at a maximum when the valve is wide open and reduced when the valve is partially closed.

Correct Decision Speed (CDS)

Carroll (1993) and Horn (1991) both include a factor that refers to the speediness by which a person decides on solutions or answers to problems that are of moderate difficulty. Carroll refers to this ability as Processing Speed or Reaction Time Decision Speed, while Horn uses the term Correct Decision Speed. As presented in Table 2-1, the WJTCA-R does not include measures of this ability.

Although the inclusion of the term *speed* in both the Correct Decision Speed and Processing Speed factor labels may suggest strong commonalities, research has indicated that these abilities are distinct and independent. The primary characteristic that distinguishes Correct Decision Speed from Processing Speed is that the former is typically measured with tasks that are used to measure other *Gf-Gc* abilities (i.e., Fluid Reasoning, Comprehension-Knowledge, Visual Processing, etc.), while the latter is typically measured by clerical tasks of trivial difficulty. The measurement of Correct Decision Speed does not focus on the number of correct answers but on the amount of time taken to generate the answers. Correct Decision Speed reflects how quickly one reacts and produces answers, either correct or incorrect.

Auditory Processing (Ga)

Auditory Processing includes the ability to comprehend, analyze, and synthesize patterns among auditory stimuli. These abilities are called Broad Auditory Perception by Carroll (1993) and Broad Auditory Processing or Auditory Intelligence by Horn (1991). Auditory Processing abilities do not require the comprehension of language *(Gc)* but are important in the development of such skills as language and music achievement. This broad ability includes a number of abilities, such as perceiving speech under distorted or distracting conditions, facility in "chunking" or perceiving the flow of sounds, blending isolated sounds into a whole, detecting differences in tones and pitch, localizing sounds, judging rhythms, and discriminating sounds, to name but a few.

Visual Processing (Gv)

Visual Processing refers to the ability to perceive, analyze, synthesize, and think with visual patterns. Broad Visual Perception and Broad Visual Intelligence are the terms used by Carroll (1993) and Horn (1991) to refer to these broad visual abilities. Frequently these abilities are measured by tasks that require the perception and manipulation of visual shapes and forms, typically when figural or geometric in nature. Individuals are typically required to perform reversals or rotations of figures, interpret how objects change as they move through space, find hidden figures, manipulate and perceive spatial configurations, and identify incomplete or distorted figures. Individuals high in this ability may demonstrate exceptional talent in painting, photography, sculpture, architecture, or engineering (Horn, 1988; Snow, 1986; Snow & Swanson, 1992).

Visual Processing also refers to tasks that are visual in the "mind's eye." Stimuli do not necessarily need to be presented visually to require Visual Processing. For example, the oral stimulus to repeat a series of digits (e.g., 3-7-1-6-7-9) is often approached visually when individuals use visual imagery to picture the sequence of numbers that they then read backwards. However, most Visual Processing tests typically present visual stimuli.

Visual Processing tests are frequently confounded by the use of speeded test administrations or by using test stimuli that require the use of reasoning to infer relationships between visual patterns. Such visual tests may be influenced by Processing Speed *(Gs)* and Fluid Reasoning *(Gs)* abilities.

Comprehension-Knowledge (Gc)

Comprehension-Knowledge abilities represent the breadth and depth of a person's knowledge and the effective application of the stored knowledge. These abilities represent one of the two major stores of acquired knowledge that have been isolated in the extant factor-analytic literature. Carroll (1993) and Horn (1991) both refer to these abilities as Crystallized Intelligence.

This ability represents the breadth and depth of acquired declarative or procedural knowledge that a person has appropriated from the dominant culture. Crystallized Intelligence is described as the "broad mental ability that develops througy 'investment' or general intelligence into learning through education and experience" (Carroll, 1993, p. 599). Comprehension-Knowledge is often the ability most laypeople think of when they use the term "intelligence" (Horn, 1988).

The declarative and procedural knowledge distinction reflects a basic difference in the extent to which knowledge is relatively static or dynamic. Declarative knowledge refers to knowledge "*that* something is the case, whereas procedural knowledge is knowledge of *how* to do something" (Gagné. 1985, p. 48). Both are components of Comprehension-Knowledge.

Declarative knowledge is held in long-term memory and is activated when related information is in short-term memory. Declarative knowledge includes factual information, comprehension and knowledge, concepts, rules, and relationships, especially information that is verbal in nture. Procedural knowledge reflects the use of reasoning based on previously learned procedures to transform knowledge. Children's knowledge of their street address would reflect declarative knowledge, while demonstrating the ability to find their way home from school would require procedural knowledge (Gagné, 1985).

A common controversy regarding Comprehension-Knowledge abilities is their relationship to school achievement (McGrew et al., 1991; Woodcock, 1993). As originally conceptualized by Cattell (1971), Comprehension-Knowledge or Crystallized Intelligence is distinct from school achievement. McGrew et al. (1991) and Woodcock (1993) maintain that in adequately designed factor-analytic studies, measures of basic academic skills in reading, mathematics, and written language *do not* load together on a common factor with measures of verbal knowledge (e.g., vocabulary or information tests). However, Carroll (1993) includes measures of reading and writing in the Comprehension-Knowledge or Crystallized Intelligence domain. Additional research is needed to clarify the relationship between these abilities.

Fluid Reasoning (Gf)

Carroll (1993) and Horn (1991) both use the term Fluid Intelligence when referring to the broad ability to reason. In more recent writings, Woodcock (1993) has called this ability Novel Reasoning. Fluid Reasoning refers to many different mental operations that an individual may use when faced with a relatively novel task that cannot be performed automatically. These include forming and recognizing concepts, identifying relations, perceiving relationships among patterns, drawing inferences, comprehending implications, problem solving, extrapolating, and reorganizing or transforming information. Many tasks have been designed to measure Fluid Reasoning, with the major design characteristics being the use of figural or symbolic stimuli and the minimization of task components that draw upon a person's store of acquired knowledge (i.e., Comprehension-Knowledge or Quantitative Abilities).

Quantitative Ability (Gq)

Quantitative Ability, or what Horn (1991) and Woodcock (1993) now refer to as Quantitative Knowledge, refers to a person's store of acquired quantitative declarative and procedural knowledge. This store of acquired knowledge is similar to Comprehensive-Knowledge *(Gc),* with the difference being that Quantitative Ability refers to the ability to use quantitative information and to manipulate numeric symbols.

As can be seen in Table 2-1, Carroll (1993) does not list a separate quantitative factor. Carroll includes quantitative reasoning as a part of Fluid Reasoning or Fluid Intelligence. As noted by Horn (1988, 1991), McGrew et al. (1991), and Woodcock (1993), the measurement of Quantitative Ability is easily confounded by tasks that measure Fluid Reasoning *(Gf)* and Comprehension-Knowldge *(Gc).* Quantitative Reasoning is distinguished from Fluid Reasoning when the task requires the application of previously learned mathematical procedural skills to solve a problem. Furthermore, Quantitative Ability is evident when a task requires mathematical skills rather than general knowledge about the field of mathematics. Knowledge about the field of mathematics would be considered to be within the Comprehension-Knowledge *(Gc)* domain.

THE RELATIONSHIP BETWEEN *Gf-Gc* THEORY AND OTHER IMPORTANT THEORIES OF INTELLIGENCE

The history of psychology reports numerous endeavors to explicate theories of intelligence. A thorough treatment of the various theories and their relationships to the development and interpretation of intelligence tests is beyond the scope of this book. However, some comments regarding how popular theories of intelligence (those that have been used to develop or interpret intelligence tests) relate to modern *Gf-Gc* theory are provided here. The reader is referred to Kamphaus (1993) and Sattler (1988) for a more detailed treatment of each individual intelligence theory and its use in psychological assessment.

General Intelligence or "g" Theories

The general intelligence or *g* theory has its roots in the work of Spearman (1904). This theory suggests that there is a very general mental ability or energy that underlies, in various degrees, almost all types of intellectual activity. This general ability involves the apprehension of experience, the education of correlates, and the education of relations (Carroll, 1993). In addition to a general factor, specific *(s)* factors also account for performance on different mental tasks, although to a much lessor degree than the large general factor.

According to Carroll (1993), the general intelligence factor at the apex of his three-stratum (narrow-broad-general) theory (see Figure 2-1) is analogous to Spearman's *g*. Spearman's specific factors, or what were later called "group" factors, are similar to Carroll's narrow or Stratum I factors. Thus, Spearman's theory contains abilities at two levels (narrow and general) of the three-stratum *Gf-Gc* theory. The primary difference between the general intelligence and modern *Gf-Gc* theories is the recognition of and emphasis on the intermediate broad *Gf-Gc* abilities that lie between the general and narrow abilities in modern Gf-Gc theory. Intelligence tests designed to measure only a general intelligence factor ignore the most basic characteristics and building blocks of intelligent behavior (i.e., the broad *Gf-Gc* abilities).

Not all *Gf-Gc* theorists agree on the presence of a large general intelligence factor. Horn (1991) disagrees that there is a large general intelligence ability above the broad *Gf-Gc* abilities. The debate regarding the existence of a large general intellectual ability above the broad *Gf-Gc* abilities has existed for many years and will continue to be debated for many more.

Verbal/Nonverbal Theories

Given the historical dominance of the Wechsler series of intelligence batteries in psychological and psychoeducational assessment, it is understandable why many clinicians come to view intelligence as consisting of verbal and nonverbal abilities. However, there is no such thing as "nonverbal" abilities (Kamphaus, 1993).

The Verbal and Performance (nonverbal) design of the original Wechsler scales was not based on any empirically supported verbal/nonverbal theory of intelligence. Rather, Wechsler designed his first scale based on a combination of clinical, practical, and empirical considerations (Kaufman, 1990; Zachary, 1990). Wechsler did not consider the Verbal and Performance dichotomy to represent two different types of intelligence. Rather, the intent of David Wechsler was to organize the tests to reflect the two different ways (i.e., two different "languages") intelligence can be expressed (Kamphaus, 1993; Reynolds & Kaufman, 1990; Zachary, 1990).

Given that the Wechsler verbal/nonverbal model was not based on any empirically derived theory of intelligence, the failure of a verbal/nonverbal model to emerge in comprehensive reviews of the extant factor-analytic research (e.g., Carroll's review summarized in Figure 2-1) should not be surprising. Carroll (1993) concluded that the Wechsler Verbal scale is an approximate measure of crystallized intelligence *(Gc)* and the Performance scale is an approximate measure of broad visual perception *(Gv)* and, somewhat less validly, fluid intelligence *(Gf)*. As discussed in Chapter 4, Woodcock's (1990) joint confirmatory studies support Carroll's *Gf-Gc* analysis of the Wechsler scales, with the exception of Woodcock's studies suggesting that the Wechsler Performance scales are primarily measures of visual abilities *(Gv)*.

Although the Wechsler verbal/nonverbal dichotomy may be clinically useful, it does not represent a valid theory of intelligence. The best available evidence suggests that the Wechsler Verbal and Performance scales measure only two of the eight to nine broad *Gf-Gc* abilities that have been identified in the extant factor-analytic research literature (Carroll, 1993; Woodcock, 1990). Tests developed according to a verbal/nonverbal model are not constructed according to the best available evidence regarding the theoretical structure of human cognitive abilities.

Luria-based Theories

Since the early to mid-1980s there has been considerable interest in developing tests that have their roots in the neuropsychological model advanced by the Soviet neuropsychologist A. R. Luria. The work of Luria, plus additional experimental and cognitive psychological research, has suggested a model of cognitive processing based on two distinct mental operations (Kamphaus, 1990, 1993; Kamphaus & Reynolds, 1984; Kaufman, 1984; Kaufman & Kaufman, 1983; Naglieri & Das, 1990). As summarized by Naglieri, Kamphaus, and Kaufman (1983), "one mental process is analytic and sequential and deals mainly with the ordering of linguistic stimuli; the other is multiple and holistic and carries out many actions simultaneously, or at least independently" (p. 25). Although different researchers have used different terms to describe this processing dichotomy, the successive/simultaneous dichotomy has been the most frequently used terminology in the psychoeducational literature.

The Kaufman Assessment Battery for Children (K-ABC) (Kaufman & Kaufman, 1983) was the first norm-referenced test to operationalize the measurement of the successive/simultaneous processing dichotomy. According to Carroll's (1993) review of the K-ABC-related factor-analytic research, "there is little if anything that is new in the K-ABC test" (p. 703). Both Carroll's and Woodcock's (1990) *Gf-Gc* structured empirical analyses suggest that the K-ABC Successive and Simultaneous processing scales are primarily measures of short-term memory *(Gsm)* and visual processing *(Gv)*, respectively. Similar to the Wechsler Verbal and Performance scales, Successive/Simultaneous scales appear to measure a limited number (i.e., two) of the eight to nine broad *Gf-Gc* abilities included in modern *Gf-Gc* theory.

Recently, Naglieri and Das (1990) have expanded this model to also include attentional and planning processes. Naglieri and Das refer to their Luria-based conceptualization as the Planning, Attention, Simultaneous, and Successive (PASS) model and are developing tests to operationally measure the model. Joint analysis of the PASS measures with other good *Gf-Gc* marker tests have yet to be completed. How the four major PASS components correspond to the broad *Gf-Gc* abilities cannot be determined at this time.

Using the comprehensive *Gf-Gc* framework as a guide, and focusing just on research that has used the K-ABC tests, Carroll (1993) concluded that Luria-based tests are generally limited in variety and do not assess the total range of mental abilities. Empirical studies grounded in the modern *Gf-Gc* framework (Carroll, 1993; Woodcock, 1990) suggest that the Luria-based successive/simultaneous model and scales may only be representing two broad *Gf-Gc* abilities, and not new, unique processes.

Gardner's Theory of Multiple Intelligences

The description of *Gf-Gc* theory as a multiple intelligences theory occasionally causes confusion when individuals try to reconcile this model with the multiple intelligences model advanced by Gardner (1983). Although Gardner's theory of multiple intelligences has yet to serve as the foundation for an individually administered norm-referenced battery of tests, Gardner's concepts have received considerable attention in the popular press.

Gardner describes seven types of intelligence—logical-mathematical, linguistic, musical, spatial, bodily-kinesthetic, interpersonal, and intrapersonal. The terms Gardner uses to label his seven intelligences are dramatically different than the terminology of *Gf-Gc* theory.

Although yet to be investigated empirically, the fundamental differences between the *Gf-Gc* and Gardner multiple intelligences theories is that *Gf-Gc* theory is concerned with *describing the basic domains or building blocks of intelligent behavior* in the cognitive domain, while Gardner's theory focuses on *how these different domains or building blocks are combined,* together with other personal competencies, in patterns representing different forms of aptitude or expertise (R. W. Woodcock, personal communication, April 27, 1993). For example, Gardner's logical-mathematical intelligence reflects a sensitivity to and capacity to process logical and/or numerical patterns and the ability to handle long sequences or chains of reasoning. Scientists and mathematicians would be high on logical-mathematical intelligence. Logical-mathematical intelligence may accurately describe individuals high in fluid reasoning *(Gf)*, quantitative ability or reasoning *(Gq)*, and the ability to visualize relationships *(Gv)*. It is the specific combination of *Gf-Gc* strengths that individuals exhibit that defines them as being high in logical-mathematical intelligence. Gardner's theory does not attempt to isolate the basic domains or elements of intelligence, a function performed by *Gf-Gc* theory; rather, it is an attempt to describe different patterns of expertise or aptitude based on specific combinations of *Gf-Gc* abilities and other personal competencies.

A model of personal competence was briefly described in Chapter 1 (see Figure 1-3) that included the broad domains of physical competence, conceptual intelligence, social competence, practical intelligence, and emotional competence. *Gf-Gc* theory represents a portion of the conceptual intelligence domain. When Gardner talks about such intelligences as bodily-kinesthetic and interpersonal, he is describing individuals who may have combinations of specific strengths in these other personal competence mains (e.g., physical competence, social competence, emotional competence).

Thus, Gardner's theory of multiple intelligences attempts to describe a different aspect of human performance, namely, expertise or aptitude. Individuals with specific expertise or aptitudes probably have unique combinations of certain *Gf-Gc* abilities together with abilities in the other domains of personal competence.

Gf-Gc THEORY AND THE DEVELOPMENT OF THE WJTCA-R

The authors of the WJ-R decided to revise the original 1977 WJ to reflect the convergence of the extant factor-analytic research literature on modern *Gf-Gc* theory. The Horn-Cattell model of *Gf-Gc* theory served as the guiding framework for revising the WJTCA-R. The use of a comprehensive data-based theory as a framework for the WJTCA-R's development is consistent with recent recommendations for using more theory in assessment research and development activities (Keith, 1987).

After selecting the Horn-Cattell *Gf-Gc* model of intelligence, the developers of the WJTCA-R followed a series of steps (McGrew et al., 1991). First, the factor-analytic research completed with the original WJ was reviewed in the context of *Gf-Gc* theory. Second, a test blueprint was developed based on the results of the factor study review. Finally, a series of exploratory and confirmatory factor analyses was completed. What follows is a brief summary of these steps. Detailed information regarding the development can be found in McGrew et al. (1991).

Review of the 1977 WJ Factor Studies

The first step undertaken in the development of the WJTCA-R was to review the factor analysis research completed with the original WJ from the perspective of *Gf-Gc* theory. This step was completed to determine the extent to which the original WJ measured the different components of the Horn-Cattell *Gf-Gc* model.

Although not using the language of *Gf-Gc* theory, independent factor-analytic studies of the original WJTCA (Kaufman & O'Neal, 1988; McGrew, 1987; McGue, Shinn, & Ysseldyke, 1979, 1982; Rosso & Phelps, 1988), as well as those reported by Woodcock (1978), consistently indicated that the WJTCA contained multiple tests of the Comprehension-Knowledge *(Gc)*, Fluid Reasoning *(Gf)*, and Processing Speed *(Gs)* abilities (McGrew et al., 1991). These factors were typically labeled the Verbal, Reasoning, and Perceptual Speed factors in these studies.

Two additional factors were identified on a less consistent basis, with the differences between studies being due to a number of different methodological and data analysis strategies (McGrew et al., 1991). When the WJ achievement tests were used together with the cognitive tests, J. B. Carroll (personal communication, March 1986) and Woodcock (1978) both identified a quantitative *(Gq)* dimension. Finally, a WJTCA factor measuring either Short-Term Memory *(Gsm)* or Auditory Processing *(Ga)* abilities was also identified.

Development of a Test Blueprint

A synthesis of all WJ factor analysis studies indicated that the complete battery (i.e., cognitive and achievement sections combined) included tests of seven of the nine *Gf-Gc* factors. Based on this synthesis, a *Gf-Gc* model of the factorial structure of the original WJ was developed to serve as a revision blueprint. An adapted version of this blueprint is presented in Table 2-2.

A review of Table 2-2 indicates that the original WJTCA included two or more tests of the *Gf-Gc* abilities of Short-Term Memory *(Gsm)*, Processing Speed *(Gs)*, Comprehension-Knowledge *(Gc)*, and Fluid Reasoning *(Gf)*. In contrast, only single tests of Long-Term Storage and Retrieval *(Glr)*, Auditory Processing *(Ga)*, and Quantitative Ability *(Gq)* were present in the WJTCA. Finally, no tests of Visual Processing *(Gv)* were found in the original WJTCA.

The test blueprint served as a guide for the development of new tests, as well as revisions to original tests. For example, the information summarized in Table 2-2 indicated that in order to provide for complete measurement of the Horn-Cattell *Gf-Gc* model, new tests were needed to measure Long-Term Storage and Retrieval, Auditory Processing, and Visual Processing. The empirical results that were used to develop the test blueprint were also reviewed to identify those existing WJ tests that needed to be modified to become "purer" measures of *Gf-Gc* abilities. The only Horn-Cattell *Gf-Gc* factor missing from the test blueprint was Correct Decision Speed *(CDS)*. The measurement of this ability has been difficult (Horn, 1988; Woodcock, 1993) and was not attempted in the development of the WJTCA-R.

Exploratory and Confirmatory WJ-R Factor Studies

After the existing tests were revised and new tests were designed, a series of exploratory and confirmatory factor analysis studies was completed at the one-quarter point of the data collection process. These preliminary analyses resulted in a number of modifications to some of the WJTCA-R tests (McGrew et al., 1991). A WJTCA-R *Gf-Gc* conceptualization was then finalized and retained throughout the remainder of the data collection. The final

TABLE 2-2   *Gf-Gc* **Cognitive Factors Measured by the 1977 Woodcock-Johnson**

	Cognitive Factors							
WJ Subtests	*Glr*	*Gsm*	*Gs*	*Ga*	*Gv**	*Gc*	*Gf*	*Gq*
Visual-Auditory Learning	x	—	—	—	—	—	—	—
Memory for Sentences	—	o	—	—	—	o	—	—
Numbers Reversed	—	o	—	—	—	—	—	—
Spatial Relations**	—	—	x	—	—	—	—	—
Visual Matching	—	—	x	—	—	—	—	—
Blending	—	—	—	x	—	—	—	—
Picture Vocabulary	—	—	—	—	—	x	—	—
Antonyms-Synonyms	—	—	—	—	—	x	—	—
Analysis-Synthesis	—	—	—	—	—	—	x	—
Concept Formtion	—	—	—	—	—	—	x	—
Analogies	—	—	—	—	—	o	o	—
Quantitative Concepts	—	—	—	—	—	—	—	x
Word Attack	—	—	—	o	—	—	—	—
Calculation	—	—	—	—	—	—	—	x
Applied Problems	—	—	—	—	—	—	—	x
Science	—	—	—	—	—	x	—	—
Social Studies	—	—	—	—	—	x	—	—
Humanities	—	—	—	—	—	x	—	—

x = High Factor Loadings

o = Moderate Factor Loadings

  *There are no measures of *Gv* in the 1977 WJ

**Spatial Relations is a highly speeded test in the 1977 WJ

Adapted from the *WJ-R Technical Manual* (p. 162) by K. McGrew, J. Werder, and R. Woodcock, 1991, Chicago, IL: The Riverside Publishing Company. Copyright 1991 by The Riverside Publishing Company. Adapted by permission.

hypothesized WJTCA-R *Gf-Gc* model evaluated at the completion of the data collection is presented in Figure 2-2.

The model in Figure 2-2 is presented in the standard path diagram format used to present the results of confirmatory factor analysis studies. The circles represent the *Gf-Gc* factors. The rectangles represent the tests hypothesized to be indicators of each *Gf-Gc* factor. The single-headed arrows from each factor (i.e., circle) to different combinations of tests (i.e., rectangles) designate those tests believed to be indicators of each *Gf-Gc* factor. To reduce the complexity of the model presented in Figure 2-2, the visual symbols traditionally used to indicate the test residuals and correlations between the factors have been omitted.

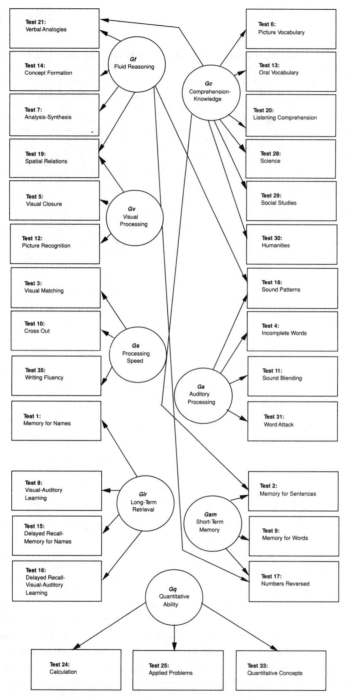

FIGURE 2-2 Hypothesized *Gf-Gc* Model of the WJ-R

Adapted from the *WJ-R Technical Manual* (p. 170) by K. McGrew, J. Werder, and R. Woodcock, 1991, Chicago, IL: The Riverside Publishing Company. Copyright 1991 by the Riverside Publishing Company. Adapted by permission.

A review of the model in Figure 2-2 indicates that the WJTCA-R contains multiple tests of each of the eight *Gf-Gc* factors. For example, it is hypothesized that the WJTCA-R Visual Matching and Cross Out tests and the Writing Fluency test from the WJ-R achievement section are all indicators of Processing Speed *(Gs)*. Comprehension-Knowledge *(Gc)* is measured by a minimum of five cognitive tests (Picture Vocabulary, Oral Vocabulary, Listening Comprehension, Verbal Analogies, and Memory for Sentences). Additional Comprehension-Knowledge information can be found in three tests from the achievement portion of the WJ-R battery (Science, Social Studies, and Humanities).

A review of Figure 2-2 indicates that certain WJ-R achievement tests provide additional indicators of certain *Gf-Gc* factors. This is the case for the *Gf-Gc* abilities of Processing Speed, Comprehension-Knowledge, and Auditory Processing. It is important to note that the model presented in Figure 2-2 does not contain all of the WJ-R reading and writing tests. The exclusion of these achievement tests from the model and subsequent analyses was based on the fact that at the time of the test revision, theory and research had not thoroughly analyzed and integrated these achievement domains into the Horn-Cattell *Gf-Gc* theory (McGrew et al., 1991).

The 29-test model presented in Figure 2-2, as well as reduced models based on only 16 and 27 tests, was evaluated with confirmatory factor methods in six age-differentiated samples and in a single sample collapsed across ages (McGrew et al., 1991). The results provided strong support for the *Gf-Gc* factor structure of the WJTCA-R. Ysseldyke (1990) was "extremely impressed with the convincing job that Woodcock has done fitting the WJ-R to the Horn-Cattell *Gf-Gc* model of intelligence" (p. 269). Reschly (1990) reached a similar conclusion when he stated that "the WJ-R provides generally sound, factorially clean measures of eight of the nine Horn-Cattell factors" (p. 260). Detailed results of these confirmatory factor studies can be found in McGrew et al. (1991). The results of these confirmatory factor studies, as well as other construct related evidence, are summarized in Chapter 4.

CONCLUDING COMMENTS

Much has been learned about the major factors of intelligence during the past 50 to 60 years. Comprehensive reviews of the extant factor-analytic research literature have converged on a multiple intelligences conceptualization, with modern *Gf-Gc* theory being the best available synthesis of this knowledge base. The Horn-Cattell model of *Gf-Gc* theory accurately reflects most of this empirical knowledge base and served as the guiding force behind the development of the WJTCA-R. As noted by Ysseldyke (1990), "the Horn-Cattell *Gf-Gc* theory provides the most salient and promising model of intelligence and the one around which cognitive measures ought to be developed" (p. 272).

A systematic theory-based test development process was used to develop the WJTCA-R. The original WJ was reanalyzed from the perspective of *Gf-Gc* theory, with the results used to develop a test revision blueprint. The blueprint guided the development of new tests as well as the revision of existing tests. A hypothesized Horn-Cattell *Gf-Gc* model of the WJTCA-R was specified and extensively evaluated with confirmatory factor analysis methods. The results of this process suggest that the WJTCA-R has significantly narrowed the gap between applied assessment technology and the best available evidence from cognitive science. A similar conclusion was reached by Ysseldyke (1990) when he stated:

> The WJ-R represents a significant milestone in the applied measurement of intellectual abilities. The manner in which theory and prior research were used in the development of the WJ-R and in the analysis of other major measures of intelligence should serve as a model for future research and development in the fields of applied psychometrics and psychoeducational assessment. (p. 272)

3

THE INDIVIDUAL
WJTCA-R TESTS

Prior to engaging in clinical interpretation of the WJTCA-R, clinicians should examine the major features of the individual tests. Although this requires an immediate focus on the individual tests, the philosophy of this text is that individual tests are best interpreted in combination with other tests. The goal of this chapter is to acquaint the clinician with the raw material necessary for the global shared-ability interpretive approach outlined in later chapters.

This chapter presents a test-by-test analysis of the 21 WJTCA-R tests. Since this text assumes that the reader is well versed in the administration and scoring of the twenty-one tests, such information is not covered. However, a brief description of each test's task requirements is included for those who may be unfamiliar with the WJTCA-R. The abilities measured by each test and the factors that may influence test performance are also presented.

Consistent with a data-based interpretive philosophy, the test-by-test analyses include summaries of the major empirical test characteristics that should guide individual test interpretation. Norm-based information regarding individual test reliability, uniqueness (test specificity), and general and common factor loadings provide the empirical foundations of interpretation. The need for clinicians to be cognizant of these empirical properties has clearly been articulated by Kaufman (1979, 1990). To reinforce the importance of the empirical test characteristic information in interpretation of the WJTCA-R tests, that information is presented first.

EMPIRICAL CHARACTERISTICS
INFLUENCING INTERPRETATION

Four empirical test characteristics are presented in this chapter: reliability, general factor loadings, uniqueness (specificity), and common factor abilities. Working knowledge of these test characteristics is required for responsible interpretation of intelligence tests such as the WJTCA-R. Otherwise, interpretation of tests becomes an idiosyncratic enterprise dependent on the whims of different clinicians. All clinicians who are serious about appropriate, competent, and professional interpretation of intelligence tests must take it upon themselves to "know thy instrument."

This belief is consistent with the writings of Matarazzo and Reynolds and Kaufman. Reynolds and Kaufman (1990) stated that "the clinical evaluation of test performance must be directed by careful analyses of the statistical properties of the test scores, the internal psychometric characteristics of the test, and the data regarding its relationship to external factors" (p. 131). Although speaking primarily about assessment by clinical neuropsychologists, Matarazzo (1990) conveyed a similar message when he stated that "published information on the psychometric properties of the tests is . . . too infrequently used by some clinicians" (p. 1004).

Unfortunately, important empirical test information is frequently presented in technical research articles or in tables upon tables of numbers in lengthy technical manuals. Often such information is not easily translated and used except by the most diligent of clinicians. To facilitate the use and internalization of this basic empirical information by clinicians, unique graphic empirical summaries are provided for each WJTCA-R test. These summaries are designed to overcome the discomfort or difficulty some clinicians find in locating and digesting detailed empirical information as it relates to clinical test interpretation.

Test Reliability

Reliability "refers to the degree to which test scores are free from errors of measurement" (APA, 1985, p. 19). Although a review of test reliability will not shed light on the abilities tapped by the WJTCA-R tests, knowledge of this information is critical for competent interpretation (Salvia & Ysseldyke, 1991). Clinicians must know whether the data generated by a test are accurate and constant and not reflecting random variation. For in-depth treatment of reliability concepts, the reader is referred to Anastasi (1988), APA (1985), Crocker and Algina (1986), Lord and Novick (1968), Saliva and Ysseldyke (1991), and Sattler (1988).

The WJTCA-R technical manual (McGrew et al., 1991) contains an extensive discussion of basic reliability concepts as well as the specific reliability information for each WJTCA-R test. The WJTCA-R test reliability coefficients (internal consistency reliability, except for the speeded tests that are test-retest reliability) reported for up to 26 different age groups are summarized graphically for each test. An example summary for the Memory for Names test is presented in Figure 3-1.

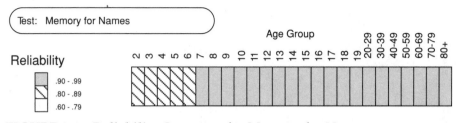

FIGURE 3-1 Reliability Summary for Memory for Names

For each age group the reliability coefficient for a test is categorized into one of three reliability categories (.60 to .79; .80 to .89; .90 to .99). The resulting graphic reliability summary easily communicates the basic reliability characteristics of each test, as well as any noticeable changes in reliability as a function of age. Memory for Names (Figure 3-1) consistently demonstrates high (.90 or above) reliability from ages 7 through late adulthood, with slightly lower reliability (.80 to .89) under 7 years of age.

The reliability classifications presented in Figure 3-1 are based on *smoothed* reliability estimates and not the original values reported in the WJ-R technical manual. As is the case with any sample-based statistical estimate, each of the different sample reliability coefficients contain sampling error. Sampling error is noticeable when reviewing a plot of the original Memory for Names reliability coefficients as a function of age. Such a plot is presented in Figure 3-2.

Although the original sample-based reliability coefficients presented in Figure 3-2 (connected by a dashed line) demonstrate a systematic age-related trend, the values demonstrate noticeable variation or "bounce" between adjacent age groups. This variation most likely reflects sampling error. Therefore, a reliability coefficient at a specific age may be a biased estimate that either over- or underestimates the true reliability. In order to provide an estimate of the population reliability free from the distracting effects of sample-based "noise" or error, a smoothed curve (based on the LOWESS smoothing function) (Goodall, 1990; Wilkinson, 1990) was fitted to the original values.

The smoothed curve provides better estimates of the population reliability parameters. The values represented by the smoothed curve in Figure 3-2 were used to complete the reliability summary for Memory for Names in Figure 3-1. A smoothing function to provide estimates of the population parameters was also used in the development and categorization of the other WJTCA-R test empirical characteristics (i.e., uniqueness; general factor loading) presented later in this chapter.

A set of minimum criteria are required for evaluating the adequacy of the reliability values reported for each test. Salvia and Ysseldyke (1991) have presented standards for the evaluation of test reliability coefficients.

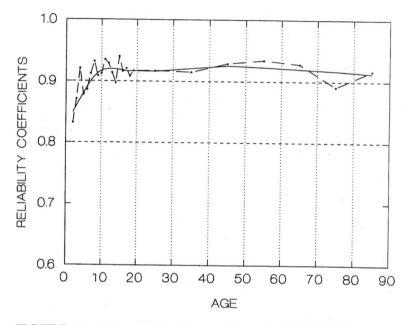

FIGURE 3-2   Memory for Names Smoothed Reliabilities

For data used for critical educational decisions (e.g., special class placement) reliability coefficients of .90 or above are recommended. The second criterion (.80 or above) is applicable for screening measures. The top two reliability categories in the reliability summary illustrated in Figure 3-1 correspond to these two standards.

Since the *individual* WJTCA-R tests are not recommended for critical educational decisions, and since individual test interpretation as recommended in this text focuses on the commonality among groups of tests for clinical hypothesis formation, the .80 or above criterion seems most appropriate. Thus, those WJTCA-R tests whose graphic reliability summaries are characterized by many shaded or striped classifications should be viewed as possessing adequate reliability for clinical interpretation.

Test General Factor Loadings

Measures of intellectual functioning have often been interpreted as reflecting a *general* mental ability referred to as *g* (Bracken & Fagan, 1990; French & Hale, 1990; Horn, 1988; Jensen, 1984; Kaufman, 1979; Sattler, 1988). The *g* concept is originally associated with Spearman (1904, 1927) and is considered to represent an underlying general intellectual ability that is the basis for most intelligent behavior.

The *g* concept has been one of the more controversial topics in psychology for decades (French & Hale, 1990; Jensen, 1992; Kamphaus, 1993; McDermott, Fantuzzo, & Glutting, 1990; Zachary, 1990). As presented in Chapter Two, the concept of multiple intelligences contradicts the idea of a single general intellectual ability being responsible for most intelligent behavior. Given the variety of positions regarding the nature and existence of this construct (Bracken & Fagan, 1990; Kamphaus, 1993), resolution of the issue is beyond the scope of this text.

Despite the inability to resolve the theoretical arguments surrounding the concept of g, an appreciation of each individual test's relationship to a general intelligence factor may be useful in interpretation (Bracken & Fagan, 1990; Kaufman, 1979, 1990; Roid & Gyurke, 1991). Historically in the field of intelligence testing each individual test's loading on the single general factor identified through some variant of factor analysis has been labeled as the test's g loading.

The primary value of knowing individual test g loadings is being able to anticipate those tests within an intelligence battery that may vary frequently from the remainder of the test profile (Kaufman, 1979). Tests that are high in their loading on the single general factor present in an intelligence battery may be expected to be at a similar level of performance as most of the other tests and the global full scale score. Tests loading high on the general factor that are markedly discrepant from the middle of a test profile may suggest the need to examine noncognitive variables (Kaufman, 1979; McGrew, 1984).

Tests that load at low levels on the general factor should be expected to vary frequently from the other tests within an intelligence battery. Such tests are less related to the general factor measured by the collection of tests in the battery. Any significant departure from the other tests within the same battery may not be abnormal. A working knowledge of each test's loading on the general factor within the intelligence battery can help clinicians identify unusual test deviations that may increase one's understanding of an examinee's functioning.

Similar to the debate surrounding the existence and definition of g, a variety of methods have been suggested for determining the g characteristics of tests (Elliott, 1990; Woodcock, 1990). Regardless of the specific method employed, they all suffer from the problem of providing test g estimates that are a function of a specific collection of tests. An individual test's loading on a single general factor will depend on the specific variety and mixture of tests used in the analysis (Woodcock, 1990).

If a single verbal test (e.g., vocabulary test) is combined with nine nonverbal/visual-spatial tests, the verbal test will have a low g loading since the general factor will most likely be defined by the nonverbal tests. In contrast, if the verbal test is included in a battery of tests that is an even mixture of verbal and nonverbal measures, the loading of this test on the general factor will most likely be different. Thus, test g loadings only reflect a test's relationship to the general factor *within a specific intelligence battery.*

A test's *g* loading may change if recomputed in the context of a different collection of tests.

Application to the WJTCA-R

Given the controversies surrounding the theoretical concept of *g* and its calculation, this test characteristic will not be labeled *g* in this text. Instead, this empirical test characteristic will be referred to as each test's *general factor loading,* minimizing the association with the notion of theoretical *g.* In a nontechnical sense each test's general factor loading is the average correlation between the test and every other WJTCA-R test (Jensen, 1992).

McGrew and Murphy's (1993) analysis provided the information needed for the development of the WJTCA-R general factor loading test summaries. They used the principal component method to calculate these WJTCA-R test characteristics.

The general factor loading summary for Concept Formation is presented in Figure 3-3. This summary is organized the same as the previously described test reliability graphic summaries. Each test's general factor loading at each age level was used to classify each test as being a *high, medium,* or *low* measure of the general factor. The criteria used to make these classifications parallel those employed in similar classifications of other intelligence tests (Kaufman, 1979, 1990; Sattler, 1990). However, the verbal labels have been changed to be less value-laden. The *high, medium,* and *low* classifications are used in place of the traditional *good, fair,* and *poor* classifications. These traditional terms convey value judgments. A test that is *low* in its loading on the general factor is not necessarily a "poor" test. Such a test may serve many other valuable functions and may not be so classified if included in a factor analysis with a different collection of tests. The less value-laden terms of *high, medium,* and *low* are used to minimize the possibility of negative generalizations being formed from the more traditional terms.

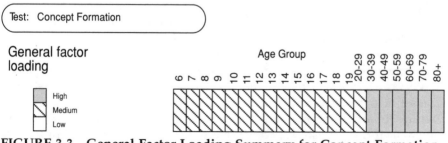

FIGURE 3-3   General Factor Loading Summary for Concept Formation

A *high* general factor loading is present when a test's loading on the first principal component equals or exceeds .70, a *medium* classification is represented by values from .51 to .69, and *low* is defined by loadings less than or equal to .50. In the general factor loading summary presented in Figure 3-3, it can easily be seen that Concept Formation is primarily a *medium* measure of the general factor through age 29, and more of a *high* measure of the general factor from age 30 and beyond.

Test Uniqueness

If clinicians plan to interpret an individual WJTCA-R test as measuring an ability unique to that test, clinicians need to be familiar with each test's specificity or uniqueness characteristics. Test *specificity* refers to the portion of a test's variance that is reliable and unique to the test (Kaufman, 1979, 1990)—"that is, not shared or held in common with other subtests of the same scale" (Reynolds & Kaufman, 1990, p. 151). Although this test property is most commonly referred to as specificity, the more meaningful term *uniqueness* will be used in this text since it better communicates the essential nature of this empirical test characteristic.

Test uniqueness reflects the degree to which a test can be interpreted as measuring a unique ability that is not accounted for by abilities shared with other tests *within a specific intelligence battery*. If a test has high statistical uniqueness values, it can be interpreted as measuring an ability distinct and specific to that test. Conversely, tests with low uniqueness values should not be interpreted as reflecting something unique, as the test score is probably more a function of measurement error, in the case of tests with low reliability, or a function of other broad abilities measured by the intelligence battery. Thus, knowledge of a test's uniqueness properties is critical for determining when, if appropriate, to interpret individual tests as reflecting distinct abilities within an intelligence battery.

McGrew and Murphy (1993) calculated and presented the empirical test uniqueness information for the WJTCA-R tests in the norm sample. Similar to the calculation of general factor loading test characteristics, a number of different methods have been suggested for the calculation of test uniqueness (Kaufman, 1990; Keith, 1990). McGrew and Murphy used the method most frequently used to calculate test uniqueness, a method based on the calculation of squared multiple correlations (Kaufman, 1979, 1990; Silverstein, 1976). Their analysis served as the basis for the development of the WJTCA-R uniqueness test summaries. The test uniqueness summary for Visual Closure is presented in Figure 3-4. This summary is organized in the same manner as previously described for the test reliability and general factor loading graphic summaries. Smoothed values were used to develop each WJTCA-R test's uniqueness summary.

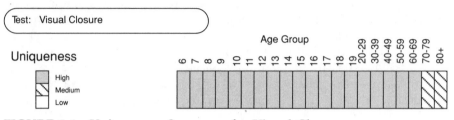

FIGURE 3-4   Uniqueness Summary for Visual Closure

Similar to the general factor loading classifications, each test's uniqueness at each age level is classified as being *high, medium,* or *low.* These labels differ from the traditionally used *ample, adequate,* or *inadequate* terms for the same reason mentioned for the test general factor loadings—these traditional terms are value-laden and may result in negative generalizations about certain individual tests. Although a test may be *low* in uniqueness within a specific intelligence test battery, the test may still serve other valuable functions. Furthermore, such a classification may change if calculated with a different combination of tests. Both the uniqueness and general factor loadings are situationally dependent on the specific battery of tests that are used in the calculation of these empirical characteristics.

Although using different terms, this three category uniqueness classification system parallels that used for reporting the uniqueness characteristics of other intelligence tests (Cohen, 1959; Kaufman, 1979, 1990; Sattler, 1988). These criteria state that a test can be interpreted individually if the test's uniqueness value equals or exceeds 25% of the total test variance, and if this value exceeds the test's error variance. Tests that meet this criteria are *high* in uniqueness. Tests that meet one of these criteria, but not both, are classified as *medium.* Finally, the remaining tests are considered to have *low* uniqueness.

A review of the Visual Closure uniqueness summary in Figure 3-4 indicates that this test can be individually interpreted at all age levels, although slightly more caution may be necessary at ages 70 and beyond. With the aid of the graphic uniqueness summaries for all WJTCA-R tests, clinicians should be able to determine when it is appropriate to interpret an individual test. Tests with either high or medium classifications can be considered legitimate for individual interpretation, although the latter should be more discrepant from the total WJTCA-R test profile before one considers individual interpretation.

Abilities Shared With Other Tests

The final empirical characteristic bearing on test interpretation is the degree to which each test measures broader common abilities. This information is

important given the test interpretation philosophy of this text that empha-
sizes the grouping of tests that measure common abilities.

Through extensive exploratory and confirmatory factor analyses of the
WJTCA-R norm data, McGrew et al. (1991) provided detailed information
on the factor structure of the WJTCA-R. As described in Chapter 2, these
analyses provide support for a seven-factor *Gf-Gc* interpretation of the
WJTCA-R. The confirmatory factor analyses results presented in Table 6-32
of the WJ-R technical manual (McGrew et al., 1991) provided the information necessary to develop the shared ability test summaries. The shared
ability test summary for Numbers Reversed is presented in Figure 3-5.

In Figure 3-5 six different age groups are presented similarly to previous summaries. Since the three youngest samples analyzed by McGrew et
al. (1991) were described according to grades in school (i.e., Grades K–3;
Grades 4–7; Grades 8–12) rather than by age, the approximate ages corre-
sponding to these grade groups were used to construct the graphic summaries. This conversion from grade to age was done to be consistent with the
other empirical test characteristic summaries.

The magnitude of Numbers Reversed's factor loadings at each of the
six age groups is presented vertically in Figure 3-5 in five categories that
range from *weak* to *strong*. The five vertical sections in Figure 3-5 correspond to factor loadings in the ranges of 0.0 to .19, .20 to .39, .40 to .59, .60 to
.79, and .80 to 1.0. For those unfamiliar with factor analysis, the higher a
test's factor loading the more the test is interpreted as a stronger measure of
the ability attributed to the factor. A review of the shared ability summary
for Numbers Reversed clarifies this information.

In Figure 3-5, two different summaries are presented. The first is the
"primary common ability" which represents the broad *Gf-Gc* ability that is
primarily measured by Numbers Reversed (i.e., *Gsm* or Short-Term Memory).
The "secondary common ability" section reflects the degree to which Numbers Reversed also measures a second *Gf-Gc* ability (i.e., *Gf* or Fluid Reasoning). For the first age group (ages 5 to 8 years), the vertical shading is greater
for *Gf* than for *Gsm*. Numbers Reversed's *Gf* factor loading for this age
group is within the .40 to .59 range (.521), while its loading on the *Gsm*
factor is appreciably lower (.167). The summary in Figure 3-5 visually por-

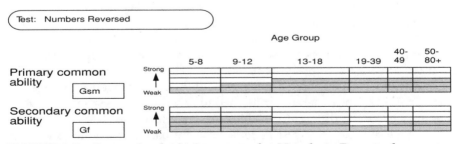

FIGURE 3-5   Factor Analysis Summary for Numbers Reversed

trays the finding that Numbers Reversed is a test that measures two *Gf-Gc* abilities, with a greater emphasis on fluid reasoning *(Gf)* up to age 12 and a greater emphasis on short-term memory *(Gsm)* after age 12.

The shared ability summary in Figure 3-5 easily communicates the major *Gf-Gc* abilities measured by Numbers Reversed across the six age groups. Clinicians can consult the shared ability summaries for each WJTCA-R test to quickly determine the *Gf-Gc* abilities measured by each test, the degree to which a test measures a common ability (reflected in the amount of vertical shading), and the extent to which these test characteristics vary as a function of age.

The following test analysis summaries are organized into three sections that correspond to the three WJTCA-R test strands that are summarized in Table 3-1 (i.e., Standard tests 1–7 and Supplemental tests 8–14 and 15–21).

TEST-BY-TEST ANALYSES AND SUMMARIES: STANDARD BATTERY

A number of sources provided information for the following individual test analyses and summaries. Each test's task requirements are drawn from the WJTCA-R's examiner's manual (Woodcock & Mather, 1989). Information regarding each test's reliability and abilities shared with other tests was drawn from the WJ-R technical manual (McGrew et al., 1991). The test characteristics of general factor loadings and uniqueness were drawn from McGrew and Murphy's (1993) analysis of the WJTCA-R norm data.

The most critical information for interpreting each test is presented in the shared ability (i.e., primary and secondary common ability) section of each test's empirical analysis graphic summary. This information indicates which of the *Gf-Gc* factor-based abilities a test measures. (Definitions of these abilities are presented in Chapter 2.) Since this information is empirically based (McGrew et al., 1991; Woodcock, 1990) and accounts for the majority of the variance of a test's score, *these abilities are those that should be considered primary in the interpretation of each WJTCA-R test.* However, as reflected in the uniqueness information, each individual test also measures unique abilities not accounted for by the broader *Gf-Gc* factors. These are referred to as the *hypothesized unique abilities.*

The hypothesized unique ability analyses for each individual test is not yet supported by empirical research. Clinicians must only use this information tentatively for hypothesis formation. The unique abilities listed for each test are based on clinical analyses by this author, as well as analyses by Mather (1991). The different terms used to describe each test's unique abilities, as well as the different variables that may influence test performance (i.e., *Variables Influencing Test Performance*), are based on common vocabulary that has evolved in the intelligence test and factor analytic literature

TABLE 3-1   Organization of WJTCA-R Cognitive Tests

Cognitive Factor	Standard Battery	Supplemental Battery	
Long-Term Memory *(Glr)*	1. Memory for Names (ED)	8. Visual-Auditory Learning	15. Delayed Recall-Memory for Names 16. Delayed Recall-Visual-Auditory Learning
Short-Term Memory *(Gsm)*	2. Memory for Sentences (ED)	9. Memory for Words	17. Numbers Reversed
Processing Speed *(Gs)*	3. Visual Matching	10. Cross Out	
Auditory Processing *(Ga)*	4. Incomplete Words (ED)	11. Sound Blending	18. Sound Patterns
Visual Processing *(Gv)*	5. Visual Closure (ED)	12. Picture Recognition	19. Spatial Relations
Comprehension Knowledge *(Gc)*	6. Picture Vocabulary (ED)	13. Oral Vocabulary	20. Listening Comprehension *(21. Verbal Analogies)*
Fluid Reasoning *(Gf)*	7. Analysis-Synthesis	14. Concept Formation	*(19. Spatial Relations)* 21. Verbal Analogies

ED = suitable for use as an early development measure.

(Horn, 1988, 1991; Kaufman, 1979, 1990; Sattler, 1988). These terms are used since they are common to many clinicians.

The following test-by-test summaries should be viewed as the foundational information upon which clinicians can build with experience. Exhaustive task analyses of each individual test, as well as the potential instructional implications based on each test's performance, are not presented. The works of Mather (1991) and Mather and Jaffe (1992) should be consulted for such information. Additional information regarding the relationship between the individual WJTCA-R tests and the individual tests in other intelligence batteries (e.g., Wechsler subtests) is presented in Chapter 4. After each test name is an abbreviation for that test that will be used in certain summary figures.

Test 1: Memory for Names (MN)

Task Requirements
Memory for Names measures the ability to learn associations between unfamiliar auditory and visual stimuli (an auditory-visual association task). At each step in the test, the subject is shown a picture of a space creature and told the creature's name. Then the subject is shown a page of nine space

creatures and is asked to point to the creature just introduced and to other previously introduced space creatures as named by the examiner. The subject's errors are corrected in this controlled-learning task. The level of difficulty increases as more "creature-name" associations are introduced (Woodcock & Mather, 1989, p. 20).

Empirical Characteristics

The empirical analysis summary for Memory for Names is presented in Figure 3-6. This test has adequate reliability for interpretation, especially at age 7 and beyond. Memory for Names is a medium measure of the general factor and a strong measure of long-term retrieval *(Glr)* at all age levels. Individual interpretation of this test can be completed with confidence given its high test uniqueness classification at all ages. Memory for Names is characterized by relatively consistent empirical characteristics across the entire range of the test.

Gf-Gc *ability*
- Long-Term Retrieval *(Glr)*

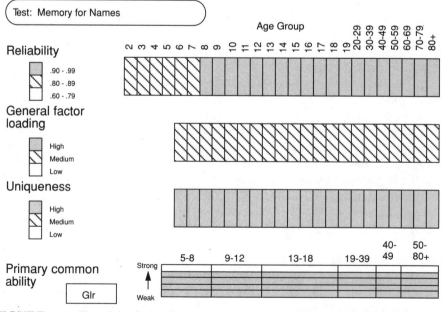

FIGURE 3-6 Empirical Analysis Summary for Memory for Names

Hypothesized Unique Abilities
- Associative memory
- Auditory-visual associational learning/memory
- Paired-associative learning/memory
- Integrated visual-auditory processing
- Short-term visual memory
- Recognition memory

Variables Influencing Test Performance
- Concentration
- Cognitive response style (reflective/impulsive)
- Ability to use feedback to modify performance
- Cognitive strategies (mnemonics; elaboration)
- Frustration tolerance (response to corrective feedback)

Test 2: Memory for Sentences (MS)

Task Requirements

Memory for Sentences measures the ability to remember and repeat single words, phrases, and sentences presented auditorily by use of a tape player or, in special cases, by an examiner. In this task, the subject makes use of sentence meaning to aid recall. (Woodcock & Mather, 1989, p. 20)

Empirical Characteristics

The empirical analysis summary for Memory for Sentences is presented in Figure 3-7. This test has adequate reliability at all ages and is most reliable at the extreme age ranges (i.e., 5 years and younger; 60 years and above). Memory for Sentences is consistently a medium measure of the general factor at all ages. Individual interpretation of this test is possible at all age levels due to consistently high uniqueness classifications. Memory for Sentences is one of a handful of WJTCA-R tests that measures two *Gf-Gc* abilities. This test measures both short-term memory *(Gsm)* and comprehension-knowledge *(Gc)*, with a tendency toward being more of a measure of short-term memory at early adolescence and beyond (beyond age 12).

Gf-Gc *abilities*
- Short-Term Memory *(Gsm)*
- Comprehension-Knowledge *(Gc)*

Hypothesized Unique Abilities

- Short-term auditory memory
- Meaningful memory

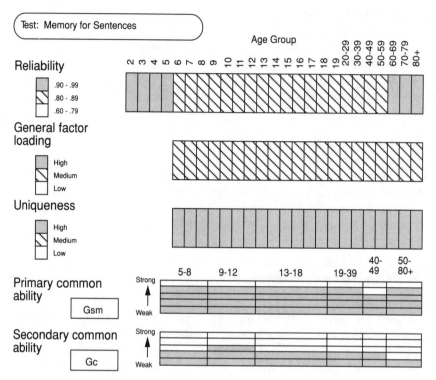

FIGURE 3-7   Empirical Analysis Summary for Memory for Sentences

- Recall memory
- Span memory
- Semantic memory
- Listening comprehension
- Receptive/expressive language
- Successive/sequential processing
- Verbal knowledge and comprehension

Variables Influencing Test Performance
- Attention span/distractibility
- Concentration
- Cognitive strategies (rehearsal; visualization; use of contextual cues/clues)
- Anxiety
- Ability to passively receive stimuli
- Hearing acuity

Test 3: Visual Matching (VM)

Task Requirements

Visual Matching measures the ability to locate and circle the two identical numbers in a row of six numbers. The task proceeds in difficulty from single-digit numbers to triple-digit numbers and has a 3-minute time limit. (Woodcock & Mather, 1989, p. 20).

Empirical Characteristics

The empirical analysis summary for Visual Matching is presented in Figure 3-8. On first inspection the reliability of Visual Matching appears poorer than most of the other WJTCA-R tests. However, the reliability of this timed test is calculated differently than that for all other WJTCA-R tests (except for the other timed test, Cross Out). Instead of reliability being calculated by the internal consistency method, this timed test must have its reliability computed via the test-retest method.

Test-retest correlations typically produce lower estimates than the internal consistency method, as instability in the underlying trait, rather than the precision of the test, may change between the two testings (Thorndike, 1982). A test-retest correlation is usually considered as the lower-bound estimate of the theoretical reliability coefficient (Crocker & Algina, 1986). Thus,

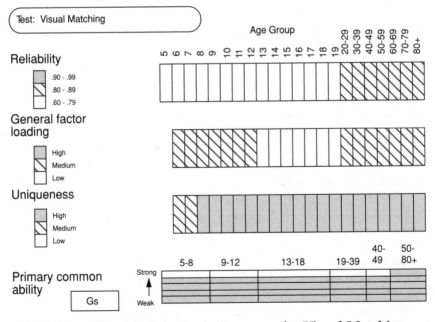

FIGURE 3-8   Empirical Analysis Summary for Visual Matching

it is inappropriate to compare the reliability of Visual Matching to that of all other WJTCA-R tests except Cross Out.

Visual Matching is a medium measure of the general factor at the youngest (i.e., 6 to 12 years) and oldest (i.e., 20 years and above) age levels and a low measure of the general factor for the intervening years. This test is a very strong measure of processing speed *(Gs)* across all ages. If examiners find that an alternative interpretation to processing speed is required for a specific case, the test has the necessary uniqueness (i.e., high) at all ages except age 5 and 6 years.

Gf-Gc *ability*
   • Processing Speed *(Gs)*

Hypothesized Unique Abilities
   • Perceptual speed
   • Visual scanning
   • Visual-perceptual fluency
   • Rapid visual discrimination
   • Visual pattern recognition
   • Clerical speed and accuracy
   • Paper-and-pencil skill
   • Psychomotor speed
   • Perception of abstract stimuli
   • Numerical ability/fluency
   • Symbolic processing

Variables Influencing Test Performance
   • Attention span/distractibility
   • Concentration
   • Cognitive response style (reflective/impulsive; field dependence/independence)
   • Efficiency/automaticity of problem-solving strategies
   • Ability to perform under time pressure
   • Anxiety
   • Perfectionistic tendencies
   • Visual-motor coordination

Test 4: Incomplete Words (IW)

Task Requirements

Incomplete Words is a tape-recorded test that measures auditory closure. After hearing a recorded word that has one or more phonemes missing, the subject identifies the complete word (Woodcock & Mather, 1989, p. 21).

Empirical Characteristics
The empirical analysis summary for Incomplete Words is presented in Figure 3-9. A review of Figure 3-9 reveals that this test's reliability varies as a function of age. The test demonstrates adequate reliability at the extreme age levels (5 years and below; 30 years and above). More cautious interpretation due to lower reliability is required from ages 6 through 29. A similar pattern is evident in Incomplete Words' general factor loading classifications, which vary from high at ages 9 and below and 17 and above to medium during the intervening years.

Despite relatively low reliability characteristics, Incomplete Words has sufficient uniqueness at all ages to allow for individual interpretation. Incomplete Words is primarily a measure of auditory processing *(Ga)* at all ages, with a slight trend towards stronger *Ga* characteristics at 40 years and beyond.

Gf-Gc ability
- Auditory Processing *(Ga)*

Hypothesized Unique Abilities
- Auditory/verbal closure
- Auditory analysis and synthesis
- Auditory/sound discrimination
- Memory for sound patterns
- Perception of distorted speech
- Short-term auditory memory
- Recall memory
- Successive/sequential processing
- Word knowledge/vocabulary

Variables Influencing Test Performance
- Educational experiences/instruction (reading approaches emphasizing sound analysis and synthesis)
- Attention span/distractibility
- Concentration
- Cognitive strategies (rehearsal; visualization)
- Anxiety
- Ability to passively receive stimuli
- Hearing acuity
- History of chronic ear infections

Test 5: Visual Closure (VC)

Task Requirements
Visual Closure is designed to measure the ability to identify a drawing or picture that is altered in one of several ways. The picture may be

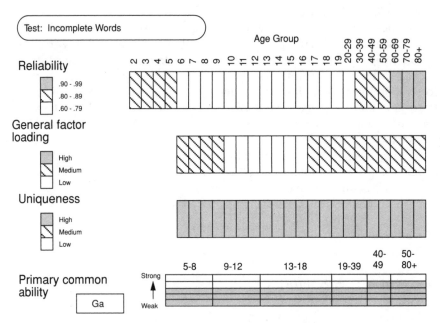

FIGURE 3-9   Empirical Analysis Summary for Incomplete Words

distorted, having missing lines or areas, or have a superimposed pattern. (Woodcock & Mather, 1989, p. 21).

Empirical Characteristics
The empirical analysis summary for Visual Closure is presented in Figure 3-10. Visual Closure is similar to Incomplete Words in its relatively low reliability and general factor loading characteristics. This test has adequate reliability only at the extreme ages (i.e., 4 years and below; 50 years and above). Visual Closure is a low measure of the general factor except at 40 years and above where it is classified as a medium measure. Visual Closure has high uniqueness characteristics at all ages except 70 years and above where it is classified as medium. In terms of the *Gf-Gc* theory of intelligence, Visual Closure is a consistent measure of visual processing *(Gv)* across all ages.

Gf-Gc *ability*
- Visual Processing *(Gv)*

Hypothesized Unique Abilities
- Visual closure
- Gestalt closure
- Visual recognition

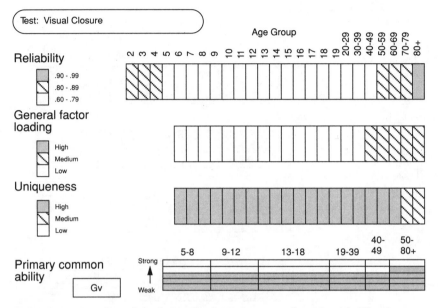

FIGURE 3-10   Empirical Analysis Summary for Visual Closure

- Visual scanning
- Visual analysis and synthesis
- Visualization/visual imagery
- Perceptual organization (visual)
- Simultaneous processing

Variables Influencing Test Performance
- Cognitive style (field dependence/independence)
- Experiences/interests in the visual/graphic arts

Test 6: Picture Vocabulary (PV)

Task Requirements

   Picture Vocabulary measures the ability to recognize or to name familiar and unfamiliar pictured objects. Six of the beginning items are in a
   multiple-choice format that only requires a pointing response from the
   subject (Woodcock & Mather, 1989, p. 21)

Empirical Characteristics

Picture Vocabulary's empirical analysis summary is presented in Figure
3-11. The reliability for Picture Vocabulary is adequate for individual inter-

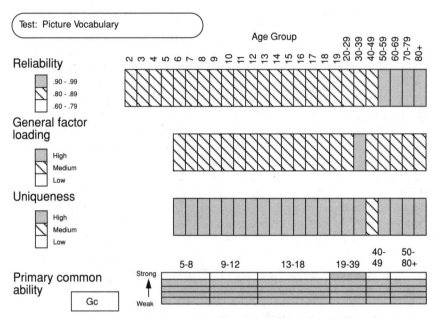

FIGURE 3-11   Empirical Analysis Summary for Picture Vocabulary

pretation as it is consistently above .80. With one exception at ages thirty to thirty-nine, this test is a medium measure of the general factor. Individual interpretation of Picture Vocabulary is acceptable as evidenced by all but one high uniqueness classification. Picture Vocabulary is consistently a strong measure of the comprehension-knowledge *(Gc)* ability in the *Gf-Gc* model of intelligence.

Gf-Gc *ability*
• Comprehension-Knowledge *(Gc)*

Hypothesized Unique Abilities
• Word knowledge/vocabulary
• Verbal knowledge and comprehension
• Fund of information/knowledge
• Verbal retrieval/word finding ability
• Recall memory
• Expressive language
• Long-term memory
• Visual recognition

Variables Influencing Test Performance
• Cultural opportunities
• Extent of outside reading

- Language stimulation
- Environmental stimulation
- Orientation/alertness to the environment
- Educational experiences/instruction
- Interests
- Intellectual curiosity and striving

Test 7: Analysis-Synthesis (AS)

Task Requirements
Analysis-Synthesis is designed to measure the ability to analyze the presented components of an incomplete logic puzzle and to determine the missing components. This is a controlled-learning task in which the subject is given instructions on how to perform an increasingly complex procedure. In addition, the subject is given feedback regarding the correctness of his or her response. The task involves learning a miniature system of mathematics—although this is not pointed out to the subject. (Woodcock & Mather, 1989, p. 21)

Empirical Characteristics
The empirical characteristics of Analysis-Synthesis are summarized in Figure 3-12. This test has adequate reliability at all age levels. Analysis-Synthesis displays a tendency to be most reliable at the extreme age levels (i.e., 9 years and below; 30 years and above). Analysis-Synthesis is a medium measure of the general factor from ages 6 to 49, after which it is a high measure of the general factor. Although interpretation of Analysis-Synthesis as a measure of fluid reasoning *(Gf)* at all age levels is the most appropriate interpretation of this test, all but one high uniqueness classification indicates that interpretation of unique abilities is appropriate when necessary.

Gf-Gc *Ability*
- Fluid Reasoning *(Gf)*

Hypothesized Unique Abilities
- Cognition of symbolic relations
- Deductive thinking
- Logical thinking
- Quantitative logic
- Rule-learning ability
- Conceptual thinking
- Abstract and concrete reasoning
- Learning ability (nonmeaningful material)
- Nonverbal reasoning

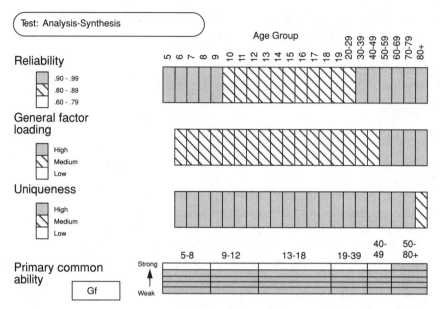

FIGURE 3-12   Empirical Analysis Summary for Analysis-Synthesis

Variables Influencing Test Performance
- Concentration
- Cognitive response style (reflective/impulsive)
- Cognitive flexibility
- Ability to use feedback to modify performance
- Cognitive strategies (problem-solving strategies)
- Frustration tolerance (response to corrective feedback)

TEST-BY-TEST ANALYSES AND SUMMARIES: SUPPLEMENTAL BATTERY (TESTS 8–14)

Test 8: Visual-Auditory Learning (VAL)

Task Requirements

Visual-Auditory Learning measures the ability to associate new visual symbols (rebuses) with familiar words in oral language and to translate a series of symbols into verbal sentences (a visual-auditory association task). The test presents a controlled-learning situation. The subject's errors are always corrected and the situation simulates a learning-to-read task. (Woodcock & Mather, 1989, p. 21)

Empirical Characteristics

Visual-Auditory Learning's empirical analysis summary is presented in Figure 3-13. This test has adequate reliability for interpretation across all ages,

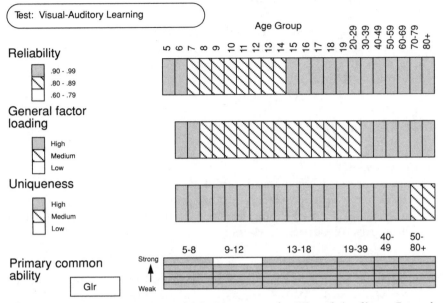

FIGURE 3-13   Empirical Analysis Summary for Visual-Auditory Learning

with consistently the highest levels of reliability from ages 15 and beyond. Visual-Auditory Learning is a high measure of the general factor at ages 7 and below and 30 and above, with medium classifications for the intervening ages. The very consistent and strong long-term retrieval *(Glr)* factor loadings indicate that this is the most appropriate interpretation for performance on this test across all ages. However, if interpretation of unique abilities is deemed appropriate, Visual-Auditory Learning possesses the necessary uniqueness at all age levels, especially before 60 years of age.

Gf-Gc *Ability*
  • Long-Term Retrieval *(Glr)*

Hypothesized Unique Abilities
  • Associative memory
  • Symbolic transformation
  • Visual-auditory associational learning/memory
  • Paired-associative learning/memory
  • Integrated visual-auditory processing
  • Short-term visual memory
  • Recall memory
  • Learning ability (meaningful material)
  • Perception of abstract stimuli

Variables Influencing Test Performance
- Concentration
- Cognitive response style (reflective/impulsive)
- Ability to use feedback to modify performance
- Cognitive strategies (mnemonics; elaboration)
- Frustration tolerance

Test 9: Memory for Words (MW)

Task Requirements
Memory for Words measures the ability to repeat lists of unrelated words in the correct sequence. The words are presented by means of an audio tape. The difficulty of the items proceeds from single words to lists of eight words (Woodcock & Mather, 1989, p. 22)

Empirical Characteristics
The empirical analysis summary for Memory for Words is presented in Figure 3-14. Memory for Words possesses adequate levels of reliability for individual interpretation at ages 8 and below and 40 and beyond. Memory for Words is a medium measure of the general factor at all ages except 20 through 49 where it is low. The most consistent empirical characteristics of Memory for Words are it's uniqueness and *Gf-Gc* factor loadings. Memory for Words demonstrates the highest level of uniqueness classification (high) at all ages. This test also demonstrates very strong and consistent loadings on the short-term memory *(Gsm)* factor at all ages.

Gf-Gc *Ability*
- Short-Term Memory *(Gsm)*

Hypothesized Unique Abilities
- Short-term auditory memory
- Auditory sequential memory
- Word span
- Semantic memory
- Recall memory
- Successive/sequential processing

Variables Influencing Test Performance
- Attention span/distractibility
- Concentration
- Cognitive strategies (rehearsal; visualization)
- Anxiety
- Ability to passively receive stimuli
- Hearing acuity

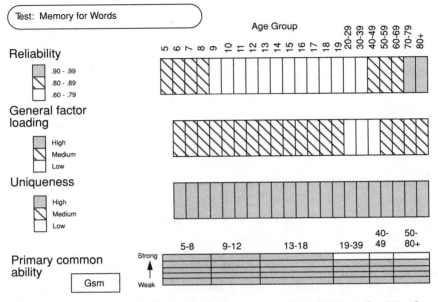

FIGURE 3-14   Empirical Analysis Summary for Memory for Words

Test 10: Cross Out (CO)

Task Requirements

Cross Out measures the ability to scan and compare visual information quickly. The subject must mark the five drawings in a row of 20 drawings that are identical to the first drawing in the row. The subject is given a 3-minute time limit to complete as many rows of items as possible. (Woodcock & Mather, 1989, p. 22)

Empirical Characteristics

The empirical analysis summary for Cross Out is presented in Figure 3-15. Since Cross Out is the other WJTCA-R speeded test (the other being Visual Matching), the comments made previously about the test-retest nature of the Visual Matching's reliability are also appropriate for Cross Out. The Cross Out and Visual Matching test-retest reliability estimates will be lower than those reported for the other WJTCA-R tests that are computed via the internal consistency method. It is inappropriate to compare the reliability of Cross Out to that of the other WJTCA-R tests, except Visual Matching.

Cross out is consistently a medium measure of the general factor and a very strong measure of processing speed *(Gs)* at all ages. When considering interpretation of this test as measuring other than processing speed *(Gs)*,

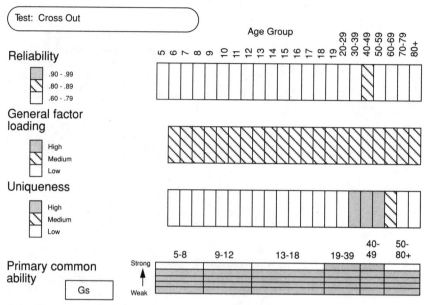

FIGURE 3-15   Empirical Analysis Summary for Cross Out

clinicians need to be cognizant of the changing uniqueness classification of Cross Out, which are low up through age 29 and 70 and above, and medium or high for ages 30 through 69.

Gf-Gc *Ability*
- Processing Speed *(Gs)*

Hypothesized Unique Abilities
- Perceptual speed
- Visual scanning
- Visual-perceptual fluency
- Rapid visual discrimination
- Visual pattern recognition
- Clerical speed and accuracy
- Paper-and-pencil skill
- Psychomotor speed
- Perception of abstract stimuli

Variables Influencing Test Performance
- Attention span/distractibility
- Concentration
- Cognitive response style (reflective/impulsive; field dependence/independence)

- Efficiency/automaticity of problem-solving strategies
- Ability to perform under time pressure
- Anxiety
- Perfectionistic tendencies
- Visual-motor coordination

Test 11: Sound Blending (SB)

Task Requirements

Sound Blending measures the ability to integrate and then say whole words after hearing parts (syllables and/or phonemes) of the words. An audio tape is used to present word parts in their proper order for each item. (Woodcock & Mather, 1989, p. 22)

Empirical Characteristics

The empirical analysis summary for Sound Blending is presented in Figure 3-16. A review of Figure 3-26 reveals that Sound Blending has adequate reliability for interpretation at all age levels. It displays its highest level of reliability at the extreme age levels (i.e., 6 years and below; 50 years and above). Sound Blending is a medium measure of the general factor across all ages. This test is best interpreted as a strong and consistent measure of

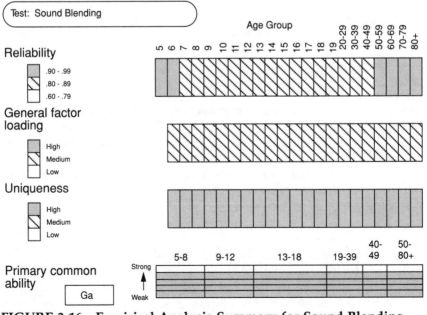

FIGURE 3-16 Empirical Analysis Summary for Sound Blending

auditory processing *(Ga)* at all age levels. When alternative interpretations are suggested, Sound Blending displays the necessary high uniqueness at all age levels.

Gf-Gc *Ability*
- Auditory Processing *(Ga)*

Hypothesized Unique Abilities
- Sound blending
- Auditory synthesis
- Auditory/sound discrimination
- Memory for sound patterns
- Short-term auditory memory
- Recall memory
- Successive/sequential processing
- Word knowledge/vocabulary

Variables Influencing Test Performance
- Educational experiences/instruction (reading approaches emphasizing sound analysis and synthesis)
- Attention span/distractibility
- Concentration
- Cognitive strategies (rehearsal; visualization)
- Anxiety
- Ability to passively receive stimuli
- Hearing acuity
- History of chronic ear infections

Test 12: Picture Recognition (PR)

Task Requirements
Picture Recognition measures the ability to recognize a subset of previously presented pictures within a field of distracting pictures. In order to eliminate verbal mediation as a memory strategy, varieties of the same type of object (several different bowls or several different windows) are used as the stimuli and distractors for each item. The difficulty of the items increases as the number of pictures in the stimulus set increases. (Woodcock & Mather, 1989, p. 22)

Empirical Characteristics
The empirical analysis summary for Picture Recognition is presented in Figure 3-17. Picture Recognition displays adequate reliability from ages 15 and above. More cautious interpretation is appropriate below age 15. Picture Recognition is consistently a medium measure of the general factor. This test is best interpreted as a relatively strong and consistent measure of

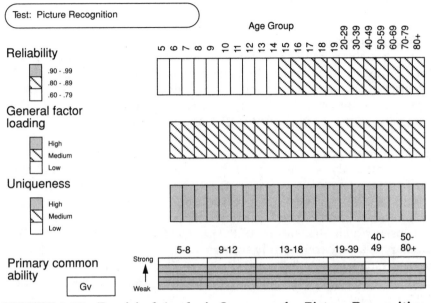

FIGURE 3-17   Empirical Analysis Summary for Picture Recognition

visual processing *(Gv)* at all age levels. When alternative interpretations are suggested, Picture Recognition displays the necessary high uniqueness at all age levels.

Gf-Gc *Ability*
- Visual Processing *(Gv)*

Hypothesized Unique Abilities
- Short-term visual memory
- Visual recognition
- Recognition memory
- Perceptual organization (visual)
- Visual analysis
- Simultaneous processing

Variables Influencing Test Performance
- Concentration
- Cognitive style (reflective/impulsive)
- Efficiency/automaticity of problem-solving strategies
- Cognitive strategies (mnemonics)

Test 13: *Oral Vocabulary (OV)*

Task Requirements

Oral Vocabulary measures knowledge of word meanings. The stimulus words are presented orally by the examiner. In Part A: Synonyms, the subject must state a word similar in meaning to the word presented. In Part B: Antonyms, the subject must state a word that is opposite in meaning to the word presented. (Woodcock & Mather, 1989, p. 22)

Empirical Characteristics

The empirical analysis summary for Oral Vocabulary is presented in Figure 3-18. This test demonstrates adequate reliability for individual interpretation, with a trend toward the highest reliability classification level (.90 or above) at age 15 and beyond. Oral Vocabulary is one of the WJTCA-R's most consistently high measures of the general factor at all age levels. Oral Vocabulary is a very consistently strong measure of comprehension-knowledge or crystallized intelligence *(Gc)* across all ages. With only two high exceptions from ages 50 to 69, this test is medium in uniqueness classification across all ages.

Gf-Gc *Ability*

- Comprehension-Knowledge *(Gc)*

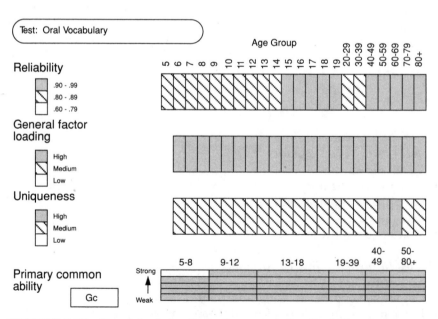

FIGURE 3-18   Empirical Analysis Summary for Oral Vocabulary

Hypothesized Unique Abilities
- Evaluation of semantic relations
- Word knowledge/vocabulary
- Verbal reasoning
- Verbal knowledge and comprehension
- Fund of information/knowledge
- Verbal retrieval/word finding ability
- Receptive/expressive language
- Long-term memory

Variables Influencing Test Performance
- Cultural opportunities
- Extent of outside reading
- Language stimulation
- Environmental stimulation
- Orientation/alertness to the environment
- Educational experiences/instruction
- Interests
- Intellectual curiosity and striving
- Cognitive flexibility (shift between Part A and B; response set)

Test 14: Concept-Formation (CF)

Task Requirements
Concept Formation measures the ability to identify the rules for concepts when shown illustrations of both instances of the concept and non-instances of the concept. This controlled-learning task involves categorical reasoning based on principles of formal logic. Unlike some concept formation tasks that require a subject to remember what has happened over a series of items, this test does not include a memory component. The subject is presented with a complete stimulus set from which to derive the rule for each item. The subject is given feedback regarding the correctness of each response. (Woodcock & Mather, 1989, p. 22)

Empirical Characteristics
The empirical characteristics of Concept Formation are summarized in Figure 3-19. With the exception of the general factor loading classifications, Concept Formation displays consistently high empirical test classifications across all ages levels. Concept Formation displays the highest level of reliability classification at all age levels, is high in necessary uniqueness for individual interpretation at all but the two oldest age levels (medium), and is consistently a strong measure of fluid reasoning *(Gf)* at all ages. This test is primarily a medium measure of the general factor up through age 29, and then shifts to being a high measure of the general factor from age 30 and above.

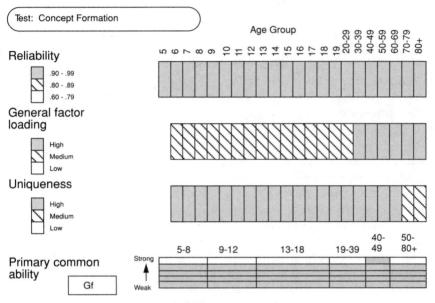

FIGURE 3-19   Empirical Analysis Summary for Concept Formation

Gf-Gc *Ability*
- Fluid Reasoning *(Gf)*

Hypothesized Unique Abilities
- Concept formation
- Conceptual thinking
- Cognition of figural relations
- Logical thinking
- Deductive thinking
- Rule-learning ability
- Abstract and concrete reasoning
- Learning ability (nonmeaningful material)
- Nonverbal reasoning

Variables Influencing Test Performance
- Concentration
- Cognitive response style (reflective/impulsive)
- Cognitive flexibility (shifting between different concept rules)
- Ability to use feedback to modify performance
- Cognitive strategies (problem-solving strategies)
- Frustration tolerance

TEST-BY-TEST ANALYSES AND SUMMARIES: SUPPLEMENTAL BATTERY (TESTS 15–21)

Test 15: Delayed Recall-Memory for Names (DRMN)

Task Requirements

Delayed Recall-Memory for Names measures the ability to recall (after 1 to 8 days) the space creatures presented in Test 1: Memory for Names. The subject is not told that subsequent testing will occur. (Woodcock & Mather, 1989, p. 23)

Empirical Characteristics

Only the reliability for Delayed Recall-Memory for Names is presented in Figure 3-20. The absence of other empirical analysis information is due to the relatively small number of individuals in the WJTCA-R norming sample who took this test (McGrew et al., 1991). Insufficient numbers of norming subjects precluded the inclusion of this test in the various age-related analysis reported by McGrew et al. (1991) and McGrew and Murphy (1993) that served as the basis for the test empirical summaries. In the factor analyses that included this test, Delayed Recall-Memory for Names was found to be a strong measure of long-term retrieval *(Glr)*.

A review of Figure 3-20 finds that Delayed Recall-Memory for Names has adequate reliability for all ages for which this information is available. This test's reliability is most consistently strong at ages thirteen and beyond.

Gf-Gc *Ability*

- Long-Term Retrieval *(Glr)*

Hypothesized Unique Abilities

- Associative memory
- Auditory-visual associational learning/memory

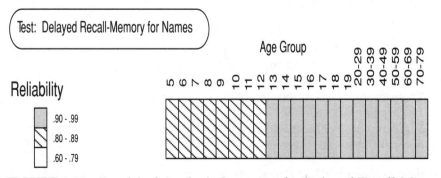

FIGURE 3-20   Empirical Analysis Summary for Delayed Recall-Memory for Names

- Paired-associative learning/memory
- Cross-modal association/integration
- Recognition memory
- Name recognition
- Learning ability (nonmeaningful material)

Variables Influencing Test Performance
- Cognitive response style (reflective/impulsive)
- Cognitive strategies (mnemonics)

Test 16: *Delayed Recall-Visual-Auditory Learning (DRVAL)*

Task Requirements
Delayed Recall-Visual-Auditory Learning measures the ability to recall (after 1 to 8 days) the symbols (rebuses) presented in Test 8: Visual-Auditory Learning. The subject is not told that subsequent testing will occur. (Woodcock & Mather, 1989, p. 23)

Empirical Characteristics
The empirical characteristics of Delayed Recall-Visual-Auditory Learning are summarized in Figure 3-21. Similar to Delayed Recall-Memory for Names, only reliability information was available for the construction of this test's empirical analysis summary. A review of Figure 3-21 finds that Delayed Recall-Visual-Auditory Learning has adequate reliability for all ages for which this information is available. This test displays its highest level of reliability classifications between 10 years of age and late adulthood. In the factor analyses that included this test, Delayed Recall-Memory for Names was found to be a moderately strong measure of long-term retrieval *(Glr)*.

Gf-Gc *Ability*
- Long-Term Retrieval *(Glr)*

Hypothesized Unique Abilities
- Associative memory
- Visual-auditory associational learning/memory
- Paired-associative learning/memory
- Cross-modal association/integration
- Recall memory
- Learning ability (meaningful material)
- Perception of abstract stimuli

Variables Influencing Test Performance
- Cognitive response style (reflective/impulsive)
- Cognitive strategies (mnemonics)

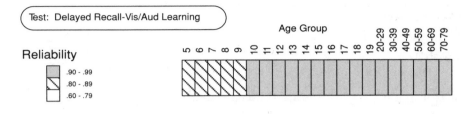

FIGURE 3-21 Empirical Analysis Summary for Delayed Recall-Visual/Auditory Learning

Test 17: Numbers Reversed (NR)

Task Requirements

Numbers Reversed measures the ability to say a series of random numbers backwards. After hearing the items from the audio tape, the subject must say the numbers in the opposite order. The subject must hold each sequence of numbers in memory while reorganizing that sequence. Item difficulty increases as more numbers are added to the sentences. (Woodcock & Mather, 1989, p. 23)

Empirical Characteristics

The empirical analysis summary for Numbers Reversed is presented in Figure 3-22. This test demonstrates adequate reliability for interpretation across all ages. Numbers Reversed's general factor and uniqueness characteristics are extremely stable as evidenced by medium general factor loadings and high uniqueness characteristics for all age levels. When necessary, individual interpretation of Numbers Reversed is appropriate. However, the *Gf-Gc* interpretation of Numbers Reversed is complex. This test appears to measure both short-term memory *(Gsm)* and fluid reasoning *(Gf)*, but at different degrees as a function of age. Numbers Reversed appears to be a relatively stronger measure of fluid reasoning from age 5 through 12, and a relatively stronger measure of short-term memory after age 12.

Gf-Gc *Abilities*
- Short-Term Memory *(Gsm)*
- Fluid Reasoning *(Gf)*

Hypothesized Unique Abilities
- Short-term auditory memory
- Auditory sequential memory
- Span Memory

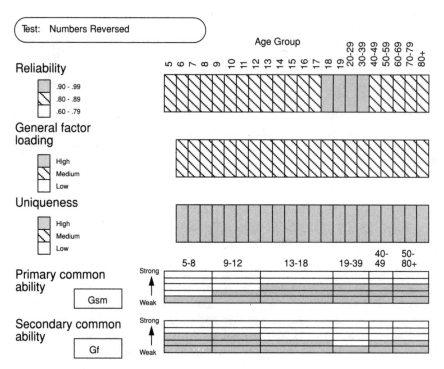

FIGURE 3-22   Empirical Analysis Summary for Numbers Reversed

- Perceptual reorganization
- Successive/sequential processing
- Visualization/visual imagery
- Numerical ability/fluency

Variables Influencing Test Performance
- Attention span/distractibility
- Concentration
- Cognitive strategies (rehearsal; visualization)
- Anxiety
- Ability to passively receive stimuli
- Hearing acuity

Test 18: Sound Patterns (SP)

Task Requirements

Sound Patterns measures the ability to indicate whether pairs of complex sound patterns are the same or different. The patterns may differ in pitch, rhythm, or sound content. Because of the nature of the items, an audio tape must be used when the test is given. (Woodcock & Mather, 1989, p. 23)

Empirical Characteristics

The empirical analysis summary for Sound Patterns is presented in Figure 3-23. Sound Patterns' reliability is adequate for individual interpretation, with high levels of reliability (.90 or above) occurring primarily at the most extreme age groups. This test is primarily a medium general factor measure with the exception of low classifications below age 10. Sound Patterns is the most unique test in the WJTCA-R battery. Inspection of the factor loading summaries (Figure 3-23) indicates that this test loads at low to moderate levels on both the auditory processing *(Ga)* and fluid reasoning *(Gf)* factors. The relatively low factor loadings, coupled with consistently high uniqueness classifications at all ages, indicates that Sound Patterns has considerable unique variance that is not shared with the other WJTCA-R tests.

Gf-Gc Abilities
- Auditory Processing *(Ga)*
- Fluid Reasoning *(Gf)*

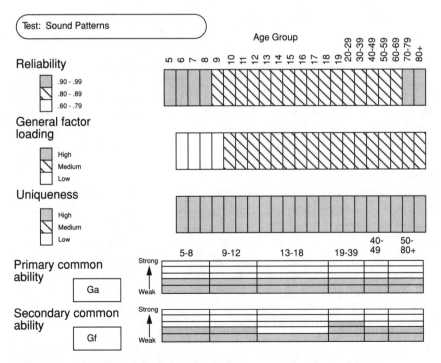

FIGURE 3-23 Empirical Analysis Summary for Sound Patterns

Hypothesized Unique Abilities
* Sound pattern recognition
* Auditory analysis
* Auditory/sound discrimination
* Memory for sound patterns
* Short-term auditory memory
* Recall memory
* Successive/sequential processing

Variables Influencing Test Performance
* Hearing acuity
* History of chronic ear infections
* Attention span/distractibility
* Concentration
* Vigilance
* Frustration tolerance
* Anxiety
* Ability to passively receive stimuli

Test 19: Spatial Relations (SR)

Task Requirements
Spatial Relations measures the ability to match shapes visually. The subject must select, from a series of shapes, the component parts needed to make a given whole shape. Item difficulty increases as the shapes become progressively more abstract and complex. (Woodcock & Mather, 1989, p. 23)

Empirical Characteristics
The empirical analysis summary for Spatial Relations is presented in Figure 3-24. Spatial Relations demonstrates adequate reliability for individual interpretation at ages 12 and above. Cautious individual interpretation is suggested below age 12. Spatial Relations is consistently a medium measure of the general factor at all ages. Individual interpretation of Spatial Relations is also appropriate, as evidenced by high uniqueness for all but the two oldest age groups. Spatial Relations is a complex test as evidenced by its relationship to fluid reasoning *(Gf)* and visual processing *(Gv)* abilities. A review of Figure 3-24 indicates that Spatial Relations is a mixed measure of fluid reasoning *(Gf)* and visual processing *(Gv)* below age 13, and a relatively stronger measure of fluid reasoning *(Gf)* from age 13 through late adulthood.

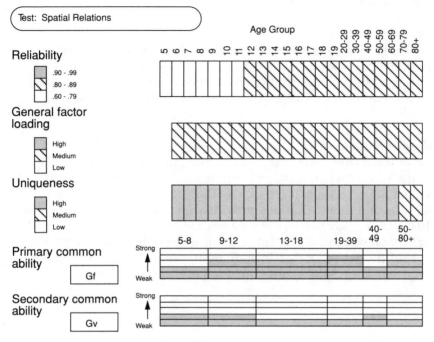

FIGURE 3-24   Empirical Analysis Summary for Spatial Relations

Gf-Gc *Abilities*
- Visual Processing *(Gv)*
- Fluid Reasoning *(Gf)*

Hypothesized Unique Abilities
- Visual-spatial ability
- Visual analysis and synthesis
- Spatial scanning
- Visualization/visual imagery
- Perceptual organization (visual)
- Nonverbal reasoning
- Abstract and concrete reasoning
- Perception of abstract stimuli
- Simultaneous processing

Variables Influencing Test Performance
- Cognitive response style (reflective/impulsive; field dependence/independence)
- Experiences/interests in the visual/graphic arts

Test 20: Listening Comprehension (LC)

Task Requirements

Listening Comprehensive measures the ability to listen to a short tape-recorded passage and supply the single word missing at the end of the passage. The subject must exercise a variety of vocabulary and comprehension skills in this oral cloze procedure. (Woodcock & Mather, 1989, p. 24)

Empirical Characteristics

The empirical analysis summary for Listening Comprehension is presented in Figure 3-25. Listening Comprehension displays adequate reliability for individual interpretation at the extreme age ranges of 9 years and below and 40 years and above. Cautious individual interpretation is necessary from age 10 through 39 given the relatively weaker reliability at these levels. Listening Comprehension appears to fluctuate between being a medium to high measure of the general factor. In addition to cautious interpretation due to relatively weaker reliability, interpretation of this test as a measure of

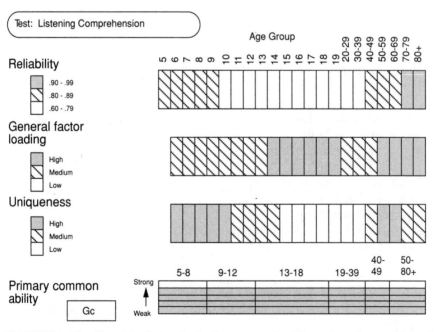

FIGURE 3-25   Empirical Analysis Summary for Listening Comprehension

unique abilities appear most appropriate from 5 to 14 years of age and 40 years and above. Listening Comprehension is consistently a strong measure of the *Gf-Gc* ability of comprehension-knowledge or crystallized intelligence *(Gc)*.

Gf-Gc *Ability*
- Comprehension-Knowledge *(Gc)*

Hypothesized *Unique Abilities*
- Listening comprehension
- Understanding of oral communication
- Verbal knowledge and comprehension
- Short-term auditory memory
- Receptive language
- Fund of information/knowledge
- Verbal reasoning

Variables *Influencing Test Performance*
- Cultural opportunities
- Extent of outside reading
- Language stimulation
- Environmental stimulation
- Orientation/alertness to the environment
- Educational experiences/instruction
- Interests
- Intellectual curiosity and striving
- Attention span/distractibility
- Concentration
- Anxiety
- Ability to passively receive stimuli

Test 21: Verbal Analogies (VA)

Task *Requirements*
Verbal Analogies measures the ability to complete phrases with words that indicate appropriate analogies. Although the vocabulary remains relatively simple, the relationships among the words become increasing complex. (Woodcock & Mather, 1989, p. 24)

Empirical *Characteristics*
The empirical analysis summary for Verbal Analogies is presented in Figure 3-26. This test demonstrates adequate reliability for individual interpretation at all ages. Verbal Analogies is one of the most consistently high measures of the general factor in the WJTCA-R, with only two medium classifications at the youngest ages of 6 and 7. This test demonstrates consistently

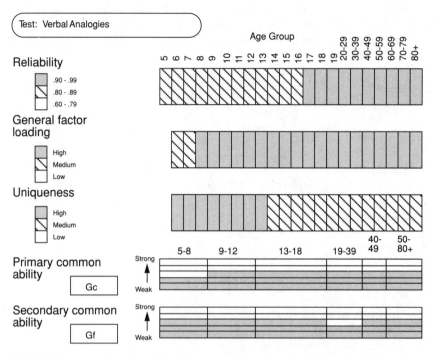

FIGURE 3-26   Empirical Analysis Summary for Verbal Analogies

high uniqueness below age 14, after which it is consistently medium in uniqueness. Verbal Analogies is a mixture measure of comprehension-knowledge or crystallized intelligence *(Gc)* and fluid reasoning *(Gf)* across all ages.

Gf-Gc *Abilities*
- Comprehension-Knowledge *(Gc)*
- Fluid Reasoning *(Gf)*

Hypothesized Unique Abilities
- Analogic reasoning
- Verbal reasoning
- Cognition of semantic relations
- Abstract and concrete reasoning
- Word knowledge/vocabulary
- Verbal knowledge and comprehension
- Fund of information/knowledge
- Verbal retrieval/word-finding ability
- Receptive and expressive language

Variables Influencing Test Performance
- Cultural opportunities
- Extent of outside reading
- Language stimulation
- Environmental stimulation
- Orientation/alertness to the environment
- Educational experiences/instruction
- Interests
- Intellectual curiosity and striving

4

THE WJTCA-R COGNITIVE CLUSTERS

The structure of the WJTCA-R is based on a comprehensive model of intelligence (i.e., the *Gf-Gc* model) that provides the foundation for Type II or intra-cognitive interpretation of the cognitive tests. Although intra-cognitive interpretation with the individual tests is possible, each of the *Gf-Gc* cognitive clusters are based on a combination of two tests. These diads provide a more reliable and valid framework than the individual tests for this type of interpretation.

TECHNICAL CONSIDERATIONS

Cluster Composition

The composition of each WJTCA-R cognitive cluster is based on the results of exploratory and confirmatory factor analyses in the standardization sample (McGrew et al., 1991). These procedures identified the two cognitive tests that when combined in equal proportions provided for the best *Gf-Gc* cognitive clusters. These 14 tests are listed in Table 4-1.

The procedures used to construct the seven WJTCA-R cognitive clusters differed from those used in the development of the 1977 WJTCA cognitive clusters. The WJTCA clusters were based on unequally weighted combinations of two to four tests. Two of the WJTCA clusters included suppressor tests (McGrew, 1986; Woodcock, 1978). The differential weighting of the tests, as well as the inclusion of suppressor tests, frequently produced results that were difficult to interpret (McGrew, 1986). Although these problems were addressed by using two alternative clusters (McGrew, 1986;

TABLE 4-1 Composition of WJTCA-R Cognitive Clusters

Cluster	Tests
Long-Term Retrieval *(Glr)*	Memory for Names
	Visual-Auditory Learning
Short-Term Memory *(Gsm)*	Memory for Sentences
	Memory for Words
Processing Speed *(Gs)*	Visual Matching
	Cross Out
Auditory Processing *(Ga)*	Incomplete Words
	Sound Blending
Visual Processing *(Gv)*	Visual Closure
	Picture Recognition
Comprehension-Knowledge *(Gc)*	Picture Vocabulary
	Oral Vocabulary
Fluid Reasoning *(Gf)*	Analysis-Synthesis
	Concept Formation

Woodcock, 1985) or special interpretative logic (Hessler, 1982), the problems in the original WJTCA cognitive clusters, as well as the lack of a comprehensive theoretical foundation for the WJTCA, resulted in the development of alternative frameworks for combining and interpreting the 12 WJTCA tests (Hessler, 1982; McGrew, 1986). The elimination of differential test weights and suppressor tests in the development of the WJTCA-R cognitive clusters has eliminated the problems that occasionally hindered intra-cognitive interpretation of the 1977 WJTCA.

Reliability

Table 4-2 summarizes the WJTCA-R cognitive cluster reliability figures reported in the technical manual (McGrew et al., 1991). The values reported for the seven clusters were computed with a formula for calculating the reliability of composite scores (Mosier, 1943). The reader is encouraged to consult the technical manual (McGrew et al., 1991) for the specific procedures used to calculate these reliability estimates.

Since the WJTCA-R cognitive clusters are to be used for generatiang strength and weakness hypotheses (i.e., Type II or intra-cognitive discrepancy analysis), the reliability criterion of .80 or above is an appropriate yardstick for evaluating these clusters. As reported in Table 4-2, the median reliability for each cluster meets this criterion. The median reliabilities range from .816 (Visual Processing) to .946 (Fluid Reasoning). The WJTCA-R cognitive clusters possess adequate reliability for generating hypotheses about

TABLE 4-2 Reliability of WJTCA-R Cognitive Clusters From Age 5 to 80+

Cluster	Range	Median
Long-Term Retrieval *(Glr)*	.92–.96	.94
Short-Term Memory *(Gsm)*	.82–.96	.89
Processing Speed *(Gs)*	.81–.96	.87
Auditory Processing *(Ga)*	.77–.97	.89
Visual Processing *(Gv)*	.73–.94	.82
Comprehension-Knowledge *(Gc)*	.89–.98	.94
Fluid Reasoning *(Gf)*	.92–.97	.95

Reliability coefficients as reported in the *WJ-R Technical Manual* (McGrew et al., 1991).

intra-cognitive strengths and weaknesses. The lack of consistent reliability at or above the .90 level argues against the use of a single WJTCA-R cognitive cluster score as the sole basis for an important educational decision (e.g., special class placement).

Validity

A network of evidence supports the interpretation of the WJTCA-R cognitive clusters as measures of seven unique human abilities. Evidence is available in the form of exploratory and confirmatory factor analysis studies (McGhee, 1993; McGrew et al., 1991; Woodcock, 1990), comparison of cluster growth curves (McGrew et al., 1991), correlations with measures of similar abilities in other intelligence batteries (McGhee, 1993; McGrew et al., 1991; Woodcock, 1990), and differential patterns of correlations between the seven cognitive factors and measures of reading, mathematics, and written language (McGrew, 1993a, 1993c; McGrew and Knopik, 1993).

Portions of this validity evidence are summarized below. The reader is encouraged to consult the original sources for a thorough treatment of the findings. The results of these studies provide important interpretive insights into the WJTCA-R clusters. The relevance to interpretation will be addressed later in this chapter as each WJTCA-R cognitive cluster is reviewed.

Factor Analysis Studies in the Norm Samples
Factor analysis refers to a set of statistical procedures that analyze the intercorrelations or covariances among a set of variables (tests) to identify a smaller number of dimensions or factors that explain the various patterns of test correlations. *Exploratory* factor studies are used primarily when the structure or dimensionality of a set of tests is unknown, and the researcher is attempting to determine what the structure may be. In contrast, *confirmatory* approaches focus on testing hypotheses based on prior theory or research about the structure presumed to be inherent in the intercorrelations.

Both exploratory and confirmatory analysis studies of the WJTCA-R provide support for the seven cognitive factors (McGhee, 1993; McGrew et al., 1991; Woodcock, 1990). Since the WJTCA-R structure is based on the *Gf-Gc* model that is derived from prior research and theory, the confirmatory factor analysis studies are most important.

The most important test of the validity of the seven cognitive cluster structure was a series of confirmatory factor analyses of the 14 cognitive tests that make up the clusters. McGrew et al. (1991) reported these analyses for six different age groups in the WJTCA-R standardization sample. The results of these analyses, which also included 2 quantitative tests (*Gq* factor) from the WJ-R achievement battery, are summarized in Table 4-3. These analyses tested the "fit" of a hypothesized structure where the two tests making up each WJTCA-R cognitive cluster, as well as the two quantitative achievement tests, were specified to be indicators only of their respective cognitive factor. This was a stringent test of the WJTCA-R cognitive cluster structure since it did not allow any of the tests to be secondary measures of other cognitive factors.

A review of the "fit statistics" in Table 4-3 supports the cognitive cluster organization of the WJTCA-R. This conclusion is based on the observation that almost all of the *Goodness-of-Fit* (GFI) and *Adjusted Goodness-of-Fit* (AGFI) statistics are above .90 or .80 respectively, and the *root-mean-square residual (rmr)* values are small and below .10. All of these values suggest good fit between the hypothesized structure and the data (Cole, 1987; Kamphaus, 1993). In addition, all the factor loadings are high and positive, another indication that the tests do measure the specified factors. The results presented in Table 4-3 provide strong support for the first 14 WJTCA-R tests being organized into the seven *Gf-Gc* cognitive clusters across the entire age range of the WJTCA-R. The only exception is slightly weaker support for the model in the oldest adult sample.

Additional support for the seven cluster WJTCA-R structure is provided by a series of confirmatory factor analyses that included 19 cognitive tests (the 2 Delayed Recall tests were not included due to significant missing data) and 8 related WJ-R achievement tests (McGrew et al., 1991). The results of these confirmatory studies in six norm subsamples are summarized in Table 4-4.

The fit statistics in Table 4-4 provide support for the eight factor *Gf-Gc* structure of the complete WJ-R and the seven cognitive clusters included in the WJTCA-R. Similar to the results presented in Table 4-3, there is a trend for the WJ-R structure to fit the data the strongest in the school-age groups, with slightly weaker fit with increasing age. The combined results presented in Tables 4-3 and 4-4 support the conclusion that the WJTCA-R tests measure seven unique factors of human intelligence. Although other WJTCA-R tests measure various aspects of the *Gf-Gc* abilities, the confirmatory factor studies provide support for the WJTCA-R cognitive clusters. Independent reviewers (Kaufman, 1990; Reschly, 1990; Ysseldyke, 1990) have reached a similar conclusion.

TABLE 4-3   Factor Loadings and Model Fit Statistics for Eight-Factor Confirmatory Factor Analysis of 14 WJ-R Standard Cognitive Tests and 2 Related Achievement Tests Across Six Samples

	Grades K–3 (n = 667)	Grades 4–7 (n = 439)	Grades 8–12 (n = 545)	Young Adult (n = 297)	Middle Adult (n = 177)	Older Adult (n = 136)
Long-Term Retrieval (Glr)						
Memory for Names	.539	.729	.696	.713	.766	.784
Visual-Auditory Learning	.821	.669	.848	.849	.904	.808
Short-Term Memory (Gsm)						
Memory for Sentences	.908	1.018	.858	.853	.771	.793
Memory for Words	.698	.516	.696	.583	.616	.699
Processing Speed (Gs)						
Visual Matching	.815	.844	.733	.763	.838	.947
Cross Out	.776	.799	.782	.897	.906	.797
Auditory Processing (Ga)						
Incomplete Words	.747	.723	.776	.819	.720	.661
Sound Blending	.655	.500	.527	.619	.788	.871
Visual Processing (Gv)						
Visual Closure	.505	.458	.540	.533	.689	.740
Picture Recognition	.559	.620	.511	.614	.600	.784
Comprehension Knowledge (Gc)						
Picture Vocabulary	.679	.673	.734	.813	.851	.862
Oral Vocabulary	.879	.915	.953	.921	.882	.934
Fluid Reasoning (Gf)						
Analysis-Synthesis	.691	.691	.771	.780	.859	.834
Concept Formation	.726	.638	.703	.727	.727	.859
Quantitative Ability (Gq)						
Calculation	.632	.767	.820	.794	.889	.898
Applied Problems	.833	.860	.907	.963	.812	.921
Fit Statistics						
GFI =	.953	.954	.957	.954	.928	.892
AGFI =	.916	.918	.923	.919	.871	.806
rmr =	.036	.039	.031	.032	.035	.049

Young adult = <40 years
Middle adult = 40–59 years
Older adult = 60+ years
Adapted from the *WJ-R Technical Manual* (p. 168) by K. McGrew, J. Werder, and R. Woodcock, 1991, Chicago: The Riverside Publishing Company. Copyright 1991 by The Riverside Publishing Company. Adapted by permission.

TABLE 4-4　Factor Loadings and Model Fit Statistics for Eight-Factor Confirmatory Factor Analysis of 19 WJ-R Cognitive and 8 Related Achievement Tests in Six Samples

	Grades K–3 ($n = 894$)	Grades 4–7 ($n = 690$)	Grades 8–12 ($n = 783$)	Young Adult ($n = 352$)	Middle Adult ($n = 202$)	Older Adult ($n = 142$)
Long-Term Retrieval (*Glr*)						
Memory for Names	.611	.702	.709	.724	.738	.625
Visual-Auditory Learning	.830	.727	.821	.861	.865	.875
Short-Term Memory (*Gsm*)						
Memory for Sentences	.526	.472	.510	.605	.557	.685
Memory for Words	.842	.869	.801	.656	.653	.732
Numbers Reversed	.167	.275	.463	.582	.503	.472
Processing Speed (*Gs*)						
Visual Matching	.783	.765	.764	.781	.787	.881
Cross Out	.701	.760	.738	.802	.801	.740
Writing Fluency	.641	.668	.607	.685	.752	.620
Auditory Processing (*Ga*)						
Incomplete Words	.521	.410	.484	.549	.629	.680
Sound Blending	.739	.619	.647	.698	.709	.675
Sound Patterns	.230	.293	.362	.212	.341	.279
Word Attack	.768	.697	.721	.740	.792	.703
Visual Processing (*Gv*)						
Visual Closure	.478	.531	.476	.440	.584	.600
Picture Recognition	.637	.695	.669	.637	.593	.652
Spatial Relations	.310	.203	.187	.027	.388	.151
Comprehension-Knowledge (*Gc*)						
Picture Vocabulary	.769	.767	.757	.832	.792	.743
Oral Vocabulary	.783	.870	.880	.866	.847	.860
Listening Comprehension	.771	.725	.775	.794	.722	.793
Verbal Analogies	.301	.409	.419	.545	.546	.460
Memory for Sentences	.362	.432	.364	.222	.264	.131
Science	.847	.833	.810	.778	.796	.806
Social Studies	.811	.833	.853	.843	.836	.817
Humanities	.801	.784	.829	.825	.861	.771
Fluid Reasoning (*Gf*)						
Analysis-Synthesis	.670	.663	.692	.746	.732	.820
Concept Formation	.677	.717	.710	.723	.824	.768
Verbal Analogies	.427	.439	.488	.337	.404	.443
Spatial Relations	.384	.420	.485	.713	.291	.543
Numbers Reversed	.521	.455	.310	.156	.267	.265
Sound Patterns	.224	.245	.165	.418	.311	.308
Quantitative Ability (*Gq*)						
Calculation	.670	.739	.805	.849	.852	.820
Applied Problems	.818	.848	.876	.902	.860	.846
Quantitative Concepts	.822	.863	.880	.914	.942	.899
Fit Statistics						
GFI =	.911	.918	.920	.875	.857	.813
AGFI =	.884	.894	.897	.837	.814	.757
rmr =	.045	.044	.042	.051	.048	.070

Alternative Factor Models

Although the confirmatory factor studies support the seven cognitive cluster WJTCA-R structure, these analyses do not prove that this is the best possible organizational structure for the WJTCA-R tests. Thus, the evaluation of alternative models is important.

McGrew et al. (1991) compared four models in a combined kindergarten-to-adult group in the WJ-R norm sample. The models included all 21 WJTCA-R tests as well as 8 related achievement tests. The models were: (a) a *first-order g* model where all 29 tests were hypothesized to measure only one general intelligence factor, (b) a *verbal/nonverbal* model where the tests were organized along verbal and nonverbal stimulus and response characteristics, (c) a *Gf-Gc* model that corresponded to the eight-factor model (including the *Gq* factor from the achievement section of the WJ-R) hypothesized by the WJ-R authors, and (d) a *hierarchical g* model that was identical to the *Gf-Gc* model with the exception of the addition of a general intelligence factor above the eight *Gf-Gc* factors. The fit statistics for the four models are presented in Table 4-5.

A review of the fit statistics in Table 4-5 indicates that the two models *(hierarchical g* and *Gf-Gc)* that hypothesized that the WJTCA-R measures seven cognitive abilities, with an eighth cognitive factor *(Gq)* present in the achievement battery, provide a better fit to the WJ-R norm data than do models that hypothesize a general intelligence or verbal/nonverbal structure. The similarity of the fit statistics for the *hierarchical g* and *Gf-Gc* models leaves open the question of the presence of a higher-order general intelligence factor. The most important finding is "that when a sufficiently diverse pool of tests that tap a wide variety of human abilities is available, models based on first-order *g* or Verbal/Nonverbal frameworks do not provide a plausible representation of human abilities" (McGrew et al., 1991, p. 172). Although the evaluation of additional alternative models is necessary, the results presented in Table 4-5 provide strong support for seven unique factors being present in the WJTCA-R.

TABLE 4-5   Select Model Fit Statistics for WJ-R 29 Variable Gf-Gc and Three Alternative Models in the Kindergarten–Adult Sample (*n* = 1,425)

Model	GFI	AGFI	*rmr*
First-order *g*	.749	.710	.069
Verbal/nonverbal	.805	.768	.065
Hierarchical *g*	.908	.890	.053
Gf-Gc	.922	.902	.045

Adapted from the *WJ-R Technical Manual* (p. 171) by K. McGrew, J. Werder, and R. Woodcock, 1991, Chicago: The Riverside Publishing Company. Copyright 1991 by The Riverside Publishing Company. Adapted by permission.

Gf-Gc *Cluster Intercorrelations*
Additional support for the seven WJTCA-R cognitive clusters being measures of distinct abilities is found in the intercorrelations between the cognitive cluster scores. The average cognitive cluster intercorrelations across seven age groups are summarized in Table 4-6.

The average cognitive cluster intercorrelations are low to moderate (ranging from .20 to .54). These correlations indicate that each of the seven WJTCA-R cognitive clusters only shares 4% to 29% common variance (determined by squaring the correlations) with the other clusters. Such values indicate that the WJTCA-R cognitive clusters are measuring seven unique abilities.

Joint Analyses With Other Intelligence Tests
A traditional source of validity information for a new test is its correlation with previously validated tests. This form of validity evidence can be found in the convergent and divergent patterns of correlations between related and unrelated tests. Such analyses can range from the informal "eyeballing" of correlation matrices to complex statistical analyses of the patterns of correlations.

Woodcock (1990) has provided a comprehensive example of the latter approach. Woodcock reported results from the joint confirmatory factor analyses of the WJ-R tests and tests from the Kaufman Assessment Battery for Children (K-ABC); (Kaufman & Kaufman, 1983), the Stanford-Binet IV (SB-IV); (Thorndike, et al., 1986), and two of the Wechslers (WISC-R, WAIS-R); (Wechsler, 1974, 1981). These analyses were based on an extensive collection of data from a number of different WJ/WJ-R validity and norm samples. The evaluation of the different tests ranged from being based on 2 to 15 different analyses.

McGhee (1993) completed a similar kind of joint confirmatory factor analysis of the WJTCA-R and the Detroit Tests of Learning Aptitude-3

TABLE 4-6   Average (Median) Intercorrelation of WJTCA-R Cognitive Clusters Across Seven Age Groups

	Cognitive Cluster						
Cognitive Cluster	*Glr*	*Gsm*	*Gs*	*Ga*	*Gv*	*Gc*	*Gf*
Long-Term Retrieval *(Glr)*	1.00						
Short-Term Memory *(Gsm)*	.37	1.00					
Processing Speed *(Gs)*	.42	.30	1.00				
Auditory Processing *(Ga)*	.46	.41	.40	1.00			
Visual Processing *(Gv)*	.46	.20	.38	.35	1.00		
Comprehension-Knowledge *(Gc)*	.49	.50	.36	.52	.33	1.00	
Fluid Reasoning *(Gf)*	.52	.41	.41	.49	.41	.54	1.00

Correlations as reported in the *WJ-R Technical Manual* (McGrew et al., 1991)

(DTLA-3) (Hammill & Bryant, 1991) and the school-age version of the Differential Abilities Scale (DAS) (Elliott, 1990) in a sample of 100 school-age children. The McGhee (1993) and Woodcock (1990) analyses provide comprehensive information on the relationships between the WJTCA-R cognitive cluster tests and tests from other intelligence batteries.

These combined analyses provide evidence supporting the validity of five of the seven WJTCA-R cognitive clusters. The WJTCA-R tests that made up the Short-Term Memory *(Gsm)*, Processing Speed *(Gs)*, Visual Processing *(Gv)*, Comprehension-Knowledge *(Gc)*, and Fluid Reasoning *(Gf)* clusters covaried with tests that measure similar abilities from the other intelligence batteries. For example, the two WJTCA-R tests that compose the *Gsm* cluster correlated with other memory tests such as K-ABC Word Order and Number Recall, SB-IV Memory for Digits and Memory of Sentences, Wechsler Digit Span, and DTLA-3 Sentence Imitation and Word Sequences. The lack of tests in the other intelligence batteries that measure Long-Term Retrieval *(Glr)* and Auditory Processing *(Ga)* precluded evaluating the validity of these WJTCA-R cognitive clusters. A listing of the WJTCA-R and other intelligence battery tests that were related, as well as the degree of the relationship, is given later in this chapter as each cluster is discussed.

Differential Relationships With School Achievement
If the WJTCA-R cognitive clusters measure different abilities, the relationships between different cognitive clusters and different achievement criteria (e.g., reading, mathematics, and writing) should vary. A series of multiple regression studies using the WJ-R norm data from age 5 to late adulthood confirms this hypothesis (McGrew, 1993a, 1993c; McGrew & Knopik, 1993). For example, in reading, all but the WJTCA-R Visual Processing *(Gv)* cluster demonstrated significant relationships with basic reading skills (i.e., word recognition). The important finding was that certain clusters (most notably Processing Speed, Auditory Processing, and Comprehension-Knowledge) demonstrated the strongest relationships with basic reading skills, and that each cognitive cluster's strength of association with basic reading skills varied by age. Processing Speed *(Gs)* and Auditory Processing *(Ga)* were highly associated with basic reading skills during the school-age years, with a subsequent decreasing trend with age. Conversely, the relationship between the Comprehension-Knowledge *(Gc)* cluster and basic reading skills increased in strength with age.

The individual WJTCA-R cognitive clusters displayed different relationships with subareas within the same broad achievement domain. For example, the Auditory Processing cluster was significantly related to both basic reading skills and reading comprehension during the school years. However, the strength of the relationship was relatively stronger for basic reading skills than for reading comprehension. This makes logical sense given the need to analyze and synthesize sounds during the acquisition of basic reading skills. The Fluid Reasoning *(Gf)* cluster was another example.

Fluid Reasoning demonstrated little relationship to basic reading skills but did display a significant relationship with reading comprehension. This is logical since reading comprehension requires greater use of broad reasoning abilities.

The finding of different relationships between the WJTCA-R cognitive clusters and reading, mathematics, and written language achievement, as well as different relationships for the same cognitive cluster and different achievement areas, provides additional support for the validity of the cognitive clusters. These findings reinforce Ysseldyke's (1990) conclusion that the WJTCA-R is a collection of tests that will enhance aptitude-treatment interaction (ATI) research. The specific relationships between the seven WJTCA-R cognitive clusters and reading, mathematics, and written language achievement are summarized later in this chapter as each cognitive cluster is reviewed.

Growth Curve Comparisons

The final form of validity evidence for the WJTCA-R cognitive clusters is cluster growth curve comparisons. Plots of the average WJTCA-R cognitive cluster scores in the norm sample from age 5 to 90 revealed different patterns of growth (McGrew et al., 1991). Certain cognitive clusters displayed rapid rates of early growth, an early plateau, and a steady decline with age. Other clusters showed more deliberate early growth, a later plateau, and less rapid decline with age. The existence of divergent growth curves for different measures can be considered evidence for the existence of unique abilities (Carroll, 1983).

COGNITIVE CLUSTER-BY-CLUSTER ANALYSIS

The seven WJTCA-R cognitive clusters provide for reliable and valid measurement of seven *Gf-Gc* abilities. The following summaries provide important interpretive information for the seven WJTCA-R clusters. In each summary the primary ability measured by the cluster is identified. The *Gf-Gc* factor descriptions presented in Chapter 2 should be consulted for more detailed explanation of these broad abilities. This brief definition is followed by information on the factorial strength of the two WJTCA-R tests that make up each *Gf-Gc* cognitive cluster. Additional WJ-R tests that measure the same *Gf-Gc* ability are also discussed. Also presented are hypotheses to help clinicians interpret differences that may be observed between the two WJTCA-R tests in each cognitive cluster.

A following section then summarizes the relationship between the tests in each of the WJTCA-R cognitive clusters and other intelligence tests. These summaries are based on the joint confirmatory factor studies of Woodcock

(1990), McGhee (1993), and Daniels and Elliott (1993). The eight-factor solution of McGhee was used rather than his nine-factor solution to provide comparable results with Woodcock.

Based on Woodcock's (1990) criteria, each test is classified as either a *strong, moderate,* or *mixed* measure of each *Gf-Gc* factor. These classifications specify the strength and factorial purity of each test, with strong tests being the best indicators of a factor and mixed tests being complex tests that measure more than one *Gf-Gc* ability. In a few instances where confirmatory factor analysis information is not available, tests from certain intelligence batteries are tentatively classified within the *Gf-Gc* framework based on task analysis, observed similarities with other tests, or by extrapolation from related empirical studies. Although the WISC-III has yet to be subjected to joint analysis with the WJTCA-R, the *Gf-Gc* summary tables assume that the strong similarities between the WISC-R and WISC-III argue for similar WISC-R/WISC-III test classifications (with the exception of the new WISC-III Symbol Search test).

In making the DAS and DTLA-3 *Gf-Gc* test classifications, it was noted that many of the WJTCA-R test factor loadings reported by McGhee (1993) were noticeably higher than the average values reported by Woodcock (1990). In order to ensure comparability across studies, the relationship between the WJTCA-R test factor loadings in Woodcock's and McGhee's studies were examined, and an average adjustment scaling value was developed. This value was used to adjust all the factor loadings in McGhee's study. When compared to the DAS and DTLA-3 test classifications based on the unadjusted factor loadings, the only classifications that changed (i.e., from strong to moderate) were for the Visual Processing *(Gv)* tests.

The factor-based information not only sheds on the validity of the WJTCA-R cognitive clusters, but it also provides information about other good tests of *Gf-Gc* abilities that can be used to follow up hypotheses generated from an individual's performance on the WJTCA-R cognitive clusters. When using this information, it is important to note that although certain WJ-R or other battery tests were found to correlate together and load on the same *Gf-Gc* factor in empirical studies, *this does not mean these tests are interchangeable and measure the exact same ability.* Each test is an indicator of one facet of the broader *Gf-Gc* ability and, thus, provides common information related to the broader ability as well as information unique to the test. This point was presented previously in Chapter 3 in the discussion of the major components (i.e., common abilities, uniqueness, measurement error) of each WJTCA-R test.

Finally, information is presented on the relationship between each WJTCA-R cognitive cluster and reading, mathematics, and written language achievement across the life span. This information is based on a series of multiple regression studies that used the WJ-R norm data (McGrew, 1993a, 1993c; McGrew & Knopik, 1993) to estimate the strength of relationship (i.e., standardized regression coefficients) between the seven cognitive clusters and achievement across the life span. As reported in these studies, the standardized regression coefficients for each WJTCA-R cognitive cluster were plotted by age. Smoothed curves were then fit to the coefficients to determine the systematic relationship between each WJTCA-R cognitive cluster and achievement as a function of age. An example for Processing Speed and basic reading skills is presented in Figure 4-1.

The interpretation of the information in Figure 4-1 is straightforward. The standardized regression coefficients indicate the amount of standard deviation change in basic reading skills achievement (as defined by the WJ-R Basic Reading Skills cluster) as related to each standard deviation change in the Processing Speed cognitive cluster score. A coefficient of .25 indicates that an increase in Processing Speed performance of one standard deviation is associated with a .25 standard deviation change in Basic Reading Skills. Thus, higher regression coefficients indicate a stronger relationship between Processing Speed and Basic Reading Skills. Based on practical and statistical considerations (McGrew, 1993a, 1993c; McGrew & Knopik, 1993), the following interpretative guidelines are used to summarize the relationship between each WJTCA-R cognitive cluster and achievement: (a) values below .10 are interpreted to mean no important relationship exists, (b) values

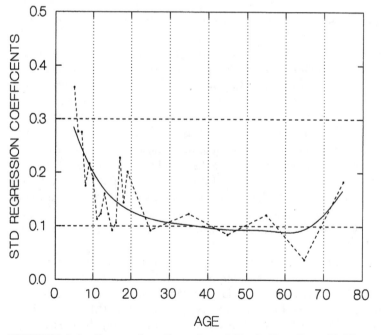

FIGURE 4-1   **Processing Speed and Basic Reading Skills**

from .10 to .29 indicate a moderate relationship exists, and (c) values at or above .30 indicate a strong relationship exists.

Using these guidelines, performance on the WJTCA-R Processing Speed cluster is moderately related to Basic Reading Skills from age 5 to approximately age forty (Figure 4-1). This relationship is strongest during the early school years and decreases with age. Processing Speed appears unrelated to Basic Reading Skills from age 40 to the mid-60s. However, Processing Speed shows an increased relationship with Basic Reading Skills during older adulthood (approximately age 65 and above). For each WJTCA-R cognitive cluster a single figure is presented that summarizes the relationship between the cluster and the following academic skills as measured by the WJ-R achievement clusters:

> *Basic Reading Skills (BRS)*—word recognition skills including sight word recognition and word analysis skills.
>
> *Reading Comprehension (RC)*—reading comprehension of single words, sentences, and passages.
>
> *Basic Writing Skills (BWS)*—basic skills in punctuation, capitalization, and word usage.
>
> *Written Expression (WE)*—ability to express ideas by producing simple and complex sentences in response to varied task demands.
>
> *Basic Mathematics Skills (BMS)*—computational skills and knowledge of mathematical concepts and vocabulary.
>
> *Mathematics Reasoning (MR)*—ability to analyze and solve practical mathematical problems.

The information used to develop these figures was extracted from the studies of McGrew (1993a, 1993c), and McGrew and Knopik (1993). This information should alert clinicians to the WJTCA-R cognitive clusters that should receive priority consideration when evaluating individuals for concerns in each academic area. The integration of this information with the cluster-specific implications presented by Mather (1991), Mather and Jaffe (1992), and Nolting (1991) provides important information for interpretation and making recommendations.

A few words of caution are necessary regarding the information describing the relationship between each WJTCA-R cognitive cluster and achievement. First, the information presented is correlational and does not prove causality. Although high regression coefficients may be reported between specific WJTCA-R cognitive clusters and specific academic areas, such findings are only suggestive and do not prove a causal relationship.

Second, the primary value of this information is the identification of specific WJTCA-R cognitive clusters that are most associated with different achievement criteria. Such findings should sensitize clinicians to those cognitive clusters that should receive the most attention when interpreting the assessment results. The failure to find significant relationships between a specific cognitive cluster and an achievement criterion should not be interpreted to mean that a specific ability is completely unrelated to the performance of the achievement criterion. For example, the results for the Visual Processing cluster indicate no significant relationship with reading achievement. One would be hard pressed to conclude that visual perceptual processing is not involved in reading, a skill that requires the reader to visually input the words. Some form of visual processing abilities are involved in the process of reading. However, the failure to find a significant relationship between the Visual Processing cluster and reading achievement in the studies reviewed means that *when considered together with other measures of* Gf-Gc *abilities, the abilities measured by other clusters accounted for most of the variance in the reading criteria.* The abilities measured by the Visual Processing cluster may be involved in reading achievement, but the relationship is small and nonsignificant when considered within the context of other *Gf-Gc* abilities that are more strongly associated with reading.

Finally, the method used to generate this information was exploratory in nature as all seven WJTCA-R cognitive cluster scores were included in a full regression model. Such a model specifies that each cognitive cluster has only one direct relationship (i.e., a single direct path in path analysis terms) with the respective achievement criterion. The possibility exists that certain of the *Gf-Gc* abilities measured by the WJTCA-R cognitive clusters may have additional indirect paths of influence that are mediated through other *Gf-Gc* abilities.

For example, long-term retrieval ability *(Glr)* may play a prominent role in the storage and retrieval of information in long-term memory (i.e., comprehension-knowledge or *Gc)*, which in turn may have a major correlation with achievement. Such an indirect relationship between long-term retrieval and reading achievement, as mediated through comprehension-knowledge, was not estimated with the research methods used by McGrew (1993a, 1993c) or McGrew and Knopik (1993). To capture the total direct and indirect influence of each *Gf-Gc* ability on different achievement criteria, a researcher would need to specify a complex causal model that would estimate both direct and indirect influences. Currently, no one has conducted such research, primarily because no clearly articulated theoretical *Gf-Gc* and achievement explanatory model has been developed that could guide such efforts.

Long-Term Retrieval (Glr)

Ability to store information and retrieve it later through association. (Woodcock, 1992, p. 45)

Interpretive Considerations

A review of Table 4-7 indicates that the WJTCA-R Long-Term Retrieval cluster consists of two strong measures of long-term retrieval, namely, Memory for Names and Visual-Auditory Learning. Additional information regarding this ability can be obtained within the WJTCA-R from the two delayed recall tests. Delayed Recall-Memory for Names is the strongest of the two supplementary measures, being classified as a moderate measure of this associative storage and retrieval ability.

Although measuring a common long-term storage and retrieval ability, differences between the two tests making up this WJTCA-R cognitive cluster can be observed. Based on a review of each test's summary analysis in Chapter 3, such differences could be attributed to the following differences between the tests:

Memory for Names	*Visual-Auditory Learning*
Auditory-Visual association	Visual-Auditory association
Recognition memory	Recall memory
Nonmeaningful material	Meaningful material (language-based)
Pointing response mode	Oral response mode

Another possible reason for differences may lie in the ease by which cognitive strategies are used when performing on each test. The use of mnemonics may be easier with the Visual-Auditory Learning test, where a number of the visual symbols look like the words they are associated with (e.g., "on" associated with a small ball *on* top of a larger ball; "horse" associated with a symbol that looks like a horse's head and neck). In contrast, using mnemonics for the associations between cartoon-like diagrams and nonmeaningful names such as "Nish," "Kiptron," and "Jawf" in Memory for Names may require much higher levels of cognitive strategy use.

Although the two WJTCA-R delayed recall tests also measure a common long-term retrieval ability, differences from the nondelayed tests (Memory for Names, Visual-Auditory Learning) may occur primarily due to the significant time delay between administrations (i.e., 1 to 8 days). Currently, no research has shed light on the specific diagnostic or educational implications of the finding of significant differences between the respective delayed and nondelayed versions of each WJTCA-R long-term retrieval test.

Relationship With Other Tests

A review of Table 4-7 indicates that, with one possible exception, no other intelligence battery includes tests that measure long-term retrieval. The listing of the DAS Recall of Objects—Immediate and Delayed test is a tenta-

TABLE 4-7   Measures of Long-Term Retrieval (Glr) in Major Intelligence Batteries

	Strong Measures	Moderate Measures	Mixed Measures
WJ-R	*Memory for Names* *Visual-Auditory* *Learning* Delayed Recall— Memory for Names	Delayed Recall— Visual Auditory Learning	
WISC-R/WAIS-R (WISC-III ?)			
SB-IV			
K-ABC			
DAS (school age)	Recall of Objects- Immediate & Delayed ?		
DTLA-3			

Tests in italics make up the WJTCA-R Cognitive cluster. Tests with question mark notations are classified based on logical/rational considerations, or limited empirical analysis.

Portions adapted from "Theoretical foundations of the WJ-R measures of cognitive ability," by R. W. Woodcock, 1990. *Journal of Psychoeducational Assessment, 8*, pp. 244–246. Copyright 1990 by the Psychoeducational Corporation. Adapted by permission.

tive classification (as indicated by the question mark in Table 4-7) based primarily on task analysis. This test was not included in McGhee's (1993) or Daniels and Elliott's (1993) confirmatory factor studies that included the DAS. In this DAS test an examinee is shown a card that displays 20 common objects that are named by the examiner. The examinee is required to recall as many objects as possible in three immediate recall trials, as well as

15 minutes later in a delayed mode. Keith's (1990) and Stone's (1992) confirmatory factor studies of the DAS found this test not to associate with the other DAS short-term memory tests. Both studies found this test to display significant uniqueness. This finding, combined with task analysis, suggests that the DAS Recall of Objects—Immediate and Delayed test could be a measure of long-term retrieval, but it failed to define such a factor in Keith's and Stone's analyses since there are no other DAS tests that measure this ability.

Relationship With Reading

The information presented in Figure 4-2 reveals important insights into the relationship between the Long-Term Retrieval cluster and reading achievement. In Figure 4-2 only smoothed curves are presented for Long-Term Retrieval and Reading Comprehension and Written Expression. The absence of a curve for Basic Reading Skills indicates that, on the average, there was no significant relationship (defined by standardized regression coefficients at or above .10) between this area of reading and the Long-Term Retrieval cluster. Similarly, long-term retrieval abilities may not be highly related to reading comprehension throughout most of the life span. The exception to this conclusion is after age 50 where the relationship between Long-Term Retrieval and Reading Comprehension demonstrates a significant increase. This finding could be related to the strong relationship reported between reading comprehension and prior acquired knowledge (Lohman, 1989; Snow & Swanson, 1992). A possible explanation is that during late adulthood decreased efficiency in retrieving acquired knowledge may hinder a person's ability to utilize prior verbal knowledge when trying to comprehend text. This hypothesis needs further study.

Closer inspection of the original research indicates that the methods used to develop the Long-Term Retrieval and Basic Reading Skills curve may have failed to capture an extremely important relationship at age 6 (McGrew, 1993c). A standardized regression coefficient of .266 was reported at a time (age 6) when most children are learning their alphabet and sounds associated with the alphabet letters. Thus, performance on the Long-Term Retrieval cluster may be particularly important for beginning reading at age 6.

Relationship With Written Language

The absence of a curve for Basic Writing Skills in Figure 4-2 indicates that there was no significant relationship between this academic area and Long-Term Retrieval across the age span presented. Performance on the Long-Term Retrieval cluster showed no important relationship with Written Expression during the school-age or young adult years. Instead, performance on the Long-Term Retrieval cluster was moderately associated with Written Expression at and beyond approximately age 40. Although only a hypothesis, the reason for this significant relationship beyond middle age may be

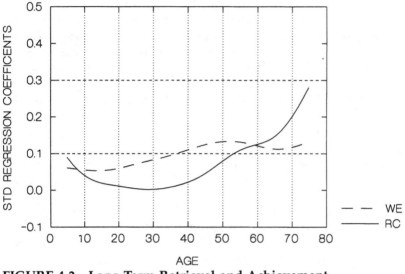

FIGURE 4-2   Long-Term Retrieval and Achievement

similar to that offered for the same pattern of findings reported for reading comprehension. Significant differences between adults in efficiency of retrieving stored verbal knowledge may account for observed differences in using this stored knowledge when writing.

Relationship With Mathematics
The absence of curves for Basic Mathematics Skills and Mathematics Reasoning in Figure 4-2 indicates that there was no reported significant relationship between performance on the Long-Term Retrieval cluster and these areas of mathematics achievement. These results suggest that performance on the Long-Term Retrieval cluster should not be over interpreted in terms of possible implications for mathematics achievement.

Short-Term Memory (Gsm)

> *Ability to hold information in immediate awareness and then use it within a few seconds.* (Woodcock, 1992, p. 44)

Interpretive Considerations
A review of Table 4-8 indicates that the WJTCA-R Short-Term Memory cluster includes one strong measure of short-term memory (viz., Memory for Words). The second test in this cluster, Memory for Sentences, is classified as a moderate measure as it was found to measure short-term memory and, to a lesser degree, comprehension-knowledge *(Gc)*. The presence of only one strong short-term memory test in this WJTCA-R cluster makes it one of

TABLE 4-8 Measures of Short-Term Memory *(Gsm)* in Major Intelligence Batteries

	Strong Measures	Moderate Measures	Mixed Measures
WJ-R	*Memory for Words*	*Memory for Sentences*	Numbers Reversed *(Gf)*
WISC-R/WAIS-R (WISC-III ?)	Digit Span		
SB-IV	Memory for Digits	Memory for Objects	Bead Memory *(Gv)* Memory for Sentences *(Gc)*
K-ABC	Number Recall Word Order		Hand Movements *(Gq)*
DAS (school age)	Recall of Digits ?		
DTLA-3	Sentence Imitation Word Sequences		

Tests in italics make up the WJTCA-R Cognitive cluster. Tests with question mark notations are classified based on logical/rational considerations, or limited empirical analysis.

Portions adapted from "Theoretical foundations of the WJ-R measures of cognitive ability," by R. W. Woodcock, 1990, *Journal of Psychoeducational Assessment, 8,* pp. 244–246. Copyright 1990 by the Psychoeducational Corporation. Adapted by permission.

the two weakest (in terms of factor purity) clusters in the cognitive battery. Additional information regarding short-term memory can be obtained from within the WJTCA-R in the form of Numbers Reversed. However, Numbers Reversed is also not a strong or pure test of short-term memory. Numbers Reversed is a mixed test that measures both fluid reasoning *(Gf)* and short-term memory *(Gsm)*.

Given the dual nature of Memory for Sentences, differences between performance on this test and Memory for Words should not be unexpected for some examinees. Based on a review of each test's summary analysis in Chapter 3, the primary reasons for possible differences may be due to the influence of language or verbal knowledge and comprehension *(Gc)* in the case of Memory for Sentences. Memory for Sentences presents the stimuli in a meaningful, language-based context, in contrast to the unrelated words with limited meaningful context in the case of Memory for Words (Mather, 1991). Although the administration of the WJTCA-R Numbers Reversed test may help clarify the nature of an examinee's short-term memory abilities, clinicians are still faced with the problem that performance on Numbers Reversed is influenced by reasoning *(Gf)* (primarily the result of the digit reversal task demand). The WJTCA-R Short-Term Memory cluster is one of two clusters where routine follow-up testing with short-term memory tests from other intelligence batteries may be appropriate. Possible tests for this purpose are presented next.

Relationship With Other Tests

A review of Table 4-8 indicates that there is no shortage of short-term memory tests in other intelligence batteries. Most take the form of repeating either digits, words, or sentences, similar to the task demands of the WJTCA-R short-term memory tests. The finding that the short-term memory tests in other batteries correlate with the two WJTCA-R Short-Term Memory cluster tests provides support for the validity of this cluster.

The selection of supplementary short-term memory tests to follow up performance on the WJTCA-R Short-Term Memory cluster depends on the specific hypothesis in question. If additional information is required about an individual's short-term memory devoid of the influence of language, then one of the digit repetition tests from the other batteries should be selected (i.e., Wechsler Digit Span; SB-IV Memory for Digits; K-ABC Number Recall; DAS Recall of Digits). If information is needed to verify the score on the WJTCA-R Memory for Words test, then one of the other tests that also uses words for stimuli (e.g., K-ABC Word Order; DTLA-3 Word Sequences) should be considered. Additional information similar to that measured by the WJTCA-R Memory for Sentences test would best be obtained from a similar sentence repetition test (i.e., DTLA-3 Sentence Imitation; SB-IV Memory for Sentences).

Relationship With Reading

As summarized in Figure 4-3, the Short-Term Memory cluster demonstrates a moderate relationship with Basic Reading Skills from age 5 to the mid-50s. The relationship between Short-Term Memory and Basic Reading Skills increases gradually from age 5 to its highest level between approximately adolescence and middle age, after which there is a noticeable decreasing trend. Short-Term Memory performance follows a similar increasing and

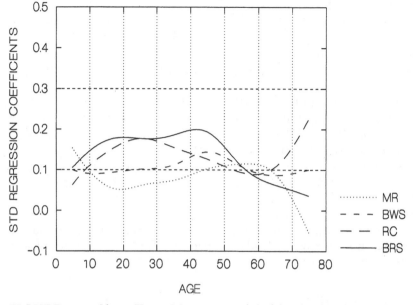

FIGURE 4-3 Short-Term Memory and Achievement

decreasing moderate trend from approximately age 10 to approximately age 50 for Reading Comprehension. The relative association between Short-Term Memory and Reading Comprehension is lower than that observed for Basic Reading Skills. After approximately age 65 Short-Term Memory demonstrates an increasing relationship with Reading Comprehension. Performance on the Short-Term Memory cluster should be considered when evaluating individuals for reading related issues throughout most of the life span. This conclusion is consistent with a body of research that has found significant relationships between short-term memory skills and reading (Brandys & Rourke, 1991; Mather, 1991).

Relationship With Written Language
The relationship between Short-Term Memory and written language appears weaker than that observed for reading. No systematic relationship was found between the Short-Term Memory cluster and Written Expression. Although Short-Term Memory was found to be moderately associated with Basic Writing Skills between approximately ages 30 and the late 50s, this one noticeable "bump" is in the context of an otherwise nearly straight line across the life span. This finding should not be overinterpreted, and needs further empirical study to determine its significance. The complete written language findings argue against placing major significance on the Short-Term Memory score for individuals assessed for written language–related concerns.

Relationship With Mathematics

As summarized in Figure 4-3, the only significant relationship between Short-Term Memory and mathematics is from age 5 to age 10 for Mathematics Reasoning, a relationship that systematically decreases over this 5-year age span. No significant relationship with Mathematics Reasoning is noted after age 10.

The finding of a significant relationship between Short-Term Memory and Mathematics Reasoning is consistent with other research (Cooney & Swanson, 1990; Mather, 1991). Nolting (1991) suggests that short-term memory may facilitate performance on mathematics reasoning tasks as individuals low in short-term memory may need to spend significant time rereading the mathematics reasoning problems that are typically presented in a story format. The results presented in Figure 4-3 suggest that this explanation may only be relevant for individuals younger than 10 years of age. The absence of a curve for Basic Mathematics Skills indicates that no significant relationship was found between this area of achievement and performance on the Short-Term Memory cluster.

Processing Speed (Gs)

Ability to rapidly perform automatic cognitive tasks. (Woodcock, 1992, p. 45)

Interpretive Considerations

The information presented in Table 4-9 reveals that the two tests that compose the WJTCA-R Processing Speed cluster (i.e., Visual Matching and Cross Out) are both strong measures of processing speed. Additional information regarding this cognitive ability can be found in the achievement section of the WJ-R battery. The Writing Fluency test, a test requiring examinees to write simple sentences within a 7-minute time frame, is a moderate measure of processing speed.

Although performance on Visual Matching and Cross Out will typically be similar, the tests do differ slightly in task demands that may result in different results. The major differences are the use of numbers in the case of Visual Matching and abstract visual designs in Cross Out and the Cross Out requirement that the correct answers match a correct or "key" stimulus. Visual Matching only requires the identification of two number sequences that match, while Cross Out requires the identification of five figures that match a key. The specific diagnostic implications of differences in performance on these two tests, for the preceding reasons, have yet to be fully investigated.

Given that both Visual Matching and Cross Out require sustained concentration under fixed time constraints, the most likely reasons for performance differences on the two tests (if they do occur) may lie in noncognitive explanations. Temporary distractibility, a lapse in concentration or motiva-

TABLE 4-9   Measures of Processing Speed (*Gs*) in Major Intelligence Batteries

	Strong Measures	Moderate Measures	Mixed Measures
WJ-R	*Visual Matching* *Cross Out*	Writing Fluency (Ach)	
WISC-R/WAIS-R (WISC-III ?)	Coding/Digit Symbol Symbol Search (WISC-III)?		
SB-IV			
K-ABC			Spatial Memory (*Gv*)
DAS (school age)	Speed of Information Processing ?		
DTLA-3			Story Sequences (*Gv*)

Tests in italics make up the WJTCA-R Cognitive cluster. Tests with question mark notations are classified based on logical/rational considerations, or limited empirical analysis.

Portions adapted from "Theoretical foundations of the WJ-R measures of cognitive ability," by R. W. Woodcock, 1990, *Journal of Psychoeducational Assessment, 8*, pp. 224–246. Copyright 1990 by the Psychoeducational Corporation. Adapted by permission.

tion, or increased anxiety during one test and not the other should be considered likely hypotheses for any observed differences between performance on these two Processing Speed tests.

Relationship With Other Tests

A review of Table 4-9 reveals a limited number of processing speed tests in other intelligence batteries that are related to the WJTCA-R processing speed tests. The Wechsler Coding/Digit Symbol tests are the only tests with known empirical relationships to Visual Matching and Cross Out. Although joint analysis with the WJTCA-R and WISC-III has yet to be published, logical analysis of the WISC-III Symbol Search test, its loading together with Coding on a separate factor in the WISC-III norm data, and its similarity to the WJTCA-R Cross Out test suggest that Symbol Search most likely will be found to be a strong measure of processing speed. The hypothesized versus empirical nature of this possibility is indicated by the question mark after the Symbol Search listing in Table 4-9.

Task analysis of the DAS Speed of Information Processing test, a timed test with rows of figures or numbers where the examinee must mark the circle with the most boxes or the highest number, suggests this test may also measure processing speed. Stone's (1992) joint confirmatory factor study of the DAS and WISC-R, where this test loaded together with the WISC-R Coding test, reinforces this hypothesis. Thus, clinicians may have three additional measures of processing speed in other intelligence batteries that could be used for follow-up testing of performance on the WJTCA-R Processing Speed cluster. To date, only the Wechsler Coding and Digit Symbol tests have demonstrated a known relationship with the WJTCA-R Processing Speed tests.

Relationship With Reading
A review of the information presented in Figure 4-4 reveals exciting information regarding the relationship between performance on the Processing Speed cluster and reading. Performance on the Processing Speed cluster is moderately related to both Basic Reading Skills and Reading Comprehension, with the strength of the association appearing stronger for the former. This is particularly true during the early years of school where the smoothed curves for Basic Reading Skills and Reading Comprehension are their highest.

The relative strength of association with Processing Speed decreases with age, with nonsignificance occurring earlier for Reading Comprehension (approximately age 15) than for Basic Reading Skills (approximately age 35). The relationship between Processing Speed and Basic Reading Skills was found to increase during late adulthood (beyond approximately age 65).

These significant findings most likely reflect the importance of learning to rapidly and fluently recognize or analyze words when reading. Individuals who quickly "automatize" mental operations may find it easier to rapidly automatize the processes involved in basic reading skills. This hypothesis is consistent with research that has demonstrated that rapid automatic processing of letters, syllables, and words frees up attentional processes for higher-level aspects of reading, such as comprehension (Fiedorowicz & Trites, 1991; LaBerge & Samuels, 1974). It is also consistent with a growing body of research that suggests that processing speed may

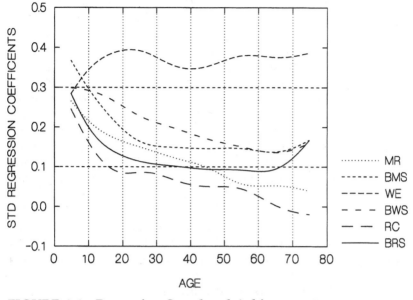

FIGURE 4-4   Processing Speed and Achievement

represent a fundamental mechanism that influences many cognitive and achievement related developmental changes (Kail, 1991; Lohman, 1989; Snow & Swanson, 1992). In sum, performance on the Processing Speed cluster should be carefully reviewed during the primary and elementary school years for reading related assessments.

Relationship With Written Language

A review of Figure 4-4 shows that Processing Speed is even more strongly associated with written language than with reading achievement. The Processing Speed cluster demonstrates a moderate relationship with Basic Writing Skills, a relationship that decreases systematically with age. Not unexpectedly, given the timed nature of the Writing Fluency test that is included in the WJ-R Written Expression cluster, the Processing Speed cluster was found to be strongly related to Written Expression across all ages. This finding could be interpreted to suggest that the WJ-R Writing Fluency test, which accounts for half of the test score used to define Written Expression in the data presented in Figure 4-4, may be measuring both writing-related behaviors and an aspect of cognitive performance (i.e., processing speed).

The findings presented in Figure 4-4 suggest that a person's processing speed may be strongly associated with automaticity or fluency in writing. Similar to reading, such findings are consistent with research that has demonstrated a relationship between processing speed and many cognitive and achievement related developmental changes (Kail, 1991; Lohman, 1989; Snow & Swanson, 1991).

Relationship With Mathematics

Performance on the Processing Speed cluster is also significantly related to mathematics performance. In the case of Basic Mathematics Skills, the relationship starts within the strong range at age 5, and systematically decreases to the moderate range starting at age 10. This Processing Speed and Basic Mathematics Skills relationship continues to decrease through the moderate range up to approximately age 30, after which it levels off in the moderate range. In contrast, the relationship between Processing Speed and Mathematics Reasoning is relatively lower. This relationship starts at a moderate level at age 5, after which it systemically declines until it is no longer significant after approximately age 45.

The "automaticity" explanation presented for reading and written language achievement may also explain the significant mathematics and Processing Speed relationship. As suggested by Mather (1991) and Nolting (1991), slow processing speed may impair a person's ability to fluently execute basic mathematics operations and computations.

Auditory Processing (Ga)

Ability to analyze and synthesize auditory stimuli. (Woodcock, 1992, p. 45)

Interpretive Considerations

A review of Table 4-10 indicates that the WJTCA-R Auditory Processing cluster is comprised of two strong measures of this *Gf-Gc* ability. A review of each test's individual summaries in Chapter 3 suggests that if differences are found between the two tests that make up the Auditory Processing cluster, these differences are most likely due to one test emphasizing auditory analysis and synthesis (i.e., Incomplete Words) while the other requires only auditory synthesis ability (i.e., Sound Blending).

Inspection of Table 4-10 indicates that additional auditory processing information can be found within the complete WJ-R battery. The Word Attack achievement test is listed as a mixed measure of auditory processing ability. This mixed classification is different from the strong classification reported by Woodcock (1990). This original classification was based on confirmatory factor studies that did not include other WJ-R reading or written language tests. When other reading and writing tests were included in exploratory analysis of the WJ-R norm data, Word Attack displayed a lower auditory processing loading and an additional loading on a language or orthographic factor (McGrew et al., 1991). Thus, Word Attack is classified as a mixed measure of auditory processing abilities and an orthographic *(Go)* or language ability. This classification is followed by a question mark in Table 4-10 to indicate the tentative nature of this classification modification, a classification needing further study.

TABLE 4-10   Measures of Auditory Processing *(Ga)* in Major Intelligence Batteries

	Strong Measures	Moderate Measures	Mixed Measures
WJ-R	*Incomplete Words* *Sound Blending*		Sound Patterns *(Gf)* Word Attack *(Go)* (Ach)
WISC-R/WAIS-R (WISC-III ?)			
SB-IV			
K-ABC			
DAS (school age)			
DTLA-3			

Tests in italics make up the WJTCA-R Cognitive cluster. Tests with question mark notations are classified based on logical/rational considerations, or limited empirical analysis.

Portions adapted from "Theoretical foundations of the WJ-R measures of cognitive ability," by R. W. Woodcock, 1990, *Journal of Psychoeducational Assessment, 8,* pp. 244–246. Copyright 1990 by the Psychoeducational Corporation. Adapted by permission.

A second supplementary measure of auditory processing is the Sound Patterns test. However, caution must be used when using Sound Patterns to follow up performance on the WJTCA-R Auditory Processing cluster since this test is a mixed measure of auditory processing and reasoning. Furthermore, as presented in Chapter 3, Sound Patterns is a test that has considerable uniqueness. Although it measures aspects of auditory processing and fluid reasoning, performance on Sound Patterns most likely is related to other unique abilities. Special studies reported by McGrew et al. (1991)

failed to clarify the specific nature of these unique abilities. Thus, the two supplementary measures of auditory processing within the WJ-R (i.e., Word Attack and Sound Patterns) must be interpreted cautiously as measures of this broad ability.

Relationship With Other Tests
As indicated in Table 4-10, there are no measures of auditory processing ability in any of the other intelligence batteries. The WJTCA-R auditory processing tests make a unique contribution to the assessment of human abilities. This contribution is noteworthy in light of the importance of auditory processing to the development of reading and writing skills.

Relationship With Reading
A review of Figure 4-5 indicates that auditory processing abilities have clear relationships with reading achievement. This is particularly noticeable for Basic Reading Skills. Auditory Processing demonstrates moderate associations with Basic Reading Skills that decrease with age from a high point at age 5 to approximately age 30. Auditory Processing then increases in its relationship with Basic Reading Skills beyond approximately age 60. The significant relationship between Auditory Processing and Basic Reading Skills makes sense, as auditory-perceptual abilities have been found to be critically related to reading (Mather, 1991; Nolting, 1991; Rourke, 1978, 1981; Rourke, Fisk & Strang, 1986; Wagner, 1986).

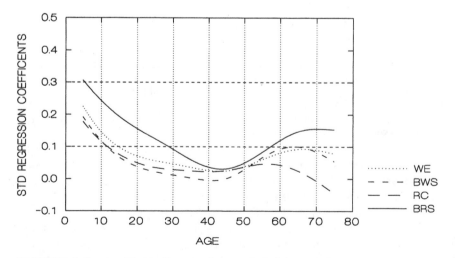

FIGURE 4-5   Auditory Processing and Achievement

Auditory Processing demonstrates a limited relationship with Reading Comprehension from approximately age 5 to age 12. The information presented in Figure 4-5 indicates that clinicians should pay particular attention to performance on the Auditory Processing cluster for reading-related assessments. This is particularly true for the development of basic word recognition and analysis skills during the primary and elementary school years.

Relationship With Written Language

The Auditory Processing cluster displays a moderate relationship with written language achievement during the early school years, but at a level lower than that noted for Basic Reading Skills. Performance on the Auditory Processing cluster is moderately related, decreasingly with age, to both Basic Writing Skills and Written Expression from age 5 to early/middle adolescence. This most likely is related to the importance of auditory skills in the analysis and synthesis of sound patterns when spelling words (Mather, 1991).

Relationship With Mathematics

The lack of smoothed curves in Figure 4-5 for Basic Mathematics Skills and Mathematics Reasoning reflects the absence of any significant relationship between auditory processing abilities and mathematics. Little significance should be attributed to performance on the Auditory Processing cluster as it relates to mathematics achievement.

Visual Processing (Gv)

Ability to analyze and synthesize visual stimuli. (Woodcock, 1992, p. 44)

Interpretive Considerations

A review of Table 4-11 indicates that the WJTCA-R Visual Processing cluster is a relatively weak cognitive cluster, as the two tests that make up this cluster are only moderate indicators of this *Gf-Gc* ability. Although interpreted as a test that may provide useful information about visual processing, the WJTCA-R Spatial Relations test is not listed in Table 4-11. Woodcock (1990) indicates that Spatial Relations is more a measure of fluid reasoning *(Gf)* abilities. No strong measures of visual processing abilities are present in the complete WJ-R battery.

Given the relatively weak association between Visual Closure and Picture Recognition, a finding that indicates that performance on each test is significantly influenced by test-specific unique abilities, clinicians should expect these two tests to frequently produce scores that are discrepant from one another. A review of each test's summary analysis in Chapter 3 suggests possible reasons for this difference. The abilities listed as "hypothesized unique abilities" for each test show little similarity. Clinicians will need to review these respective lists for possible reasons for different test

TABLE 4-11   Measures of Visual Processing (Gv) in Major Intelligence Batteries

	Strong Measures	Moderate Measures	Mixed Measures
WJ-R		*Visual Closure* *Picture Recognition*	
WISC-R/WAIS-R (WISC-III ?)	Block Design Object Assembly	Picture Completion Mazes	
SB-IV	Pattern Analysis	Copying Paper Folding & Cutting	Bead Memory *(Gsm)*
K-ABC	Triangles	Gestalt Closure	Photo Series *(Gf)* Matrix Analogies *(Gf)* Spatial Memory *(Gs)*
DAS (school age)		Pattern Construction Recall of Designs	
DTLA-3		Design Sequences Reversed Letters Design Reproduction Picture Fragments	Story Sequences *(Gs)*

Tests in italics make up the WJTCA-R Cognitive cluster.

Portions adapted from "Theoretical foundations of the WJ-R measures of cognitive ability," by R. W. Woodcock, 1990, *Journal of Psychoeducational Assessment, 8,* pp. 244–246. Copyright 1990 by the Psychoeducational Corporation. Adapted by permission.

scores. Additional follow-up testing with other measures of visual processing may be necessary to clarify performance differences on the Visual Closure and Picture Recognition tests.

Relationship With Other Tests
A review of Table 4-11 indicates that the moderate coverage of visual processing by the Visual Processing cluster can be supplemented by selecting

from a large number of moderate to strong tests in other intelligence batteries. Across the 5 other intelligence batteries listed in Table 4-11, there are 15 different moderate to strong tests that can be used to measure visual processing abilities.

Relationship With Achievement

No figure is presented to summarize the relationship between the Visual Processing cluster and reading, written language, or mathematics achievement. This omission reflects the finding that this cluster consistently failed to display any practical or statistically significant relationship with these achievement areas across the life span. Although visual processing abilities may be related to performance in some vocational and occupational domains (Horn, 1988; Snow, 1988; Snow & Swanson, 1992), the research suggests that clinicians should not dwell on the diagnostic implications of low Visual Processing scores as they relate to reading, written language, or mathematics achievements. Although knowledge of a person's visual processing performance can be useful in the formulation of general instructional strategies (Mather & Jaffe, 1991), the diagnostic importance of performance on the Visual Processing cluster should not be overinterpreted.

Comprehension-Knowledge (Gc)

Breadth and depth of knowledge including verbal communication and reasoning using previously learned procedures. (Woodcock, 1992, p. 44)

Interpretive Considerations

A review of Table 4-12 reveals no shortage of strong comprehension-knowledge measures in the complete WJ-R battery. The two tests comprised in the WJTCA-R Comprehension-Knowledge cluster (i.e., Picture Vocabulary and Oral Vocabulary) are both strong measures of this *Gf-Gc* ability. Additional strong measures can be found within both the cognitive (i.e., Listening Comprehension) and achievement (i.e., Science, Social Studies, and Humanities) sections of the complete WJ-R. Finally, Verbal Analogies can provide additional information, although interpretation of this test as a measure of comprehension-knowledge is made more complex by the influence of fluid reasoning abilities.

The strong comprehension-knowledge classifications for Picture Vocabulary and Oral Vocabulary indicate that typically an examinee's performance on these two tests should be similar. If notable differences are found, the most likely explanation may be found in the different reasoning and language demands of the two tests. As presented in Chapter 3, Oral Vocabulary requires, to a greater extent than Picture Vocabulary, both receptive and expressive language abilities. Picture Vocabulary is more a measure of expressive language with limited receptive language requirements. Finally,

TABLE 4-12   Measures of Comprehension-Knowledge (Gc) in Major Intelligence Batteries

	Strong Measures	Moderate Measures	Mixed Measures
WJ-R	*Picture Vocabulary* *Oral Vocabulary* *Listening Compre-* *hension* Science (Ach) Social Studies (Ach) Humanities (Ach)		Verbal Analogies *(Gf)*
WISC-R/WAIS-R (WISC-III ?)	Information Similarities Vocabulary Comprehension	Picture Arrangement	
SB-IV	Vocabulary Verbal Relations	Absurdities Comprehension	Memory for Sentences *(Gsm)*
K-ABC	Faces and Places (Ach) Riddles (Ach)		
DAS (school age)	Word Definitions Similarities		
DTLA-3	Word Opposites Story Construction Basic Information		

Tests in italics make up the WJTCA-R Cognitive cluster.

Portions adapted from "Theoretical foundations of the WJ-R measures of cognitive ability," by R. W. Woodcock, 1990, *Journal of Psychoeducational Assessment, 8,* pp. 244–246. Copyright 1990 by the Psychoeducational Corporation. Adapted by permission.

Oral Vocabulary requires the evaluation of semantic relations while Picture Vocabulary requires little in the way of reasoning with words.

Relationship With Other Tests
A review of Table 4-12 reveals a large number of additional comprehension-knowledge tests in other intelligence batteries. Across the 5 other intelligence batteries, there are 13 additional strong measures of comprehension-knowledge. Given that there are 6 strong WJ-R measures of comprehen-

sion-knowledge, additional testing with other intelligence tests would most likely be useful only when specific forms of verbal or comprehension-knowledge abilities need exploration.

As was the case with the original 1977 verbal tests, the WJTCA-R comprehension-knowledge tests do not require lengthy verbalization. One- to two-word answers are typically all that is required (McGrew, 1986). Because of this limited oral response requirement, comprehension-knowledge tests from other batteries may provide useful supplemental information to these WJTCA-R tests. For example, the Wechsler Vocabulary or Comprehension tests would provide a greater opportunity to clinically evaluate an examinee's syntax, grammar, detail of oral expression, phonology, and/or morphology (Hessler, 1982; McGrew, 1986).

Relationship With Reading
A review of Figure 4-6 finds that the Comprehension-Knowledge cluster is highly related to reading across most of the life span. In contrast to the other WJTCA-R clusters, the relationship between Comprehension-Knowledge and reading increases systematically with age and is primarily in the strong category (i.e., coefficients of .30 or above).

Given the importance of prior knowledge and verbal abilities in reading comprehension (Lohman, 1989; Mather, 1991; Snow & Swanson, 1991), it is not surprising to see the Comprehension-Knowledge cluster being mod-

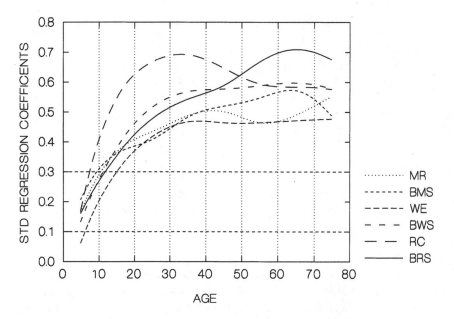

FIGURE 4-6 Comprehension-Knowledge and Achievement

erately related to Reading Comprehension from approximately age 5 to age 8 and thereafter increasing rapidly into the strong category. The Comprehension-Knowledge cluster demonstrates a similar relationship with Basic Reading Skills, although at a lower level until approximately age 50. It appears that as other *Gf-Gc* abilities decrease in their association with reading achievement with increasing age (e.g., see Auditory Processing and Processing Speed), comprehension-knowledge abilities increase in strength of association. Thus, greater attention should be paid to performance on the Comprehension-Knowledge cluster with increasing age.

Relationship With Written Language

A review of Figure 4-6 indicates that the conclusions regarding the relationship between Comprehension-Knowledge and written language parallel those for reading. The relationship between Comprehension-Knowledge and Basic Writing Skills and Written Expression systematically increases in importance across the life span. The strength of association is relatively greater for Basic Writing Skills as its curve is almost exclusively in either the moderate or strong range. The strength of association between Comprehension-Knowledge and Written Expression is relatively lower, particularly before approximately age 7 when writing consists of the development of isolated skills or simple sentences, tasks that draw less on an individual's store of acquired verbal knowledge. As with reading, clinicians should pay increased attention to performance on the Comprehension-Knowledge cluster with increasing age as it relates to written language related assessments.

Relationship With Mathematics

The relationship between performance on the Comprehension-Knowledge cluster and Basic Mathematics Skills and Mathematics Reasoning are similar. In both areas, the relationship is in the moderate range from age 5 to approximately age 10. There is a systematic increasing trend with age, with the relationship for both areas of mathematics increasing into the strong range after age 10. The strong level of association is maintained for both areas of mathematics after age 10.

Fluid Reasoning (Gf)

> *Ability to reason, form concepts, and to solve problems that often include unfamiliar information or procedures. Manifested in the reorganization, transformation, and extrapolation of information.* (Woodcock, 1992, p. 45)

Interpretive Considerations

A review of Table 4-13 shows that the two tests that make up the WJTCA-R Fluid Reasoning cluster (i.e., Analysis-Synthesis and Concept Formation) are both strong tests of this *Gf-Gc* ability. Additional information regarding fluid reasoning abilities can be gleaned from the WJTCA-R Spatial

TABLE 4-13   Measures of Fluid Reasoning (Gf) in Major Intelligence Batteries

	Strong Measures	Moderate Measures	Mixed Measures
WJ-R	*Analysis-Synthesis Concept Formation*	Spatial Relations	Verbal Analogies *(Gc)* Numbers Reversed *(Gsm)* Sound Patterns *(Ga)*
WISC-R/WAIS-R (WISC-III ?)			
SB-IV	Matrices		
K-ABC			Photo Series *(Gv)* Matrix Analogies *(Gv)*
DAS (school age)	Matrices		Sequential & Quantitative Reasoning *(Gq)?*
DTLA-3	Symbolic Relations		

Tests in italics make up the WJTCA-R Cognitive cluster. Tests with question mark notations are classified based on logical/rational considerations, or limited empirical analysis.

Portions adapted from "Theoretical foundations of the WJ-R measures of cognitive ability," by R. W. Woodcock, 1990, *Journal of Psychoeducational Assessment, 8*, pp. 244–246. Copyright 1990 by the Psychoeducational Corporation. Adapted by permission.

Relations test, and to a lesser extent, Verbal Analogies and Numbers Reversed.

The strong fluid reasoning classifications for Analysis-Synthesis and Concept Formation indicate that typically an examinee's performance on these two tests should be similar. However, differences will occasionally occur. Based on individual task analysis (see Chapter 3), the most likely explanations for performance differences between these tests are the differences in the cognition of *figural* (i.e., Concept Formation) and *symbolic* (i.e., Analysis-Synthesis) relations. Furthermore, Analysis-Synthesis is a miniature mathematics logic system and thus may be more related to quantitative reasoning than Concept Formation.

Relationship With Other Tests

Contrary to the clinical lore that has developed around many intelligence tests, a review of Table 4-13 reveals a relative absence of strong or moderate measures of fluid reasoning in other intelligence batteries. A number of mixed tests are available in other intelligence batteries. Interpretation of these other tests is problematic due to the finding that these tests also measure other *Gf-Gc* abilities. If additional information regarding fluid reasoning is needed to follow up Fluid Reasoning cluster scores, the best tests appear to be the Matrices tests from the SB-IV and DAS, or the DTLA-3 Symbolic Relations test. The tentative mixed classification for the DAS Sequential and Quantitative Reasoning test reflects significant differences in interpretation of this test (Daniels & Elliott, 1993; McGhee, 1993).

Although the information presented here focuses on interpretation of the WJTCA-R, the information summarized in Table 4-13 should discourage clinicians from interpreting certain tests as strong measures of fluid intelligence. Nonverbal or performance tests that are most often interpreted as strong measures of fluid reasoning were found to be primarily measures of visual processing (e.g., Wechsler Block Design) in joint confirmatory factor analysis studies.

Relationship With Reading

A review of Figure 4-7 finds that performance on the Fluid Reasoning cluster is moderately related to Reading Comprehension, but not Basic Reading Skills, from age 5 to approximately age 30. This finding makes sense given that reading comprehension requires the use of reasoning to understand and develop concepts and to organize and classify ideas in text (Mather, 1991). In contrast, the ability to recognize or analyze words (i.e., Basic Reading Skills) requires little in the way of fluid reasoning abilities and is more associated with other *Gf-Gc* abilities (e.g., auditory processing and processing speed). The decreased association between Fluid Reasoning and Reading Comprehension after age 30, coupled with the information presented in Figure 4-7 for Comprehension-Knowledge, suggests that prior verbal knowledge becomes more important than fluid reasoning abilities for reading comprehension beyond this age.

Relationship With Written Language

The findings presented for written language in Figure 4-7 are similar in many respects to those for reading. The aspect of written language that requires greater thinking or reasoning with ideas and thoughts (i.e., Written Expression) is moderately associated with fluid reasoning abilities from age 5 to late adolescence. Fluid Reasoning demonstrates a similar trend for Basic Writing Skills, although somewhat lower and ending earlier (i.e., at approximately age 15). The information presented in Figure 4-7 suggests that clinicians should attend to performance on the Fluid Reasoning cluster as it relates to written language development up through adolescence. After this

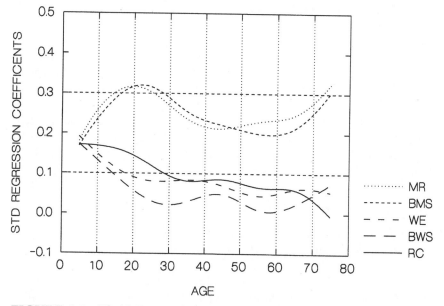

FIGURE 4-7 Fluid Reasoning and Achievement

point, performance on the Fluid Reasoning cluster does not appear to be significantly associated with written language performance.

Relationship With Mathematics

A review of Figure 4-7 indicates that performance on the Fluid Reasoning cluster is more strongly associated with mathematics achievement than with achievement in the language arts. This finding is consistent with a body of literature that suggests that individuals with specific problems in mathematics may show their most salient cognitive deficits in abstract reasoning involving concept formation, using immediate feedback, understanding causal relationships, and problem solving (DeLuca, Rourke, & Del Dotto, 1991; Nolting, 1991; Snow & Swanson, 1992).

The relationships for both Basic Mathematics Skills and Mathematics Reasoning with Fluid Reasoning are very similar. These relationships are characterized as systematically increasing with age from moderate levels at age 5 up to approximately age 15. From age 15 to the mid- to late 20s the relationship is strong, after which it systematically decreases into the moderate range. The possibility of increased relationships between fluid reasoning abilities and both areas of mathematics is suggested after approximately age 65. Performance on the Fluid Reasoning cluster should receive particular attention when evaluating individuals for concerns in the area of mathematics.

ADDITIONAL INTERPRETIVE FEATURES

In addition to the seven WJTCA-R *Gf-Gc* cognitive clusters and supplementary cognitive tests related to each cluster, other cognitive interpretive options are provided within the WJTCA-R and the complete WJ-R battery. Two features are discussed here. A third, the intra-cognitive discrepancies, are discussed in Chapter 6.

An eighth *Gf-Gc* cognitive factor (viz., Quantitative Ability, *Gq*) is measured by tests in the achievement section of the WJ-R battery. Information regarding this factor is reviewed. Information regarding a specialized Oral Language cluster is also presented.

Quantitative Ability (Gq)

> *Ability to comprehend quantitative concepts and relationships and to manipulate numerical symbols.* (Woodcock, 1992, p. 44)

As presented in Chapter 2, the complete Horn-Cattell *Gf-Gc* model includes a quantitative ability *(Gq)* factor. In the 1977 WJ battery, tests of this ability were present in both the cognitive and achievement sections. The Calculation and Applied Problems tests were in the achievement section of the battery, while the Quantitative Concepts test was in the cognitive section. Although intelligence tests have had a long history of including quantitative reasoning tests (e.g., Wechsler Arithmetic; SB-IV Quantitative, Number Series, Equation Building), this practice has not been without criticism. Research (McGrew, 1984, 1986) has suggested that the inclusion of the Quantitative Concepts test in the 1977 WJTCA may have significantly distorted certain cognitive scores (viz., two of the Scholastic Aptitude clusters) for individuals with mathematics-related learning problems.

To address this concern, Quantitative Concepts was moved to the achievement section in the WJ-R. Clinicians who need to obtain information about an individual's quantitative ability will need to turn to the WJ-R achievement battery. The Calculation and Applied Problems tests compose the WJTCA-R Broad Mathematics (Quantitative Ability) cluster score, with Quantitative Concepts providing supplementary information.

The Calculation test measures an individual's ability to perform mathematical calculations requiring the operations of addition, subtraction, multiplication, and division, as well as geometric, trigonometric, logarithmic, and calculus operations (McGrew et al., 1991). The Applied Problems test involves the solving of practical problems in mathematics. The Applied Problems items require an individual to discriminate between relevant and irrelevant information in a problem, identify the procedures that need to be used, and then perform the necessary mathematical calculations (McGrew et al., 1991). The supplementary Quantitative Concepts test is a measure of knowledge of mathematics vocabulary and concepts and does not require an individual to perform calculations or to make application decisions (McGrew et al., 1991).

Technical Considerations

A review of the reliability statistics for the WJTCA-R Broad Mathematics (Quantitative Ability) cluster finds this cluster to have strong reliability characteristics. Across 22 age groups from age 5 to 80 plus, all reliability coefficients were above the .90 criterion (range = .912 to .986; median = .953) (McGrew et al., 1991) required for interpretive purposes.

Similarly to the seven WJTCA-R cognitive clusters reviewed earlier, a network of evidence supports the validity of the Broad Mathematics (Quantitative Ability) cluster. In the norm-based confirmatory factor analysis studies (McGrew et al., 1991) that evaluated an eight-factor WJ-R *Gf-Gc* structure that included a quantitative factor (see Tables 4-3 and 4-4), the fit statistics provided strong support for the model. In addition, a review of the intercorrelations in the WJ-R technical manual finds that the average correlations between the Broad Mathematics (Quantitative Ability) cluster and the seven WJTCA-R cognitive clusters ranged from .34 (Visual Processing) to .59 (Fluid Reasoning). These correlations indicate that the Broad Mathematics (Quantitative Ability) cluster has approximately 12% to 35% shared variance or common abilities with the other seven clusters—values that support the unique contribution of this cluster.

The conclusion that the Broad Mathematics (Quantitative Ability) cluster is measuring a unique ability is further reinforced by the cluster's growth curve characteristics. As reported by McGrew et al. (1991), this curve was distinctly different from the curves of the other WJTCA-R cognitive clusters. Finally, the joint confirmatory factor studies reviewed earlier (Woodcock, 1990) found the three WJ-R mathematics tests to be strongly related to other mathematics or quantitative reasoning tests in other intelligence or achievement batteries.

Interpretive Considerations

A review of Table 4-14 finds the two tests that make up the Broad Mathematics (Quantitative Ability) cluster (i.e., Calculation and Applied Problems), as well as the supplementary Quantitative Concepts test, are all strong measures of the quantitative ability factor. However, given the differences in content of the tests, scores at different levels would not be unexpected depending on the specific nature of an examinee's mathematical skills and reasoning. Information regarding instructional implications and recommendations based on performance on the quantitative ability tests can be found in Mather (1991) and Mather and Jaffe (1992).

Relationships With Other Tests

A further review of Table 4-14 finds that the WJ-R quantitative ability tests correlate with a number of other mathematical or quantitative reasoning

TABLE 4-14   Measures of Quantitative Ability (Gq) in Major Intelligence Batteries

	Strong Measures	Moderate Measures	Mixed Measures
WJ-R	*Calculation (Ach)* *Applied Problems (Ach)* Quantitative Concepts (Ach)		
WISC-R/WAIS-R (WISC-III ?)	Arithmetic		
SB-IV	Quantitative Number Series Equation Building		
K-ABC	Arithmetic (Ach)		Hand Movements *(Gsm)*
DAS (school age)	Basic Number Skills (Ach) ?		Sequential & Quantitative Reasoning *(Gf)* ?
DTLA-3			

Tests in italics make up the WJTCA-R Cognitive cluster. Tests with question mark notations are classified based on logical/rational considerations, or limited empirical analysis.

Portions adapted from "Theoretical foundations of the WJ-R measures of cognitive ability," by R. W. Woodcock, 1990, *Journal of Psychoeducational Assessment, 8,* pp. 244–246. Copyright 1990 by the Psychoeducational Corporation. Adapted by permission.

tests. Clinicians have a number of different tests from other intelligence or related achievement batteries to use for follow-up testing if needed.

Oral Language

The Oral Language cluster is a combination of five WJTCA-R tests that cut across the standard and supplemental cognitive batteries. The Oral Language cluster is intended to be a broad-based measure of oral language or verbal abilities (McGrew et al., 1991). The reliability characteristics of this cluster are very strong and are at levels adequate for interpretation. Across the WJTCA-R norm sample, the Oral Language cluster reliabilities ranged from .938 to .989, with a median of .960. The five WJTCA-R tests that make up the Oral Language cluster, as well as an analysis of each test's stimulus, task, and expressive/receptive language requirements, are presented in Figure 4-8.

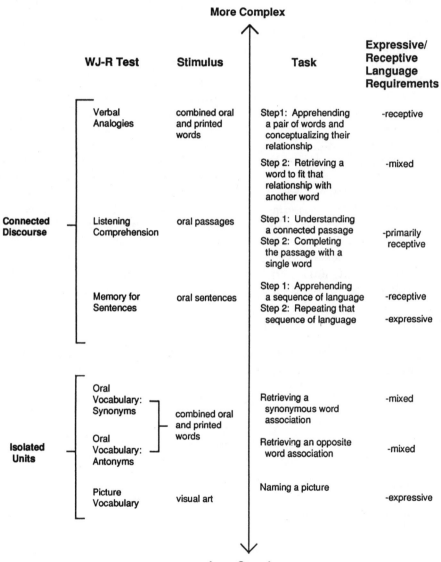

FIGURE 4-8 Skills Measured by the WJ-R Oral Language Cluster
(From the *WJ-R Technical Manual* (p. 113) by K. McGrew, J. Werder, and R. Woodcock, 1991, Chicago: The Riverside Publishing Company. Copyright by The Riverside Publishing Company. Reprinted by permission.)

A review of Figure 4-8 indicates that the WJTCA-R Oral Language cluster is a broad-based measure of language. The combined tests measure a mixture of receptive and expressive language abilities, although the expressive language demands are relatively lower. Only the Memory for Sentences test requires lengthy verbal expression, and this is in a structured format in which the examinee repeats sentences. With the exception of Memory for Sentences, examinees are only required to produce a one-word oral response to the tests in the Oral Language cluster. When an evaluation of an individual's oral language requires greater attention to lengthier oral expression, examiners should consult Table 4-12 for a listing of comprehension-knowledge tests that may possess such task requirements (e.g., Wechsler Vocabulary). Mather (1991) provides suggestions for additional formal and informal assessment methods that can also be used. Instructional implications and possible recommendations related to performance on this cluster are provided by Mather (1991) and Mather and Jaffe (1992).

Information presented by McGrew et al. (1991) provides empirical support for the validity of the Oral Language cluster. Correlations with the major scales from the Wechslers, SB-IV, and K-ABC are summarized in Table 4-14. The WJTCA-R Oral Language cluster correlated highly with the Wechsler Verbal Scale (.75 and .61). In the Grade 10 to 11 sample the Oral Language cluster correlated at a similar high level with SB-IV Verbal Reasoning score (.71). In the Grade 3 to 4 sample, Oral Language correlated higher with SB-IV Short-Term Memory (.69). This finding makes sense given that the SB-IV Short-Term Memory scale includes a sentence imitation task similar to the

TABLE 4-15   Concurrent Correlations for WJTCA-R Oral Language Cluster and Other Measures in Two Samples

Measure	Grades 3–4	Grades 10–11
WISC-R/WAIS-R		
Verbal Scale	**.75**	**.61**
Performance Scale	.36	.39
SB-IV		
Verbal Reasoning	.54	**.71**
Abstract/Visual Reasoning	.50	.49
Quantitative Reasoning	.38	.38
Short-Term Memory	**.69**	.50
K-ABC		
Sequential Processing	.56	——
Simultaneous Processing	.37	——
Achievement	**.82**	——

Correlations based on samples of 70–72 (Grades 3–4) and 50–51 (Grades 10–11) subjects as reported in the *WJ-R Technical Manual* (McGrew et al., 1991).

Memory for Sentences test that is included in the Oral Language cluster. The .82 correlation with the K-ABC Achievement scale also supports the validity of the Oral Language cluster since this scale has been interpreted to measure aspects of verbal abilities (Keith, 1985; Keith & Dunbar, 1984).

The information summarized in Table 4-15 indicates that the Oral Language cluster is the single best measure within the WJTCA-R for assessing an individual's language abilities. Although the WJTCA-R Comprehension -Knowledge cluster also correlates highly with these same measures (McGrew et al., 1991), it is only a two-test cluster in contrast to the five-test Oral Language composite. When individuals are referred for concerns about verbal or oral language, administration of the WJTCA-R Oral Language cluster should receive serious consideration.

Although Oral Language's correlations with other verbal tests are high (generally .60s to .80s), these results indicate that the Oral Language cluster is not interchangeable with these other measures. Correlations of this magnitude indicate shared variance of approximately 40% to 60% with the other verbal measures. Discrepancies between the WJTCA-R Oral Language cluster and the respective verbal scales listed in Table 4-15 will occur, most likely related to the different mix of language abilities assessed by each test.

CONCLUDING COMMENTS

The WJ-R battery provides nine cluster scores for generating hypotheses about a person's intra-cognitive strengths and weaknesses. Empirical information is available that indicates that all nine clusters possess adequate reliability and validity characteristics. Seven of the cognitive clusters are reliable and valid indicators of seven of the Horn-Cattell *Gf-Gc* factors. An eighth *Gf-Gc* factor (i.e., Quantitative Abilities) is available in the achievement section (Broad Mathematics cluster) of the WJ-R battery. A specialized Oral Language cluster is available for assessing a person's broad oral language or verbal abilities. These nine clusters are the primary scores that should be used when generating intra-cognitive hypothesis from a person's performance on the WJ-R.

A review of joint factor analysis studies (Tables 4-7 to 4-14) indicates that the WJTCA-R cognitive clusters measure abilities also measured by other intelligence batteries and measure a number of abilities that are not assessed or assessed in a limited manner by other intelligence batteries. Similar *Gf-Gc* domains are assessed in the areas of short-term memory *(Gsm)*, visual processing *(Gv)*, comprehension-knowledge *(Gc)*, and quantitative abilities *(Gq)*. In contrast, the WJTCA-R cognitive clusters make a unique contribution to the assessment of intelligence by including a number of strong measures of long-term retrieval *(Glr)*, processing speed *(Gs)*, fluid reasoning *(Gf)*, and auditory processing *(Ga)*.

The information summarized in Tables 4-7 to 4-14 highlights the unique contribution the WJTCA-R makes to intellectual assessment. These tables also provide a guide to supplemental WJ-R cognitive and achievement and other intelligence battery tests that can be administered to follow up performance on the WJTCA-R cognitive clusters. Although the specific follow-up testing that is needed will vary from case to case, the relatively weaker factor purity of the WJTCA-R Short-Term Memory and Visual Processing clusters suggests that such efforts may need to be more routine in these two areas.

Six of the WJTCA-R cognitive clusters demonstrated significant relationships that varied by age with reading, written language, and mathematics achievement. The specific cognitive clusters that were found to be significantly related to different domains of achievement are summarized in Table 4-16. The shaded boxes indicate that at some particular age range a specific cognitive cluster was found to be significantly associated with the respective achievement domain. Table 4-16 serves as a quick reference for identifying the WJTCA-R cognitive clusters that should be carefully inspected

TABLE 4-16   Summary of Relationships Between WJTCA-R Gf-Gc Cognitive Clusters and Achievement

Gf-Gc Factor	Reading — Basic Reading Skills	Reading — Reading Comprehension	Written Language — Basic Writing Skills	Written Language — Written Expression	Mathematics — Basic Math Skills	Mathematics — Math Reasoning
Long-Term Retrieval (Glr)		▓		▓		
Short-Term Retrieval (Gsm)	▓					▓
Processing Speed (Gs)	▓	▓	▓	▓	▓	
Auditory Processing (Ga)	▓	▓	▓	▓		
Visual Processing (Gv)						
Comprehension-Knowledge (Gc)	▓	▓	▓	▓	▓	▓
Fluid Reasoning (Gf)						

Shaded boxes indicate that at some age level(s), a *Gf-Gc* Cognitive Cluster was significantly related to the achievement domain.

as a function of different academic concerns. More specific information can then be found by reviewing Figures 4-2 to 4-7.

The information summarized in Table 4-17 indicates that performance on certain cognitive clusters (i.e., Processing Speed, Comprehension-Knowledge, and Fluid Reasoning) may be diagnostically significant across reading, written language, and mathematics, although to different degrees. In contrast, the Long-Term Retrieval and Auditory Processing clusters should be carefully reviewed when evaluating individuals for concerns in the language arts areas of reading and written language. Although providing useful information that may facilitate instructional planning, performance on the Visual Processing cluster appears to be largely unrelated to reading, written language, or mathematics achievement. The finding that the WJTCA-R makes a significant contribution to the inadequately assessed areas of long-term retrieval, processing speed, auditory processing, and fluid reasoning by other intelligence batteries, coupled with the significant relationship between these abilities and different types of achievement, indicates that the WJTCA-R cognitive clusters should be used by assessment personnel who routinely assess individuals for academic problems.

5

SUPPLEMENTAL WJTCA-R
TEST GROUPINGS

In-depth interpretation of *individual* high or low tests in intelligence batteries is not a sound practice. As stated by Kaufman (1979):

> Too many examiners seem to fall into the rut of interpreting high and low subtests in isolation, reciting in their case reports cookbook prose about what each subtest purportedly measures. Mindless interpretation of this sort is a cop-out, and does not usually provide information of practical value. (p.133)

Lying between the extremes of interpreting individual tests and the global full scale intelligence score is the interpretation of groups of tests that share common abilities. The interpretation of shared abilities among a group of tests provides for higher levels of reliability and validity than individual test analysis (Kamphaus, 1993). There is a greater probability of generating more valid intra-cognitive hypotheses if combinations of two or more tests are considered for interpretation.

Chapter 4 presented information on the most valid test grouping structure for interpreting intra-cognitive performance on the WJTCA-R. The seven *Gf-Gc* cognitive clusters are supported by extensive exploratory and confirmatory factor analysis studies in the WJ-R standardization sample (McGrew et al., 1991) as well as joint analyses with other intelligence batteries (McGhee, 1993; Woodcock, 1990). Given that legalities now require intelligence tests to be interpreted according to higher standards (Kamphaus, 1993; Matarazzo, 1990), the seven cognitive clusters discussed should receive priority consideration in intra-cognitive interpretation.

However, individual cases often present test profiles that defy interpretation within the organizational structure provided by the test's author. In these situations, clinicians may need alternative frameworks for organizing and interpreting patterns. This chapter presents a number of supplemental test groupings that can be used in clinical interpretation of the WJTCA-R.

The test groupings presented in this chapter all have some empirical foundation. This differs somewhat from my original book (McGrew, 1986) where two chapters were devoted to presenting alternative test groupings or theoretical models by which to interpret performance on the WJTCA tests. Although most of the original WJTCA alternative test groupings had empirical foundations, some were drawn from isolated small studies and a few were only rationally based.

The supplemental test groupings presented in this chapter are all based on empirical analyses of the WJTCA-R norming data. The results from the exploratory and confirmatory factor studies reported in the WJ-R technical manual (McGrew et al., 1991) were reinspected with a relaxed criterion for what constituted a significant or salient factor loading. In addition, relationships between tests that were unaccounted for by the factors (i.e., correlations among test residuals) in the confirmatory factor studies were closely inspected. Finally, the majority of the groupings are drawn from unpublished analyses I completed with the WJTCA-R norm data (McGrew, 1993b). Using the WJTCA-R norm data, I deliberately underfactored the WJTCA-R tests to identify groups of tests that merge together into larger groupings. In addition, the same norm data was subjected to cluster analytic methods. The results of these supplementary empirical studies have identified twelve test groupings that may facilitate clinical interpretation of the WJTCA-R.

Those familiar with my 1986 WJTCA text will notice the absence of a separate chapter on alternative theoretical models of intelligence for interpreting the WJTCA-R tests. The atheoretical nature of the original WJTCA resulted in the search for theoretical models of intelligence by which to interpret the tests. The use of *Gf-Gc* theory in the development of the WJTCA-R and the strong support for the operationalized WJTCA-R *Gf-Gc* structure (McGhee, 1993; McGrew et al., 1991; Woodcock, 1990) render such theoretical speculations largely useless. Although portions of some of these alternative models of intelligence are contained in this chapter, I leave the theoretical speculation and empirical validation regarding the fit of these different models to the WJTCA-R to others.

EXPANDED Gf-Gc TEST GROUPINGS

The organizational structure presented by the WJTCA-R authors defines certain groups of tests as measuring specific *Gf-Gc* factors. The groupings presented in this section represent certain of these *Gf-Gc* test groupings, but with additional tests added that may be consistent with the abilities measured by the factors. When appropriate, supportive information from related WJ-R achievement tests is also presented. Five *expanded* test groupings are presented.

Expanded Long-Term Retrieval (Glr)

Cognitive *Tests 1–14*	*Cognitive* *Tests 15–21*
Visual-Auditory Learning	Delayed Recall-VAL
Memory for Names	Delayed Recall-MN
Picture Recognition	
Visual Closure	

The Visual-Auditory Learning, Memory for Names, and two delayed recall tests are the primary measures of long-term storage and retrieval in the WJTCA-R. This *Gf-Gc* factor measures a person's ability to store information that is later retrieved through association. Clinicians may find the Picture Recognition and Visual Closure tests grouped with the primary long-term retrieval tests. Although Picture Recognition and Visual Closure could be interpreted separately as measures of visual processing *(Gv)*, performance on these two tests may be consistent with the abilities measured by the primary long-term storage and retrieval tests.

Given the distorted or partial visual images in Visual Closure, examinees may need to search through their store of visual images and retrieve a verbal label that is associated with the visual stimuli. In the case of Picture Recognition, examinees draw upon their memory to recognize the correct subset of previously presented pictures. Although only a brief delay occurs between the presentation of the original stimulus and the presentation of the response options in Picture Recognition, this delay may involve the beginning stages of the long-term storage process. In addition, during the Picture Recognition test examinees may use a verbal mediation strategy to associate verbal labels with the different visual stimuli, a process that may be facilitated by long-term retrieval abilities.

Performance on the Visual Closure and Picture Recognition tests may provide additional evidence of either a strength or weakness in long-term storage and retrieval. If these two tests are consistent with the primary long-term storage and retrieval tests, clinicians should entertain the hypothesis that all of these tests provide a broad base of information regarding long-term storage and retrieval abilities.

Expanded Short-Term Memory (Gsm)

Cognitive Tests 1-14	*Cognitive Tests 15-21*
Memory for Sentences	Numbers Reversed
Memory for Words	Listening Comprehension

The Memory for Sentences, Memory for Words, and Numbers Reversed test are the three best measures of short-term memory available in the WJTCA-R (see Table 4-8 in Chapter 4). The listing of the Listening Comprehension test together with these three short-term memory tests suggests that for some examinees, performance on this test may reflect more about the person's short-term memory and less about their comprehension-knowledge abilities.

As noted in the description of Listening Comprehension in Chapter 3, this test requires examinees to listen to tape-recorded passages and then supply a single word that is missing at the end of the passage. Although performance on this test is primarily influenced by a variety of vocabulary and comprehension skills, the ability to retain the orally presented information in short-term memory is involved. Many of the Listening Comprehension passages require the ability to listen to a text containing 20 to 40 words. Significant short-term memory deficits may impact an individual's ability to retain the information long enough for comprehension. A WJTCA-R profile that is characterized by a markedly high or low Listening Comprehension test together with similar levels of performance on the Memory for Sentences, Memory for Words and Numbers Reversed tests, may be providing consistent information about a very broad strength or weakness in short-term memory abilities.

Expanded Processing Speed (Gs)

Cognitive Tests 1-14	*Cognitive Tests 15-21*
Visual Matching	Numbers Reversed
Cross Out	

As noted in Chapter 4, the Visual Matching and Cross Out tests are strong measures of a person's ability to efficiently and fluently perform automatic cognitive tasks (i.e., processing speed). The association of these two tests with the Numbers Reversed test, a test with no time constraints, is on the surface inconsistent with a processing speed interpretation. Task analysis of Numbers Reversed, however, sheds light on possible reasons for its association with Visual Matching and Cross Out.

Numbers Reversed requires an examinee to auditorily receive a sequence of numbers, retain them in short-term memory, and then reorganize the digits for subsequent recall. Many individuals use covert visual imagery to aid in the perceptual reorganization of the auditory stimuli during digit reversal tasks (Mishra, Ferguson, & King, 1985). The ability to perform all of these tasks quickly, automatically, and efficiently (i.e., processing speed) may facilitate a higher level of performance on this task. Thus, the grouping of the Numbers Reversed test with Visual Matching and Cross Out could be interpreted as consistent with a processing speed interpretation. As noted in Chapter 4, the Writing Fluency test from the WJ-R achievement section also provides additional information regarding processing speed.

Two other alternative explanations for this grouping are also possible. First, the visual imagery component in Numbers Reversed, coupled with the visual stimuli of Visual Matching and Cross Out, suggests a slightly modified speed of processing interpretation. Rather than suggesting information about general processing speed, this triad may indicate a person's facility or fluency with speed of visual processing, particularly with visual symbols. Second, all three tests require examinees to focus sustained attention and concentration. Visual Matching and Cross Out require sustained concentration for three minutes each. Digit repetition tasks such as Numbers Reversed are also frequently described as being sensitive to attention and concentration variables. Consistent levels of performance on these three tests may provide insights into an individual's attention and concentration abilities.

Expanded Comprehension-Knowledge (Gc)

Cognitive Tests 1-14	*Cognitive* Tests 15-21
Picture Vocabulary	Verbal Analogies
Oral Vocabulary	Listening Comprehension
Memory for Sentences	
Visual Closure	
Incomplete Words	

As indicated earlier (see Table 4-12 in Chapter 4), the Picture Vocabulary, Oral Vocabulary, Memory for Sentences, Verbal Analogies, and Listening Comprehension tests are all measures of a person's breadth and depth of knowledge (i.e., Gc—comprehension-knowledge), with particular emphasis on verbal knowledge. The grouping of these tests in a WJTCA-R profile should be expected. A similar level of performance on the Visual Closure and Incomplete Words tests, rather than suggesting different abilities, may further reinforce the primary interpretation of an individual's comprehension-knowledge abilities.

Performance on the Visual Closure test may be related to comprehension-knowledge abilities, as examinees must retrieve the correct verbal label or word to identify the visual stimulus. The Incomplete Words test requires examinees to listen to words that have one or more phonemes missing and then identify the complete word. Fluent access to a large vocabulary may facilitate performance on this test. The fact that fluent access to a rich vocabulary may enhance performance on both the Visual Closure and Incomplete Words tests is consistent with the comprehension-knowledge factor.

Certain tests from the WJ-R achievement battery may also be similar to the cognitive tests included in this grouping. Most notable would be the three knowledge tests (i.e., Science, Social Studies, and Humanities). Even the quantitative tests of Applied Problems and Quantitative Concepts may fall at a similar level, and, rather than reflecting primarily quantitative abilities, this finding may provide additional information about a person's comprehension-knowledge abilities (McGrew, 1993b). The Applied Problems test presents mathematical problems in a largely verbal or language context, while Quantitative Concepts measures a type of vocabulary knowledge (viz., mathematics vocabulary). Finally, although not included in any of the reported empirical studies, performance on the WJ-R Reading Vocabulary and Passage Comprehension reading tests may provide support for hypotheses about an individual's comprehension-knowledge abilities.

Expanded Fluid Reasoning (Gf)

Cognitive *Tests 1-14*	*Cognitive* *Tests 15-21*
Concept Formation	Spatial Relations
Analysis-Synthesis	Verbal Analogies
Oral Vocabulary	Listening Comprehension
	Numbers Reversed
	Sound Patterns

Of all the WJTCA-R tests that load on the fluid reasoning factor, Concept Formation, Analysis-Synthesis, Spatial Relations, and Verbal Analogies are those that consistently load the highest. As reported by McGrew et al. (1991), Numbers Reversed and Sound Patterns also are associated with the fluid reasoning factor, although at much lower levels. The two remaining tests, Oral Vocabulary and Listening Comprehension, can also be interpreted as requiring reasoning abilities. Oral Vocabulary requires reasoning in the form of thinking of synonyms to words. Listening Comprehension requires examinees to understand the ideas presented in the orally presented passages at a high enough level to "figure out" the missing word.

The six major tests in this grouping (not Numbers Reversed or Sound Patterns) require complex mental processing characterized by abstract-conceptual thinking, problem solving, and deductive logic. The overriding commonality is the processing of abstract relationships, ideas, conceptualizations, "what-if" reasoning, and/or logic. In this regard, this grouping of tests is similar to the Reasoning-Thinking and Broad Reasoning test groupings presented for the 1977 WJTCA (McGrew, 1986). Given the verbal and nonverbal nature of the six tests, Broad Reasoning may be an appropriate label for this expanded fluid reasoning test grouping.

ADDITIONAL TEST GROUPINGS

Seven additional test groupings are presented here that are not expanded versions of the WJTCA-R *Gf-Gc* factors. These groupings emerged when two or more of the seven WJTCA-R *Gf-Gc* factors combined in the supplementary empirical analysis studies.

Auditory Sequential Processing/Memory

Cognitive Tests 1–14	*Cognitive Tests 15–21*
Memory for Sentences	Numbers Reversed
Memory for Words	Sound Patterns
Incomplete Words	
Sound Blending	

Across all supplementary empirical analyses, this grouping of six tests was the most consistent pattern to emerge. This grouping represents a merger of all the WJTCA-R short-term memory and auditory processing tests. Although based on a smaller number of tests, this grouping is similar to the Auditory-Sequential Processing grouping presented for interpretation of the 1977 WJTCA (McGrew, 1986).

Analysis of the six tests reveals that in all cases, auditory stimuli are presented that must be received in a successive or sequential mode, retained over a brief period of time, and subsequently recalled and processed in some way. The overriding commonality is the sequential presentation of auditory stimuli that must be processed through short-term memory. The short-term memory component of these tests is obvious. Sequential processing demands are present as maintaining the serial or temporal order of the auditory stimuli is important to performance on the tests. The requirement that the stimuli be processed sequentially, and the fact that many of the stimuli are linguistic are characteristic of the successive-sequential mode of cognitive processing that is most frequently associated with the simultaneous-successive model of cognitive processing (Kamphaus, 1990; Kamphaus & Reynolds, 1984; Kaufman, 1984; Kaufman & Kaufman, 1983; Naglieri & Das, 1990; Naglieri, Kamphaus & Kaufman, 1983).

Consistently high or low performance on this grouping of tests may reflect a strength or weakness in successive or sequential processing or auditory sequential short-term memory. Determining whether the short-term memory or successive-sequential processing component is most salient is difficult; thus the title refers to both abilities.

The observation that the WJ-R Word Attack test also associates with these cognitive tests suggests another possible interpretation. Mather (1991) has classified the WJTCA-R tests according to their different linguistic or language processing characteristics. The six cognitive tests in this grouping together with the Word Attack test represent all but one (i.e., Listening Comprehension) of the tests she classified as measuring the linguistic processing components of Verbal Attention and Memory (i.e., Sound Patterns, Memory for Words, Numbers Reversed, Memory for Sentences, Listening Comprehension) and Phonological Awareness (i.e., Sound Blending, Incomplete Words, Sound Patterns, Word Attack). Clinicians may need to consider consistent performance on these tests as providing useful information regarding a person's linguistic competency.

Visual Perceptual Fluency

Cognitive Tests 1–14	*Cognitive Tests 15–21*
Cross Out	Spatial Relations
Visual Matching	
Visual Closure	
Picture Recognition	

This grouping of tests represents the merger of the processing speed and visual processing tests. Given the visual nature of the stimuli used in the two processing speed tests (i.e., Visual Matching and Cross Out), when combined with the three visual processing tests, the most overriding commonality is the use of visual stimuli. Although the processing is not necessarily complex for the two speeded tests, all five tests require some form of visual processing that involves either visual recognition, discrimination, scanning, analysis and synthesis, or spatial manipulation. The speed requirements of Visual Matching and Cross Out, combined with their relatively low level of visual processing, suggest that this grouping may not reflect complex visual perceptual organizational ability, but more the efficiency and fluency of basic visual perceptual abilities.

This hypothesis is consistent with two WJ-R achievement tests that were found related to these five cognitive tests. As noted in Chapter 4, the Writing Fluency test requires processing speed, as individuals must write simple sentences within a seven-minute time limit. The relationship with the Calculation test is more difficult to explain, although performance on this mathematics test may be facilitated by the automaticity of a person's basic mathematics facts. Performance on these two related achievement tests may be influenced by speed of automatic processing with visual stimuli (i.e., writing letters in Writing Fluency; working with numbers in Calculation). Together with the five cognitive tests, this grouping may measure the fluency or efficiency of a person's visual perceptual processing abilities.

Auditory Attention/Listening

Cognitive Tests 1–14	*Cognitive Tests 15–21*
Incomplete Words	Sound Patterns
Sound Blending	Listening Comprehension

Three of the tests in this grouping (i.e., Incomplete Words, Sound Blending, and Sound Patterns) are the primary measures of auditory processing in the WJTCA-R. Each test requires some form of analysis and synthesis of patterns of sounds. The Listening Comprehension test has no similar requirement. Instead, examinees listen to brief, orally presented passages. This four-test grouping does not appear to be an expanded version of auditory processing.

The primary similarity among all four tests is the requirement for an examinee to passively listen to stimuli presented via a tape player. However, three other WJTCA-R tests (i.e., Memory for Words, Memory for Sentences, and Numbers Reversed) that have a similar requirement did not combine with the four tests in this grouping. The main difference between the unrelated auditory memory tests and the Incomplete Words, Sound Blending, Sound Patterns, and Listening Comprehension tests may be due to the latter tests making more significant demands on an individual's ability to attend and listen carefully.

When performing on Incomplete Words, Sound Blending, and Sound Patterns, examinees must carefully listen to isolated sound units and patterns and then either analyze or synthesize the isolated units. This task may be more demanding in terms of listening than the three unrelated auditory memory tests (i.e., Memory for Words, Memory for Sentences, and Numbers Reversed), where the stimuli are presented in complete meaningful units (i.e., words and numbers) that require no analysis and synthesis. The three auditory processing tests in this grouping may make significant demands on an examinee's ability to attend and listen.

Although the Listening Comprehension test is similar to the three unrelated auditory memory tests in the use of words and sentences as stimuli, the length of the stimuli (i.e., over 20 to 40 words in some passages) may require greater focused attention. The greater emphasis on sustained attention and listening may account for the association of the Listening Comprehension test with the three auditory processing tests. Together, the Incomplete Words, Sound Blending, Sound Patterns, and Listening Comprehension tests may reflect a person's ability to focus attention and listen to auditorily presented information.

New Learning Efficiency

Cognitive Tests 1–14

Memory for Names
Visual-Auditory Learning
Analysis-Synthesis
Concept Formation

Cognitive Tests 15–21

Despite their use as predictors of learning, intelligence tests have been criticized for not including actual learning tasks (Kaufman, 1979). The WJTCA-R is unique in the field of intellectual assessment as it contains four tests that require an examinee to learn new material during the actual test session. The Memory for Names, Visual-Auditory Learning, Analysis-Synthesis, and Concept Formation tests may provide extremely valuable insights regarding an individual's efficiency or rate of learning new material. This is the same test grouping that was presented for the 1977 WJTCA (McGrew, 1986), but with the addition of the new Memory for Names test.

More important than a generalized hypothesis about learning efficiency is the wealth of clinical information available from close observation of an examinee's behavior during performance on these four tests. Clinical observations may reveal valuable insights about an individual's use of feedback to modify performance, the amount of clues necessary to learn a task, the effect of cognitive style variables on performance, and frustration tolerance when learning.

Broad Synthesis Ability

Cognitive Tests 1–14

Incomplete Words
Sound Blending
Visual Closure

Cognitive Tests 15–21

Spatial Relations

This grouping consists of two tests each from the *Gf-Gc* factors of auditory and visual processing. The most likely shared ability is evident based on a review of the task demands of each test, as well as a review of the auditory and visual processing tests that are *not* included. Incomplete Words and Sound Blending both require the synthesis of isolated sounds. Visual Closure and Spatial Relations require the integration or synthesis of isolated visual parts into a whole. Conversely, neither of the "missing" visual (i.e.,

Picture Recognition) or auditory (i.e., Sound Patterns) tests require any closure or synthesis process. It is hypothesized that these four tests, if at a similar level in a WJTCA-R profile, may be suggestive of a strength or weakness in the broad ability to integrate or synthesize isolated parts into a whole. In a sense this is a broad Gestalt closure test grouping. Such abilities may be consistent with the simultaneous mode of processing described in the simultaneous-successive model of cognitive processing (Kamphaus, 1990; Kamphaus & Reynolds, 1984; Kaufman, 1984; Kaufman & Kaufman, 1983; Naglieri & Das, 1990; Naglieri et al., 1983).

Word Finding/Verbal Retrieval

Cognitive Tests 1–14	*Cognitive Tests 15–21*
Picture Vocabulary	
Oral Vocabulary	
Incomplete Words	
Sound Blending	
Visual Closure	

Despite being tests from such different *Gf-Gc* abilities as comprehension-knowledge and auditory and visual processing, these five tests may group together due to a common word finding or verbal retrieval ability. The ability to find or retrieve the single correct word is evident in the case of the Picture and Oral Vocabulary tests. The ability to fluently retrieve a single word that is associated with the synthesized patterns of sounds in the Incomplete Words and Sound Blending tests may facilitate performance on these two auditory processing tests. Finally, as discussed earlier regarding the Expanded Long-Term Retrieval test grouping, examinees need to retrieve a verbal label that is associated with the visual stimuli in the Visual Closure test. It is hypothesized that a similar level of performance on these five tests may be influenced by fluency of word finding or verbal retrieval.

Nonverbal Ability (nonspeeded)

Cognitive Tests 1–14	*Cognitive Tests 15–21*
Visual Closure	Delayed Recall-MN
Picture Recognition	Delayed Recall-VAL
Concept Formation	Spatial Relations
Analysis-Synthesis	
Memory for Names	
Visual-Auditory Learning	

With the exception of the two WJTCA-R speeded tests (i.e., Visual Matching and Cross Out), these nine tests are all the WJTCA-R tests that present visual stimuli to the examinee. All other WJTCA-R tests are presented orally. Although this grouping of tests does not represent a pure nonverbal grouping (i.e., verbal responses are required), consistently high or low performance on these tests, when contrasted with the remaining auditory-linguistic tests, may provide useful information about differences between a person's nonverbal/visual and auditory/linguistic abilities. This grouping of tests may prove useful when evaluating individuals with significant language-based difficulties.

CONCLUDING COMMENTS

The supplemental test groupings presented in this chapter should aid clinicians when engaging in Type II or intra-cognitive discrepancy interpretation of the WJTCA-R. Before leaving these groupings, a number of comments are necessary.

First, the usefulness of the supplemental test groupings will be determined by future clinical utility and research efforts. The accumulation of a sufficiently large knowledge and data base is a lengthy and time-consuming process. Since this knowledge building is an ongoing process, it is expected that the utility of some of the groupings presented in this chapter will pass the test of time, while others may not.

Second, a major concern in the shared ability approach to the interpretation of intelligence tests is the lack of empirical support for the validity of many hypothesized groupings (Kamphaus, 1993). Hypotheses derived from an individual's performance on an individual intelligence test need to be based on reliable and valid information. Thus, the WJTCA-R *Gf-Gc* test structure provided by the test's authors (see Chapter 4) should receive priority attention in intra-cognitive interpretation. The WJTCA-R *Gf-Gc* structure is grounded in a sound empirical foundation. Clinicians should use the supplemental WJTCA-R test groupings only after attempts are made to use the WJTCA-R *Gf-Gc* interpretive structure. Clinicians need to be cognizant of the lower level of validity of hypotheses derived from the supplemental test groupings.

Finally, although a number of supplemental test groupings are presented in this chapter, this list is by no means exhaustive. There are probably other valid test groupings, some of them based on other theoretical models of intelligence, that may help unlock WJTCA-R test profiles. It will be exciting to learn of other WJTCA-R test groupings advanced by clinicians, theoreticians, and researchers.

6

INTERPRETING THE WJTCA-R TEST PROFILE

The individual tested makes an unspoken plea to the examiner not to summarize his or her intelligence in a single, cold number; the goal of profile interpretation should be to respond to the pleas by identifying hypothesized strengths and weaknesses that extend well beyond the limited information provided by the FS-IQ and that will conceivably lead to practical recommendations that help answer the referral questions.—A. S. Kaufman (1990, p. 422)

The preceding three chapters provided the necessary material to unlock the WJTCA-R individual test profiles. Chapter 3 presented information on the characteristics of the 21 WJTCA-R tests. Chapters 4 and 5 focused on how the individual tests can be grouped to generate hypotheses about an individual's cognitive strengths and weaknesses. This chapter outlines interpretive procedures for applying this material.

The goal is to present a *mode of thinking* for clinicians to adopt when interpreting the WJTCA-R individual test profiles. The emphasis is on interpreting *shared abilities* measured by groups of WJTCA-R tests (Kamphaus, 1993; Kaufman, 1990), and not on characteristic WJTCA-R profiles. The search for characteristic intelligence test profiles for clinical groups has been largely unproductive (Kaufman, 1990). To date, no empirical WJTCA-R profile studies have been reported that could be used to guide interpretation.

In presenting a step-by-step interpretive process there is the risk of the sequential steps acquiring a mechanistic or cookbook flavor. This is an inherent constraint of the linear nature of the written word and cannot be avoided. The reader is advised that the *process for interpreting the WJTCA-R individual test profile must be interfaced with the practitioner's clinical skills*. The reader who is familiar with the work of Kaufman (1979, 1990) will detect obvious similarities between the process presented in this chapter and the interpretive process Kaufman outlined for the Wechsler batteries.

The interpretive process described here is similar to the one originally presented for interpretation of the 1977 WJTCA tests (McGrew, 1986). However, the revision and expansion of the WJTCA-R, as well as the introduction of new interpretative features (i.e., intra-cognitive discrepancy scores), require a number of significant modifications to the process.

All 21 WJTCA-R tests typically will not be administered to most individuals. Clinicians will customize the comprehensiveness and nature of the assessment to the specific referral concerns. Some referrals may only require administration of the 7-test Standard Cognitive battery, others the 14-test Extended Cognitive scale, and others a unique combination of tests. This flexibility makes it difficult to present a standard interpretive process. As a result, interpretative procedures are described that can be used with the three primary WJTCA-R administration strategies that will most likely be used.

THREE PRIMARY WJTCA-R TEST ADMINISTRATION STRATEGIES

It is anticipated that three different test administration strategies will dominate most uses of the WJTCA-R. The *Standard Battery* strategy consists of administering the 7-test Standard cognitive battery, and possibly select supplementary tests based on specific referral concerns. The *Extended Battery* strategy is the most comprehensive and consists of administering the first fourteen cognitive tests, which serve as the basis for the Extended Broad Cognitive Ability cluster, and possibly select additional tests. Finally, the *Differential Aptitude* strategy focuses on administering the 8 tests across the Standard and Supplemental batteries that allow for the calculation of the four Scholastic Aptitude clusters, and possibly select additional tests.

These three WJTCA-R administration strategies have different strengths and weaknesses in terms of available interpretative features, breadth of coverage of the *Gf-Gc* abilities, economy of testing time, and focus on broad (i.e., Broad Cognitive Ability clusters) versus narrow (i.e., Scholastic Aptitude clusters) prediction of expected achievement. A comparison of the strengths and weaknesses of the three different strategies is presented in Table 6-1.

A review of Table 6-1 indicates that the Extended Battery strategy provides the most comprehensive coverage of predictive and strength and weakness interpretive options. Both Broad Cognitive Ability and Scholastic Aptitude clusters are available in the Extended Battery strategy. In addition, the

TABLE 6-1 Comparative Features of the Three Different WJTCA-R Test Administration Strategies

| | Strategy | | |
Feature	Extended Battery	Standard Battery	Differential Aptitude
Number of tests administered	14	7	8
Prediction options			
Broad Cognitive Ability	X	X	—
Scholastic Aptitude	X	—	X
Cognitive strength and weakness interpretation			
At least 1 test per *Gf/Gc* ability	X	X	X
At least 2 tests per *Gf/Gc* ability	X	—	—
Intra-cognitive discrepancy scores	X	—	—

Extended Battery strategy provides the most comprehensive information (i.e., 2 tests per *Gf-Gc* ability; intra-cognitive discrepancy scores) for analyzing cognitive strengths and weaknesses. The comprehensiveness of the Extended Battery strategy is at the expense of economy of testing time, as a minimum of 14 tests must be administered.

The Standard Battery and Differential Aptitude strategies have the advantage of economy of testing time since each requires the administration of only seven or eight tests. The primary difference between these two strategies is the scores used for making predictions about a person's expected achievement. The Standard Battery strategy provides a broad-based score (i.e., Broad Cognitive Ability Standard cluster), while the Differential Aptitude strategy provides narrow, specialized aptitude scores (i.e., Scholastic Aptitude clusters) for prediction.

Both the Standard Battery and Differential Aptitude strategies include at least one test of each *Gf-Gc* cognitive ability, although they are not the same tests. Although the Differential Aptitude strategy focuses on administering those tests needed to obtain the four Scholastic Aptitude clusters, it is fortuitous that seven of the eight tests are drawn from seven of the Gf-Gc cognitive ability domains. The Differential Aptitude strategy provides two measures (i.e., Analysis-Synthesis and Concept Formation) of Fluid Reasoning *(Gf)*. The intra-cognitive discrepancy scores are not available for either the Standard Battery or Differential Aptitude strategies.

THE EXTENDED BATTERY STRATEGY

The Extended Battery test administration strategy is the strategy that lends itself most easily to an interpretive process similar to that outlined for the WJTCA (McGrew, 1986) and other intelligence tests (Kamphaus, 1993; Kaufman, 1979, 1990). The process for generating hypotheses about an individual's cognitive strengths and weaknesses when using the Extended Battery strategy is described below.

Step 1: Identify Significant Strengths and Weaknesses Within the WJTCA-R Test Profile

Identifying relative strengths and weaknesses within a WJTCA-R test profile is the starting point for interpretation. "Making sense of these fluctuations is the crux of the task" (Kaufman, 1990, p. 429), a task that requires in-depth knowledge of the information described in this chapter and the three previous chapters.

When using the Extended Battery strategy, there are two different approaches for evaluating intra-individual variability. The identification of significant fluctuations through either of these methods gives clinicians their "detectives licenses" (Kaufman, 1990, p.482) to engage in clinical interpretation. The failure to identify any significant strengths or weaknesses in the WJTCA-R profile should be interpreted to mean that the profile may only be reflecting normal or chance variability.

Strengths and Weaknesses at the Cluster Level

As described in Chapter 1, a separate intra-cognitive discrepancy score is provided for each of the seven WJTCA-R cognitive clusters. Each cognitive cluster score is compared to a predicted or expected score for a person that is based on the average of the person's six other cognitive cluster scores. Each intra-cognitive discrepancy score is compared against intra-cognitive discrepancy norms that are based on the WJTCA-R norm data (McGrew et al., 1991). These scores allow clinicians to quantify how discrepant each of a person's seven *Gf-Gc* cognitive clusters is from the other six cluster scores. The intra-cognitive discrepancy scores are presented in terms of percent of the population and the standard deviation of the difference scores (SD DIFF scores based on standard error of estimate units). The intra-cognitive discrepancy score scale has a mean of zero and standard deviation of ±1.0 (McGrew et al., 1991).

A WJTCA-R SD DIFF score of −1.50 for the Processing Speed cluster would mean that the person's Processing Speed score was −1.50 standard deviation units below the average of the other six cognitive cluster scores. This discrepancy is found in approximately 6.5% percent of the population. A +0.95 intra-cognitive discrepancy for the Visual Processing cluster means that the person's Visual Processing cluster score is +0.95 standard deviation units above the average of the other six WJTCA-R Cognitive cluster scores. This discrepancy is found in approximately 17% of the population. The intra-cognitive discrepancy scores are useful when evaluating cognitive strengths and weaknesses within the WJTCA-R *Gf-Gc* interpretative framework at the *cluster score level*.

When using intra-cognitive discrepancy scores to identify strengths and weaknesses between the WJTCA-R Cognitive clusters, one must operationally define a "significant" discrepancy. Based on past clinical practices for defining an unusual occurrence, intra-cognitive SD DIFF scores ranging from ±1.0 to ± 2.0 should be considered as possible criteria. The selection of a criterion will depend on the interpretative philosophy of each clinician.

In this text the ±1.5 criterion is used. The ±1.0 value is felt to be too liberal, as approximately 32% of the population will display either positive or negative intra-cognitive discrepancies in each area. In contrast, the ±2.0 criterion is judged to be too conservative because it will identify approximately 5% of the population as having either a positive or negative intra-cognitive discrepancy in each cognitive area. The ±1.5 criterion will identify approximately 13% of the population as having either a positive or negative intra-cognitive discrepancy in each cognitive area.

Strengths and Weaknesses at the Individual Test Level

Detailed analysis of strengths and weaknesses at the *individual test level* requires a different approach. In order to identify strengths and weaknesses among a person's individual WJTCA-R tests, a reference point against which all individual tests are compared must be established. In the interpretation of most intelligence tests this is some form of average score.

For reasons presented in Chapter 8, the Broad Cognitive Ability cluster standard score cannot accurately be used to represent the "average" score among the individual tests that compose the cluster score. The Broad Cognitive Ability cluster *W* score cannot be used as recommended for clinical interpretation of the WJTCA (McGrew, 1986) since no individual WJTCA-R test profile is available for the plotting of the individual tests and the Broad Cognitive cluster *with their respective confidence bands*. The WJTCA-R Developmental Level profiles are based on the W score metric, but these profiles provide for the plotting of *developmental* level bands and not *confidence* bands. The individual test profile recommended for strength and weakness interpretation of the WJTCA (McGrew, 1986) is not available for similar use in the WJTCA-R.

The best reference point is an *average* standard score against which all individual test standard scores are compared. Given that within the Extended Battery strategy some cases may require the administration of the basic 14 tests, while other cases may dictate the administration of additional tests (i.e, from 14 to 21+), the basis of the average reference point would be comprised of different mixes of abilities for different cases. A standard reference point is recommended to remedy this situation.

Regardless of the final number of tests administered in the Extended Battery strategy, an average standard score *based on the first 14 tests* that serve as the foundation for this strategy is recommended. This average score is recommended since it is based on an equal proportion of tests of each of the seven *Gf-Gc* abilities measured by the WJTCA-R. The strength and weakness worksheet presented in Figure 6-1 is provided for completing the necessary calculations.

An individual's standard scores ($M = 100$; $SD = 15$) are recorded in the "SS" (Standard Score) column after each of the first 14 tests is administered. If additional tests have also been administered they are recorded in the same column.

The sum of the standard scores *for the first 14 tests* is recorded in the large rectangle. This rectangle indicates those tests that are to be summed together to calculate an average standard score. This sum, as well as the required steps for obtaining the average standard score (labeled "Ave." on the worksheet— see Figure 6-1), is located in the large rectangle immediately under the fourteen standard score lines. Average scores that contain decimals should be rounded to the nearest whole number.

Since it is contrary to our understanding of human behavior to expect an individual's abilities to be uniformly developed, a criterion must be specified to identify tests that vary *significantly* from the average standard score. These significant values are obtained by following the arrows to the two rectangles that are labeled "+15 and "–15." The clinician should add and subtract fifteen standard score points to the average value calculated in the prior step. These two values should be recorded in the respective rectangles. These two values are the standard scores above and below which the individual WJTCA-R tests are judged to be significant strengths or weaknesses.

The choice of the ±15 standard score strength and weakness criterion is based on a similar practice advocated for other intelligence tests. Wechsler subtest scores that differ by more than 3 scaled score points (1 standard deviation according to the Wechsler subtest scaled score scale that has a mean of 10 and standard deviation of 3) from the average (mean) subtest scaled score are considered as possible strengths and weaknesses (Kaufman, 1979, 1990). The ±15 standard score criterion is of a similar magnitude to this Wechsler-based rule of thumb.

The alternative to using the ±15 standard score strength or weakness criterion is to use precise tables that indicate the exact score difference needed for each test to obtain statistical significance. Precise values for determining whether an individual test in an intelligence battery is significantly discrepant from the average score of all the individual tests are often suggested and provided in various tables for different tests. Although more precise, interpretive procedures that require numerous calculations and statistical manipulations can detract from competent clinical interpretation (Kamphaus, 1993). Precise tables are not suggested for the WJTCA-R interpretive process. I concur with Kaufman (1990) that:

SS

S W 1. Memory for Names ____

S W 2. Memory for Sentences ____

S W 3. Visual Matching ____

S W 4. Incomplete Words ____

S W 5. Visual Closure ____

S W 6. Picture Vocabulary ____

S W 7. Analysis-Synthesis ____

S W 8. Visual-Auditory Lrng ____

S W 9. Memory for Words ____

S W 10. Cross Out ____

S W 11. Sound Blending ____

S W 12. Picture Recognition ____

S W 13. Oral Vocabulary ____

S W 14. Concept Formation ____

(+15)

____ /14= ____
(Sum)

(-15)

S W 15. Delayed Recall-MN ____

S W 16. Delayed Recall-VAL ____

S W 17. Numbers Reversed ____

S W 18. Sound Patterns ____

S W 19. Spatial Relations ____

S W 20. Listening Comprehension ____

S W 21. Verbal Analogies ____

Plotting the Ave.
and +-15 lines
and the test
confidence bands
on the WJTCA-R
SS/PR profile
is recommended.

(Less than -15 value)

(Greater than + 15 value)

**FIGURE 6-1 WJTCA-R Strength/Weakness Worksheet: Extended
Strategy**

There is no rational defense for encouraging clinicians to use empirical rules that not only encourage additional clerical errors but that suggest a kind of psychometric precision that is just not obtainable in the clinical setting. Empirical rules and guidelines are needed to prevent interpretive chaos, but they should be simple and easily internalized. (p. 428)

Each individual test's standard score (recorded in the "SS" column) is then compared to the values recorded in the –15 and +15 rectangles. Test standard scores that are less than the –15 value are considered possible weaknesses. Weakness tests are so indicated by circling the capital *W* in the leftmost column before the test's name. Individual test standard scores that are greater than the +15 value are identified as possible strengths. Strength tests are indicated by circling the capital *S* at the same location on the worksheet. The completion of these procedures results in the identification of strength *(S)* and weakness *(W)* tests that will be used in subsequent steps. A completed worksheet for a case study is presented in Figure 6-2. This case study (hereafter called "John") represents the performance of a male student who was referred for academic concerns in first grade.

John was administered 17 WJTCA-R tests. The average of the first 14 tests is 97.1, a value that is rounded to 97. The respective values 15 standard score points below (i.e., 82) and above (i.e., 112) the average of 97 are recorded in the ±15 rectangles.

Three tests (Memory for Sentences, Memory for Words, and Oral Vocabulary) have standard scores below the value of 82. These three tests are labeled weakness tests by circling the *W* indicator before each test's name. The standard scores for two tests (Cross Out and Picture Recognition) exceed the +15 criteria of 112. These two tests are labeled strength tests by circling the capital *S* in front of their respective names.

In the worksheet presented in Figure 6-2, the Listening Comprehension test is marked by a circled *W* that contains a question mark notation. This notation indicates that this test was not less than the standard score weakness criterion of 82, but that it was close (i.e., 83). Such a notation reflects the interpretive philosophy of not discarding potentially useful information at this early stage in the interpretative process. The objective of Step 1 is only to identify all information that may be relevant for subsequent interpretation. Excessive attention should not be devoted to fine-grade discriminations in test strength and weakness classifications at this point in the interpretive process. Clinicians with a more conservative philosophy may choose to not label borderline strength and weakness tests.

As noted on the worksheet presented in Figure 6-2, it is strongly recommended that the confidence bands for each test administered be plotted on the WJTCA-R Standard Score/Percentile Rank Profile provided in the WJTCA-R test record. The procedures for plotting the individual test confidence bands are described in the examiner's manual (Woodcock & Mather, 1989).

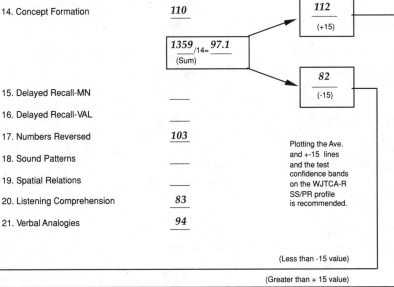

SS

S W   1. Memory for Names   *102*

S (W)   2. Memory for Sentences   *80*

S W   3. Visual Matching   *99*

S W   4. Incomplete Words   *89*

S W   5. Visual Closure   *96*

S W   6. Picture Vocabulary   *87*

S W   7. Analysis-Synthesis   *109*

S W   8. Visual-Auditory Lrng   *107*

S (W)   9. Memory for Words   *76*

(S) W   10. Cross Out   *119*

S W   11. Sound Blending   *93*

(S) W   12. Picture Recognition   *115*

S (W)   13. Oral Vocabulary   *77*

S W   14. Concept Formation   *110*

$\dfrac{1359}{14} = 97.1$
(Sum)

112
(+15)

82
(-15)

S W   15. Delayed Recall-MN   ____

S W   16. Delayed Recall-VAL   ____

S W   17. Numbers Reversed   *103*

S W   18. Sound Patterns   ____

S W   19. Spatial Relations   ____

S (W ?) 20. Listening Comprehension *83*

S W   21. Verbal Analogies   *94*

Plotting the Ave.
and +-15 lines
and the test
confidence bands
on the WJTCA-R
SS/PR profile
is recommended.

(Less than -15 value)

(Greater than + 15 value)

**FIGURE 6-2   WJTCA-R Strength/Weakness Worksheet for John:
Extended Strategy**

In addition to plotting the confidence bands, the average standard score value (i.e., "Ave." value in the worksheet) should be recorded as a single vertical line drawn from the top to the bottom of the profile page. Similar lines should be drawn on the worksheet for the -15 and +15 standard score values. Figure 6-3 presents the completion of these procedures for John's WJTCA-R performance.

The recommendation to plot the test strength and weakness results (see Figure 6-3) is based on the greater ease by which patterns of strengths and weaknesses can be comprehended when presented visually. As will be demonstrated in later steps, a careful review of the visual representation of a WJTCA-R test profile can often uncover useful insights that are difficult to detect from the numerical information summarized in the strength and weakness worksheet.

Step 2: Identify Strength and Weakness Test Groupings

The goal of this step is to identify test groupings that contain the majority of the significantly discrepant strength or weakness tests identified in Step 1. To facilitate this process the WJTCA-R Test Grouping Strength/Weakness Worksheet presented in Figure 6-4 can be used. The worksheet presented in Figure 6-4 is a modified and revised version of a similar worksheet first offered for clinical interpretation of the WJTCA (McGrew, 1986).

Organization and Description of the Test Grouping Worksheet

The WJTCA-R Test Grouping Strength/Weakness Worksheet lists all the test groupings presented in Chapters 4 and 5. The top half of the worksheet includes the *Gf-Gc* cluster groupings that form the organizational structure provided by the authors of the WJTCA-R. Also included in the Gf-Gc Groupings section are the expanded *Gf-Gc* groupings described in Chapter Five. Immediately below the *Gf-Gc* based groupings are the remaining supplemental groupings described in Chapter 5.

Across the top of the worksheet are the 21 WJTCA-R test abbreviations that were presented in Chapter 3. The tests are organized according to their placement in the three major organizational sections of the WJTCA-R (i.e., Standard Tests 1–7, Supplemental Tests 8–14, and Supplemental Tests 15–21). Immediately under each test name abbreviation is a square that is used to record the test's strength or weakness status as determined in Step 1.

Each test grouping is indicated by the presence of a square immediately underneath each respective test. For example, on the same horizontal line as the Expanded Long-Term Retrieval grouping label are squares underneath the Memory for Names (MN), Visual Closure (VC), Visual-Auditory Learning (VAL), Picture Recognition (PR), Delayed Recall—Memory for Names (DRMN), and Delayed Recall—Visual-Auditory Learning (DRVAL) tests.

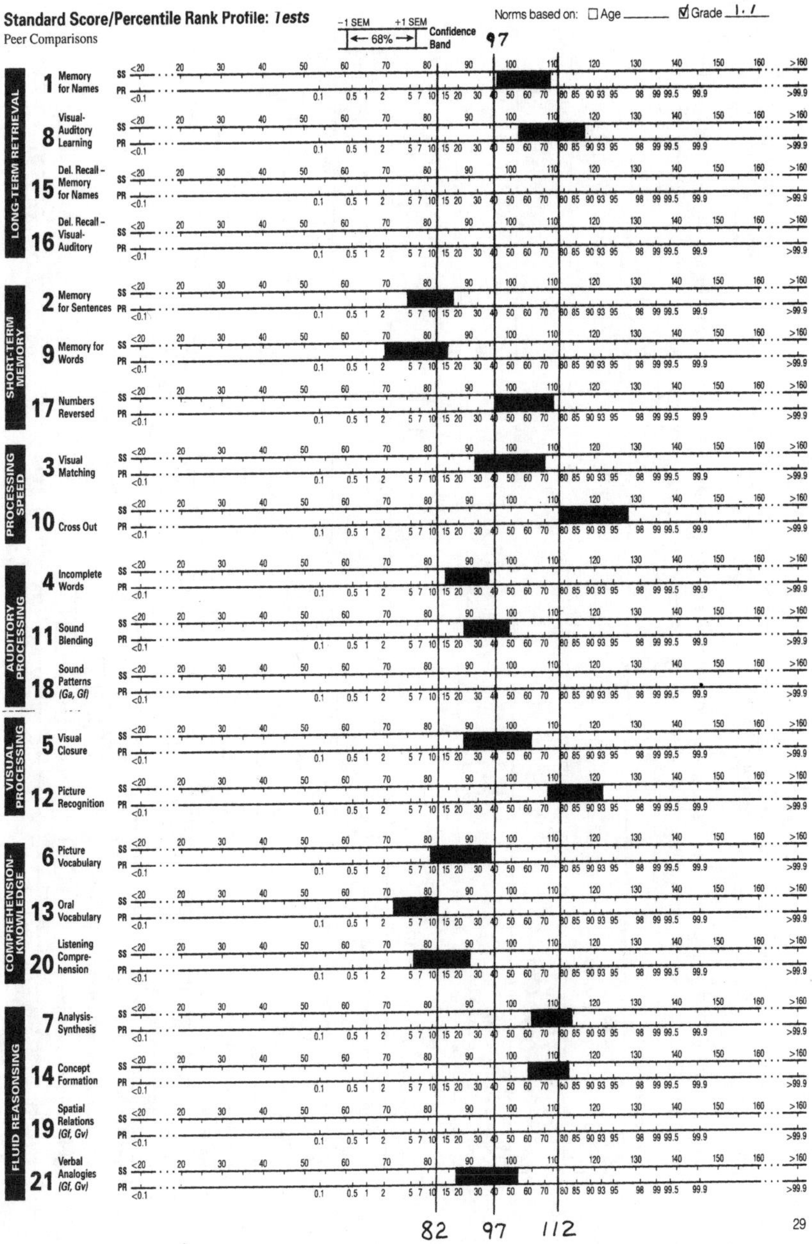

FIGURE 6-3 Standard Score/Percentile Rank Profile for John

WJTCA-R Test Grouping Strength/Weakness Worksheet
(Developed by Kevin S. McGrew)

Circle possible S or W test groupings →

Intra-Cog. Disc.

Label as S or W or + or - →

Standard Tests 1-7: MN MS VM IW VC PV AS

Supplemental Tests 8-14: VAL MW CO SB PR OV CF

Supplemental Tests 15-21: DRMN DRVAL NR SP SR LC VA

Test Grouping

Gf-Gc Groupings:

S W	Long-Term Retrieval (Glr)
S W	Exp. Long-Term Retrieval (Glr)
S W	Short-Term Memory (Gsm)
S W	Exp. Short-Term Memory (Gsm)
S W	Processing Speed (Gs)
S W	Exp. Processing Speed (Gs)
S W	Auditory Processing (Ga)
S W	Visual Processing (Gv)
S W	Comprehension-Knowledge (Gc)
S W	Exp. Comp-Knowledge (Gc)
S W	Fluid Reasoning (Gf)
S W	Exp. Fluid Reasoning (Gf)

S W	Aud. Seq. Processing/Memory
S W	Visual Perceptual Fluency
S W	Auditory Attention/Listening
S W	New Learning Efficiency
S W	Broad Synthesis Ability
S W	Word Finding/Verbal Retrieval
S W	Nonverbal Ability (nonspeeded)

FIGURE 6-4 WJTCA-R Grouping Strength/Weakness Worksheet

152

At the left-most edge of the worksheet is a column of *S's* and *W's*. These letters are used to designate the strength or weakness test groupings. Immediately to the left of the seven *Gf-Gc* test grouping clusters provided by the test authors is a place for recording a person's intra-cognitive discrepancy scores.

Identify Strength and Weakness Tests on the Grouping Worksheet

To identify test groupings that may hold the key to unlocking a profile, the following procedures should be followed. First, record the strength *(S)* or weakness *(W)* status of the tests as determined in Step 1. This involves the transferring of the *S* and *W* information summarized in the Strength/Weakness Worksheet (Figure 6-2) to the test grouping worksheet.

This is accomplished by placing an *S* (i.e, strength) or *W* (i.e., weakness) (or any other personalized notation used by a clinician such as "+" or "−" or the use of color codes) into the squares under the appropriate test abbreviation on the test grouping worksheet. Given that most assessments will not involve the administration of all 21 WJTCA-R tests, those tests that *were not administered* must be designated. Tests that were not administered are designated by a large *X* in the square for each of the tests. Figure 6-5 demonstrates the completion of these procedures for John's WJTCA-R performance.

As originally determined in Step 1 and recorded on the test grouping worksheet presented in Figure 6-5, the Memory for Sentences (MS), Memory for Words (MW), Oral Vocabulary (OV), and Listening Comprehension (LC) squares contain *W* or *W?* designations. The Cross Out (CO) and Picture Recognition (PR) tests are designated as strengths *(S)*. After the strength, weakness, and non-administered tests are appropriately labeled across the top of the grouping worksheet, the next step is to place the *S, W,* and *X* notations (as well as any *S?* or *W?* notations if used) in every square listed directly under each designated test. Figure 6-5 demonstrates the completion of this step for John.

Identify Possible Strength and Weakness Groupings

The next step is to identify possible strength and weakness groupings. This is done by horizontally inspecting the tests contained in each test grouping to determine if the majority of tests in a grouping (ignoring those that were not administered— marked by an *X*) are consistently designated as strengths and/or weaknesses.

For example, the Expanded Long-Term Retrieval grouping consists of the Memory for Names (MN), Visual Closure (VC), Visual-Auditory Learning (VAL), Picture Recognition (PR), Delayed Recall—Memory for Names (DRMN), and Delayed Recall-Visual-Auditory Learning (DRVAL) tests. Inspection of Figure 6-5 shows that the DRMN and DRVAL tests were not administered to John. Of the four tests in this grouping that were administered, only PR was identified as a strength. None of the other

WJTCA-R Test Grouping Strength/Weakness Worksheet

(Developed by Kevin S. McGrew)

Standard Tests 1-7

Supplemental Tests 8-14

Supplemental Tests 15-21

Label as S or W or + or –

Circle possible S or W test groupings

Intra-Cog. Disc.

Test Grouping

Gf-Gc Groupings

S W Long-Term Retrieval (Glr)
S W Exp. Long-Term Retrieval (Glr)

S W Short-Term Memory (Gsm)
S W Exp. Short-Term Memory (Gsm)

S W Processing Speed (Gs)
S W Exp. Processing Speed (Gs)

S W Auditory Processing (Ga)
S W Visual Processing (Gv)

S W Comprehension-Knowledge (Gc)
S W Exp. Comp-Knowledge (Gc)

S W Fluid Reasoning (Gf)
S W Exp. Fluid Reasoning (Gf)

S W Aud. Seq. Processing/Memory
S W Visual Perceptual Fluency

S W Auditory Attention/Listening
S W New Learning Efficiency

S W Broad Synthesis Ability
S W Word Finding/Verbal Retrieval
S W Nonverbal Ability (nonspeeded)

FIGURE 6-5 Recording of Strength and Weakness Information on the Grouping Worksheet for John

154

Expanded Long-Term Retrieval tests was identified as either a strength or as weakness. There is no consistency among the administered Expanded Long-Term Retrieval tests that would suggest that this should be considered a possible strength or weakness grouping.

A review of Figure 6-5 reveals that three of the four tests in the Expanded Short-Term Memory grouping are all designated as weaknesses. This consistency suggests that the Expanded Short-Term Memory grouping should be considered as reflecting a possible weakness for John. The weakness status for the Expanded Short-Term Memory grouping is designated by circling the respective W label at the left-most margin of the worksheet. This is demonstrated in Figure 6-6. There is no strong consistency among the weakness tests in any other grouping that would warrant a weakness designation.

The weakness *(W)* designation for the Short-Term Memory grouping illustrates a number of important interpretive principles. The first deals with the thorny issue of how internally consistent small test groupings must be. Consistent rules for the interpretation of test triad groupings are particularly hard to formulate. If clinicians prefer a conservative approach to profile interpretation, they may prefer to not consider triad groupings as reflecting possible strengths or weaknesses unless all three tests are so designated within the grouping. Taking the conservative approach, the Short-Term Memory grouping would not be designated as a possible weakness for John. Kaufman (1990) recommends that test triads only be considered when no more than one of the test's score equals the person's average or mean score.

In contrast, the objective of this portion of the interpretive process is to generate as many strength and weakness hypotheses as possible. The remaining steps in the interpretive process will reduce the list of groupings to a realistic number. Clinicians need not be extremely concerned about the number of groupings generated by the end of Step 2.

Given this philosophy, the Short-Term Memory grouping was designated as a possible weakness in Figure 6-6. This designation also reflects the *importance of being familiar with the detailed individual test information presented in Chapter 3*. As presented in Chapter 3, the Numbers Reversed test is a factorially complex measure of both short-term memory and fluid reasoning abilities. The observation that the Numbers Reversed test was not consistent with the primary short-term memory tests (i.e., Memory for Sentences and Memory for Words) is therefore not an unexpected finding. The *S* designation of the Short-Term Memory grouping, as well as the Expanded Short-Term Memory grouping, makes sense.

The designation of test groupings as possible strengths or weaknesses is completed for the worksheet in Figure 6-7. At this stage no noticeable strength test groupings have been identified. Although the only two strength tests (i.e., Cross Out and Picture Recognition) are both in the Visual Perceptual Fluency test grouping, the two remaining administered tests in this grouping

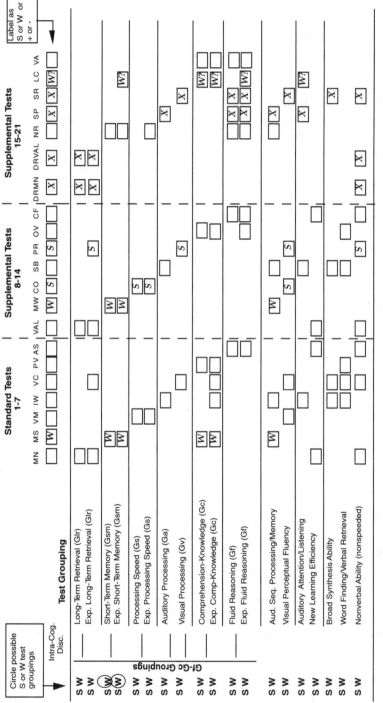

FIGURE 6-6 Recording of Strength and Weakness Test Groupings for John

(i.e., Visual Matching and Visual Closure) were not designated as strengths. Only 50% of the administered tests in the Visual Perceptual Fluency grouping are internally consistent. No other test groupings contained both of the two strength tests. No viable strength test groupings have been identified at this point in the interpretive process.

During the completion of this process, clinicians should follow the guiding principle that *the majority of tests within a grouping should be significantly discrepant in the same direction before a grouping is retained for further analysis.* If other tests in a grouping are not significantly discrepant but are in the same direction of the significantly deviant tests and are at or below (weaknesses) or at or above (strengths) the person's average test score, the grouping can still be considered (Kamphaus, 1993).

For example, it is possible for a four-test grouping to have three of its tests judged significantly discrepant as outlined in Step 1. The fourth test may be nonsignificant but may be in the same direction as the other three. Such a finding is usually revealed when inspecting the Standard Score/Percentile Rank Profile. The need for flexibility is particularly important when evaluating large test groupings. It is contrary to our knowledge of the complexity of human behavior, and the numerous potential influences on individual tests (see Chapter 3), to expect that all tests in a hypothesized grouping will be 100% consistent at all times.

It is not possible to specify strict criteria to address these decisions. In the case of two-test groupings, the dyad should be internally consistent since there is a greater risk of error when interpretation is based on a limited sample of abilities. There will always be exceptions based on case-specific circumstances, and these exceptions cannot be anticipated and can only be recognized by good clinicians. The discussion of the Short-Term Memory grouping is one example. *This worksheet process is presented only as an aid to be augmented by sound clinical judgment.*

Using the Intra-Cognitive Discrepancy Information

The WJTCA-R intra-cognitive discrepancy scores should also be used to identify possible strength and weakness groupings within the *Gf-Gc* framework. Located immediately before the *Gf-Gc* Groupings label on the worksheet is the column for recording a person's intra-cognitive discrepancy scores. John's intra-cognitive discrepancy scores are recorded on the test grouping worksheet in Figure 6-7.

Using the ±1.5 intra-cognitive discrepancy criterion, the Short-Term Memory and Comprehension-Knowledge groupings are identified as possible weaknesses. The Fluid Reasoning grouping is considered a possible strength. The significant intra-cognitive discrepancy score for the Short-Term Memory grouping is not new information. The Short-Term Memory grouping had already been designated as a possible weakness. The intra-cognitive findings result in the designation of the Comprehension-Knowledge and Fluid Reasoning groupings as *S* or *W* in the left-most portion of the worksheet (Figure 6-7).

FIGURE 6-7 Completed Grouping Worksheet for John

The identification of the Comprehension-Knowledge grouping as a possible weakness and the Fluid Reasoning as a possible strength did not occur when using the ±15 individual test strength and weakness determination method. Although the identification of strength and weakness groupings by the individual test and intra-cognitive discrepancy methods will frequently be the same (e.g., Short-Term Memory grouping), the different ways in which these two approaches identify variability within a person's test profile may often produce different results.

The test grouping worksheet (see Figure 6-7) lists five different tests in the Comprehension-Knowledge grouping. These five tests are those that were found to load on the Comprehension-Knowledge factor identified in factor analysis studies of the norm data (see Chapter 4). The Comprehension-Knowledge grouping was not originally identified as a possible weakness grouping according to the ±15 point individual test method since only three of the five Comprehension-Knowledge tests were identified as weaknesses.

In contrast, all seven of the WJTCA-R cognitive cluster scores are calculated on the basis of *only two tests*. The reason the Comprehension-Knowledge grouping was identified as a possible weakness via the intra-cognitive discrepancy method is because the two-test Comprehension-Knowledge cognitive cluster (versus the five-test grouping presented in the worksheet) was found to be discrepant from the other two-test *Gf-Gc* cognitive clusters.

The test groupings presented in the grouping worksheet provide the maximum information concerning the different abilities measured by the different tests. Although it would be simpler to not use the intra-cognitive scores and use only the individual test procedures based on the ±15 criterion, such a decision ignores potentially useful information that may point the clinician in the direction of useful hypotheses. A review of John's WJTCA-R Standard Score/Percentile Rank Profile (Figure 6-3) illustrates the value of using the intra-cognitive discrepancy scores.

John's profile (Figure 6-3) shows that a major portion of the confidence bands for the three Comprehension-Knowledge weakness tests (i.e., Memory for Sentences, Oral Vocabulary, and Listening Comprehension) are outside the –15 weakness line. Although the other two tests included in the Comprehension-Knowledge grouping (i.e., Picture Vocabulary and Verbal Analogies) were not identified as weaknesses, a review of Figure 6-3 shows that the confidence band for the Picture Vocabulary test is below the average or midpoint line drawn on the individual test profile. Although not identified as a significant weakness, the Picture Vocabulary test is relatively low (i.e., standard score = 87), is 10 points below the average standard score of 97, and is the same direction as the other three Comprehension-Knowledge weakness tests. In contrast, a review of John's profile finds the Verbal Analogies test to be within his average range.

Because the Comprehension-Knowledge intra-cognitive discrepancy score suggested a possible weakness, a closer review of John's test profile was undertaken, which found that four of the five tests in this grouping are below his average reference point. Three of the four tests were identified as being significantly weak in Step 1 (see Figure 6-2). The observation that a majority of the Comprehension-Knowledge tests (i.e., four of five) are in the weakness direction suggests that this grouping should be designated as a possible weakness in Figure 6-7. The Comprehension-Knowledge intra-cognitive discrepancy score resulted in a closer examination of John's test profile, a decision that helped identify a potentially important piece of information concerning John's cognitive functioning.

The +1.52 Fluid Reasoning intra-cognitive discrepancy score (see Figure 6-7) results in an *S* designation for this grouping. A close inspection of the grouping worksheet (Figure 6-7) reveals that none of the four Fluid Reasoning grouping tests that were administered were identified as strengths. John's profile reveals (Figure 6-3) that the two tests that compose the WJTCA-R Fluid Reasoning Cognitive cluster were both above John's average test score of 97, but not to the point that they were identified by the ±15 criterion. Both scores were either 12 to 13 standard score points above John's average standard score of 97.

Inspection of the remaining two Fluid Reasoning grouping tests that were administered found both to be at or slightly above John's average standard score (see Figure 6-3). The Verbal Analogies test is very near John's average score line, and the Numbers Reversed test is just above the average score line on the profile. This mild fluid reasoning strength is not as significant as the weakness identified for the Short-Term Memory and Expanded Short-Term Memory groupings. Nonetheless, the intra-cognitive scores, coupled with a careful visual review of the test profile, identified potentially important information about John's reasoning abilities.

Step 3: Integrate the Strength and Weakness Test Grouping Information with Other Relevant Information

At this point in the interpretive process the clinician has only a listing of possible strength and weakness test groupings. The next step is to evaluate the viability of the designated strength and weakness test groupings to determine which grouping-based hypotheses "best fit" the case under consideration. A hallmark of competent interpretation is using multiple sources of data to support test-generated hypotheses (Kamphaus, 1993).

This process can be conceptualized as a scientific approach to intelligence test interpretation, as the goal is to seek out external verification for competing test hypotheses (Kamphaus, 1993; McGrew, 1984, 1986). The clinician must consider the merits of each grouping in the context of other sources of data and information (e.g., test behavior, classroom observations, background information, teacher comments, other test scores). The goal is to use other sources of information to validate or support the hypothesized abilities underlying certain of the designated test groupings.

Behavioral Observations

A good starting point is to consider behavior observed during the assessment and in other settings (e.g., classroom). For example, if the Auditory Attention/Listening test grouping is identified as a possible weakness, this weakness should be ignored if the individual displays excellent attention and concentration. Conversely, if the individual requires constant redirection, is very distractible, and frequently requests that directions be repeated, then the Auditory Attention/Listening grouping should be retained for further consideration. General behaviors that may affect the performance of the different WJTCA-R tests, as well as the other variables that may influence test performance, are summarized in Table 6-2. The information presented in Table 6-2 is based on the individual test analysis presented in Chapter 3.

John's observed test behavior was not extremely revealing, although it was still informative. John was attentive, cooperative, and adequately motivated throughout the entire evaluation. Rapport was good, and the examiner judged the results to be a valid representation of John's functioning. Although no test behavior was judged to be unusual, this finding still provides useful information for evaluating John's possible strength and weakness test groupings.

John's completed test grouping worksheet (Figure 6-7) suggested a possible weaknesses in short-term memory abilities. Both the Short-Term Memory and Expanded Short-Term Memory ability groupings were designated as possible weaknesses. The observation of good attentiveness during the assessment suggests that John's performance on the short-term memory tests was not influenced by lapses in attention and concentration. As summarized in Table 6-2, performance on all tests in the two short-term memory groupings may be influenced by variables that disrupt a person's mental efficiency (e.g., attention and concentration; disrupting influences of anxiety). The failure to detect any lapses in John's attention and concentration allows the clinician to assume that John's relatively weak performance on the short-term memory tests may reflect weaknesses in these types of memory abilities, not other nonmemory factors.

Referral Concerns, Observations by Others, and Background Information

A clinician typically has a wealth of other information to use during this step. Specific referral concerns, observations by significant others (e.g. teachers), and background information are often useful sources of information for evaluating the designated strength and weakness test groupings.

For example, an individual could be referred by a teacher because he or she "understands new concepts and logic very easily, but has extreme difficulty retaining factual information." Even if the Fluid Reasoning test grouping was designated as a possible weakness for this person, the viability of this hypothesized weakness should be questioned based on the reported

TABLE 6-2 Variables Influencing Performance on Two or More WJTCA-R Tests

Variables	Glr				Gsm			Gs		Ga			Gv			Gc			Gf		
	MN	VAL	DRMN	DRVAL	MS	MW	NR	VM	CO	IW	SB	SP	VC	PR	SR	PV	OV	LC	AS	CF	VA
Attention span/distractability					X	X	X	X	X	X	X	X						X			
Concentration		X			X	X	X	X	X	X	X	X		X				X	X	X	
Ability to receive stimuli passively					X	X	X			X	X	X						X			
Anxiety					X	X	X	X	X	X	X	X						X			
Ability to perform under time pressure								X	X					X							
Cognitive response style (reflective/impulsive)	X		X	X				X	X					X	X				X	X	
Frustration tolerance	X	X										X							X	X	
Efficiency/automaticity of problem-solving strategies								X	X					X							
Perfectionistic tendencies								X	X												
Ability to use feedback to modify performance	X	X																	X	X	

Individual Tests

TABLE 6-2 (*Continued*)

| | Individual Tests | | | | | | | | | | | | | | | | | | | | | | | |
| | Glr | | | | Gsm | | | Gs | | Ga | | | Gv | | | Gc | | | Gf | | |
Variables	MN	VAL	DRMN	DRVAL	MS	MW	NR	VM	CO	IW	SB	SP	VC	PR	SR	PV	OV	LC	AS	CF	VA
Hearing acuity					X	X	X			X	X	X									
History of chronic ear infections										X	X	X									
Cognitive flexibility																	X		X	X	
Cognitive strategies (mnemonics; elaboration)	X		X		X					X				X							
Cognitive style (field dependence/field independence)								X	X	X			X		X						
Cognitive strategies (problem-solving strategies)																			X	X	
Cognitive strategies (rehearsal/visualization)					X	X	X			X	X				X						
Experiences/interests in the visual/graphic arts													X		X						
Cultural opportunities																X	X	X			X
Extent of outside reading																X	X	X			X

Table 6-2 (Continued)

163

TABLE 6-2 *(Continued)*

Variables	Individual Tests																				
	Glr				Gsm		Gs			Ga		Gv				Gc				Gf	
	MN	VAL	DRMN	DRVAL	MS	MW	NR	VM	CO	IW	SB	SP	VC	PR	SR	PV	OV	LC	AS	CF	VA
Language stimulation																X	X	X			X
Environmental stimulation																X	X	X			X
Orientation/alertness to environment																X	X	X			X
Educational experiences/instruction										X	X					X	X	X			X
Interests																X	X	X			X
Intellectual curiosity and striving																X	X	X			X
Visual-motor coordination								X	X												

164

ease by which this person learns new concepts and logical principles. Such a referral concern would provide support for a possible weakness in long-term retrieval and storage abilities if suggested by a weakness designation for the Long-Term Retrieval or Expanded Long-Term Retrieval test groupings.

Another example would be the strong consideration of the Expanded Short-Term Memory grouping for an individual who is significantly low on all four memory tests in the grouping and who is reported by teachers and parents to experience difficulty remembering and following directions. These are only a few examples that demonstrate how existing background and referral information, including observations made by significant others, can be very useful when evaluating the designated strength and weakness test groupings.

John's referral and background information indicated he was referred in first grade due to teacher and parent concerns about academic progress, particularly in reading and the printing of letters. John continued to experience academic difficulty despite supplementary reinforcement of his skills at home and at school. John's teacher felt that as his academic problems had increased, he was becoming slightly less motivated, and more restless in large group settings. John was described as showing adequate social relationships with other first grade students.

Informal observations of John by his teacher and parents suggested normal functioning in basic motor skills, communication abilities, and basic health. Sensory evaluations indicated normal vision. Hearing screening by the school nurse indicated that John may have a mild high frequency hearing loss, a finding that precipitated a referral to the family's physician.

A review of John's test grouping worksheet (Figure 6-7) indicated no significant problems performing on tests most influenced by problems with hearing acuity. Six tests are listed in Table 6-2 as being sensitive to problems with hearing acuity. John did not display a significant weakness on the tests in the Auditory Processing grouping, tests that are most sensitive to the effects of hearing acuity. John's ability to perform adequately on the two primary auditory tests (i.e., Incomplete Words and Sound Blending) suggests that his weakness on the auditory-based short-term memory tests was most likely not due to a possible high-frequency hearing loss.

Other Assessment Information

If additional individual or group administered assessment data are available for an individual, this information should be reviewed as the strength and weakness test groupings are evaluated.

Individuals with long histories of functional problems have often been assessed more than once, and often by different clinicians with different instruments. It is not unusual to find one or more reports of intellectual assessments in the files of individuals who have moved frequently, have had long-standing functional problems, and/or who have received special services for many years. The results of these prior assessments, particularly if they reveal a consistent pattern of strengths and weakness, can help a clinician evaluate the validity of the designated WJTCA-R strength and weakness groupings.

For example, if the completion of the test grouping worksheet identifies the Visual Processing grouping as a possible weakness, a review of the related visual processing tests on any other intelligence tests that had been previously administered to this person could be informative. As presented in Table 4-11 in Chapter 4, the Wechsler batteries, SB-IV, K-ABC, DAS, and DTLA-3 all contain measures of visual processing abilities. If an individual had been administered one or more of these intelligence batteries, and the person was consistently low on the respective visual processing tests, this information would support the viability of the Visual Processing test grouping as representing a weakness for this individual. The *Gf-Gc* analysis of the intelligence batteries presented in Tables 4-8 to 4-14 should be used in this type of analysis.

For clinicians working in educational settings, group administered intelligence test information is often available in a student's file. Although group test scores must be used with great caution, a consistent pattern of strengths and weaknesses on a group intelligence test may help the clinician evaluate competing WJTCA-R strength and weakness test groupings.

For example, the validity of a Comprehension-Knowledge or Expanded Comprehension-Knowledge test grouping weakness would be supported by poor performance on the verbal and general information sections of a group administered test. Although group administered test information may be informative when evaluating WJTCA-R test groupings, this information typically has limited usefulness given the narrow range of cognitive abilities measured by most group tests. Group test information should be used cautiously when evaluating the WJTCA-R test groupings. The effective use of group administered test information depends on the clinician's knowledge of the tests contained in a specific group battery.

With the exception of the *Gf-Gc* test summaries provided in Tables 4-8 to 4-14, a listing of possible test information (e.g., group intelligence tests, language tests, neuropsychological tests) that may be available for all possible referrals is beyond the scope of this text. The ability to use supplementary assessment information when evaluating the WJTCA-R strength and weakness test groupings depends on each clinician's familiarity with the other assessment instruments.

Given the relatively young age of John (i.e., first grader; 7 years and 6 months) and the fact that John had not been previously referred for any special services, there was no existing assessment information available. However, the *WJ-R Tests of Achievement* were administered to John together with the WJTCA-R. John's performance on the WJ-R achievement clusters was consistent with the referral concerns.

Compared to others of the same grade, John's abilities as measured by the Broad Reading (percentile rank = 7; standard score = 78) and Broad Written Language clusters (percentile rank = 5; standard score = 76) were weak. John's mathematics abilities as measured by the Broad Mathematics cluster were relatively stronger (percentile rank = 15; standard score = 84). The finding of relatively weaker language arts achievement (i.e., Broad Reading and Written Language clusters) and stronger mathematics achievement (i.e., Broad Mathematics cluster) provides some support for the Comprehension-Knowledge weakness and Fluid Reasoning strength identified for John (see Figure 6-7).

Comprehension-knowledge *(Gc)* and fluid reasoning *(Gf)* abilities are both related to language arts and mathematics achievement. However, comprehension-knowledge abilities are more strongly related to language arts, and fluid reasoning is more strongly related to mathematics (see Figures 4-6 and 4-7 and related discussion in Chapter 4). John's WJ-R achievement scores are consistent with the identification of a relative weakness by the Comprehension-Knowledge grouping and a relative strength by the Fluid Reasoning grouping. Although achievement test scores must be used cautiously, and never as the sole piece of supporting evidence, when combined with other supporting information (e.g., other intelligence test scores; referral and background information) they can help solidify a clinician's confidence in certain strength and weakness hypotheses.

Investigate New Insights

As clinicians become experienced with the WJTCA-R and the interpretive process outlined in this chapter, the general steps in the process will become more "automatized." Experienced clinicians will often find their minds freed to develop new insights, generate new hypotheses, and ask new questions as they are completing the process. For these clinicians the scientific, linear, "left-brain," sequential interpretive process has been augmented by complementary "right-brain," holistic, global insights.

Kaufman (1990) suggests that these two modes of thought reflect differences in how examiners approach the task of interpretive problem solving. Although they possibly reflect different problem-solving styles of clinicians, I believe that the more insightful, holistic, "simultaneous" interpretive insights may also reflect the movement of a clinician along the novice to expert continuum. The expert-like automatic processing of the routine sequential steps frees up the clinician's mind to hypothesize and think at a higher, global level. WJTCA-R test patterns previously detected through the step-by-step process are instantly recognized and trigger other interpretive hypothesis and thinking. The development of new insights that supplement those gleaned during the sequential interpretive steps will not occur for all cases, nor, for that matter, for all clinicians. When it does, these potential new "leads" need to be investigated.

At times these new leads may be unproductive. At other times, very important insights or hypotheses are generated about a case. It is impossible to describe this process in a structured manner. This step in the interpretive process tends to be idiosyncratic for each case, not relevant for all cases, and largely dependent on the accumulated expertise of each clinician. The experienced user of the WJTCA-R may have already generated a number of new hypotheses that beg for further investigation in the case of John's WJTCA-R test profile.

When one of the seven *Gf-Gc* Groupings is identified as a possible strength and weakness and this grouping also has a related "expanded" grouping that is not similarly designated, reasons for this difference can often be informative. John's Fluid Reasoning grouping was designated as a possible strength as a result of the intra-cognitive discrepancy score information. However, the Expanded Fluid Reasoning grouping was not identified as a strength. The experienced clinician should ask why.

Six of the eight tests in the Expanded Fluid Reasoning grouping were administered to John. Two (Oral Vocabulary and Listening Comprehension) were identified as weaknesses. The Analysis-Synthesis and Concept Formation tests were previously identified as mild strengths by the intra-cognitive discrepancy score. By being intimately familiar with the individual characteristics of each test (see Chapter 3), the astute clinician might hypothesize that the Expanded Fluid Reasoning grouping was not identified as a strength due to a possible difference in John's ability to reason with verbal and language stimuli (i.e., Oral Vocabulary and Listening Comprehension) and primarily visual and nonverbal stimuli (i.e., Analysis-Synthesis and Concept Formation).

A review of John's test profile (Figure 6-3) reveals a dichotomy between relative strengths on the Analysis-Synthesis and Concept Formation tests and weakness on the Oral Vocabulary and Listening Comprehension tests. John's Verbal Analogies test is in the same direction as Oral Vocabulary and Listening Comprehension and is also below John's average midpoint line on the profile. John's performance on Numbers Reversed, a test requiring some reasoning but not complex verbal ability, is above the average midpoint line. Such observations raise questions about a difference in John's ability to process or think with verbal/language versus visual/non-language based material.

As a result of this observation, it is logical to examine John's complete test profile for other supporting evidence of this dichotomy. A logical starting point is an examination of John's performance on the tests in the Nonverbal Ability grouping. In John's case (see Figure 6-7), six of the nine tests in this large grouping had been administered. However, only one (i.e., Picture Recognition) had been designated as a strength. A careful review of the test profile (Figure 6-3) reveals that the midpoints of the confidence bands for five of the six administered Nonverbal Ability tests (i.e., Memory for Names, Visual-Auditory Learning, Picture Recognition, Analysis-Synthesis, and Concept Formation) are consistently above the average midpoint line on the profile. Although the midpoint of the sixth test (i.e., Visual Closure) is not above the average midline, it is almost exactly on this reference point. Thus, all six of the Nonverbal Ability test's confidence bands are at or above John's average level of performance. The finding that almost all tests in a grouping are either at or above or at or below a person's average test score supports the strength or weakness hypothesis suggested by the test grouping (Kaufman, 1990; Kamphaus, 1993).

The Nonverbal Ability grouping contains only nonspeeded tests. Further inspection of John's test profile (Figure 6-3) reveals that the midpoints for the confidence bands for the two speeded visual tests (i.e., Visual Matching and Cross Out) are also above John's average level of test performance. Taken together, all of this information suggests the hypothesis that John may perform best when dealing primarily with nonverbal and visual-spatial tasks and stimuli. The generation of this hypothesis, in turn, requires a closer inspection of John's performance on the primarily auditory and verbal WJTCA-R tests.

As previously discussed, John's Comprehension-Knowledge grouping was designated as a possible weakness, although the Expanded Comprehension-Knowledge grouping was not. A close inspection of John's test profile (Figure 6-3) finds the midpoints of the confidence bands for six of the seven tests in the Expanded Comprehension-Knowledge grouping (i.e., Memory for Sentences, Incomplete Words, Picture Vocabulary, Oral Vocabulary, Listening Comprehension, Verbal Analogies) are all below John's average midpoint line. The one exception is Visual Closure, a primarily visual task.

At this stage in the interpretive process the hypothesis could be advanced that rather than reflecting specific strengths in fluid reasoning abilities and specific weaknesses in short-term memory and comprehension-knowledge abilities, John's WJTCA-R test profile may reflect distinct differences in the ease by which he receives, thinks with, and expresses himself with auditory-linguistic/verbal stimuli and tasks versus nonverbal/visual-spatial stimuli and tasks.

The advancement of this hypotheses is the direct result of following up the observations gleaned during the completion of the WJTCA-R test grouping worksheet. The identification of these broader strength and weakness hypotheses reflects the importance of inspecting a person's test profile (Figure 6-3) to identify tests within test groupings that may not be *significantly* discrepant but that are in the same direction. The hypothesis that very broad differences may exist in how John approaches tasks with different stimulus characteristics, a hypothesis not immediately suggested through the completion of the standard steps described for the test grouping worksheet, demonstrates the need to be flexible in using the worksheet.

The interpretive logic described here is only one example of this last step. Other useful hypotheses may be generated through different thinking. The generation of potentially useful insights often occurs when examining differences between the "expanded" and original *Gf-Gc* test groupings, examining inconsistencies between tests within a specific test grouping (i.e., a grouping having both strengths and weaknesses), and by spending time visually scanning the person's individual test profile.

Concluding Comments

Step 3 is the most critical step in the interpretive process. By the end of Step 3 a number of hypotheses regarding an individual's functioning should be formulated. When deciding between competing groupings, clinicians should give priority consideration to groupings that account for the largest number of strength or weakness tests. Hypotheses based on the largest test groupings will be more reliable and valid (Kamphaus, 1993; Kaufman, 1990).

The completion of this interpretive process is a challenging exercise in systematic and logical thinking. Intimate familiarity with the information presented in the preceding chapters is critical for astute application of this process. The case study of John demonstrates that the WJTCA-R Test Grouping Strength/Weakness Worksheet and Steps 1 through 3 describing its use are only presented as aids for learning a flexible interpretive framework that cannot be followed in a "cookook" manner. *Neither the test grouping worksheet nor the steps that describe its use should be used as substitutes for sound clinical judgment and expertise.*

Step 4: If Steps 1 Through 3 Fail to Generate Any Viable Hypotheses, Investigate Possible Child-Specific Hypotheses

Clinicians will frequently encounter WJTCA-R test profiles that defy clear analysis. If this point is reached after completing Steps 1 through 3, a clinician may need to adopt a flexible and eclectic search for a "one time only" grouping strategy specific to the individual case. The search for a child-specific interpretation is dependent on the expertise of the clinician, particularly the clinician's ability to draw upon background knowledge and experience. The success of this detective process depends on the clinician's knowledge in the psychology of learning, cognition, intelligence, neuropsychology, learning disability research, etc., and the clinician's ability to apply this knowledge to individual profiles.

It is not possible to outline this process since it will most often be child-specific in nature. Clinicians must be able to integrate the information obtained from the previous steps with their total knowledge base and clinical experience. If this knowledge base is limited or has gaps, clinicians should consult other professionals who possess the necessary expertise.

Step 5: Decide If Additional Supplementary Assessment Is Needed

By the time clinicians have completed the previous four steps they will typically have identified a number of potential strength and/or weakness hypotheses. When other nonassessment information is consistent with the hypotheses and when the tests within the strength or weakness groupings are very consistent, clinicians may feel confident in their hypotheses. However, clinicians often face situations where the assessment and nonassessment information is not completely convincing. When faced with these situations, clinicians should consider administering additional assessment instruments to help confirm or disconfirm the hypotheses under consideration.

Supplemental tests can be selected either from within the WJTCA-R, or from other assessment instruments. The organization of the tests in the test grouping worksheet (Figure 6-4) facilitates the identification of additional WJTCA-R tests that might be administered. In the case of John, additional WJTCA-R tests could be administered to investigate the hypotheses about his auditory-linguistic/verbal versus nonverbal/visual-spatial dichotomy. The two delayed recall tests (i.e., Delayed Recall—Memory for Names, Delayed Recall—Visual-Auditory Learning) and the Spatial Relations tests could be administered since all three are listed in the Nonverbal Ability test grouping. The Sound Patterns test would provide additional information about John's auditory abilities.

Individual tests from other intelligence batteries can also be administered. By reviewing Tables 4-7 through 4-14 in Chapter 4, clinicians can locate additional measures of the *Gf-Gc* abilities measured by the WJTCA-R. Table 4-8 indicates that a clinician could select from the Wechsler Digit Span, SB-IV Memory for Digits, K-ABC Number Recall and Word Order, DAS Recall of Digits, and DTLA-3 Sentence Imitation and Word Sequences tests for additional measures for confirming John's apparent weakness in short-term memory. Additional tests to confirm John's hypothesized weakness in comprehension-knowledge and strength in fluid reasoning can also be identified in these tables.

Clinicians will need to draw upon their own assessment knowledge base to identify additional tests for following up hypotheses not based on the *Gf-Gc* framework. For example, additional information regarding the abilities measured by the Auditory Attention/Listening and Auditory Sequential Processing/Memory test groupings could be found in the *Goldman-Fristoe-Woodcock Auditory Skills Battery* (Goldman, Fristoe, & Woodcock, 1974).

The extent to which additional supplementary assessment is pursued depends on the degree of confidence a clinician has in the hypotheses he or she has generated. Clinicians should not be pressured into drawing premature conclusions or making important decisions and recommendations based solely on time considerations (Kamphaus, 1993). At times the best practice is to defer the presentation of hypotheses and recommendations until additional assessment is completed.

Step 6: If Steps 1 Through 5 Fail to Identify Any Meaningful Grouping-Based Hypotheses, Cautiously Consider Individual Test Interpretation

If a clinician is unable to generate any grouping-based hypotheses, then a number of possibilities need to be entertained. First, one must consider the possibility that there is nothing unusual with an individual's abilities. Historically, much of psychoeducational assessment has been a hunt for a deficit within a subject (viz., deficit or medical model) (Coles, 1978). Aside from the philosophical difficulties inherent in a deficit model, this model often flies in the face of common sense. Environmental factors, including instructional deficits in the case of learning-related referrals, may often be the cause of an individual's problems. In such cases it would not be unusual for the WJTCA-R profile to reflect no major weaknesses. *Clinicians should not be driven to locate a cognitive deficit within an individual and should be willing to entertain the possibility that the individual's difficulties may lie in the environment or in noncognitive domains* (e.g., motivation, interest, social-emotional functioning). In these situations the WJTCA-R test profile may reflect nothing more than normal variability.

A second possibility is that an individual may have a unique pattern of cognitive strengths and weaknesses, but it may not be reflected by the WJTCA-R tests. It is naive to assume that everything important regarding an individual's cognitive abilities is comprehensively tapped by the 21 WJTCA-R tests. The tests are only samples from the larger domain of human abilities. The possibility exists that an individual may possess a very unique pattern of cognitive strengths and weaknesses, but these abilities are not measured by the WJTCA-R or by other tests. If a clinician considers this possibility, it either dictates the need for further assessment in other domains with other instruments or the acknowledgment that for certain individuals one may be unable to measure this cognitive pattern. In these situations it may be more appropriate to forgo further psychometric assessment and to initiate experimentation with different treatment methods while concurrently monitoring the subject's treatment response.

If after considering the above possibilities a clinician concludes that the WJTCA-R tests hold the key to interpretation, then individual test interpretation could be considered. This is mentioned only as a possibility. No space will be devoted to demonstrating individual test interpretation. This lack of discussion should not be interpreted to suggest that this level of interpretation should be ignored. Rather, it should be deemphasized (Kamphaus, 1993). Occasionally an experienced clinician, through individual test task analysis, may formulate some very perceptive hypotheses. However, individual test interpretation has frequently been found to be useless and is only recommended as a last resort (Kamphaus, 1993; Kaufman, 1979; 1990). This does not negate the usefulness of knowing detailed test information (Chapter 3), as any knowledge about the individual tests helps when completing the interpretive procedures presented in this chapter.

If individual test interpretation appears appropriate, then test unique-ness information (see Chapter 3) should play a prominent role. Test unique-ness reflects the degree to which an individual test can be interpreted as measuring a unique ability not related to other broad abilities or measure-ment error. Tests that possess medium to high uniqueness characteristics at the age level of the assessed individual (see Chapter 3) can be interpreted on an individual basis. Individual tests with low test uniqueness should only be individually interpreted when dramatically discrepant from the re-mainder of the WJTCA-R test profile.

THE STANDARD BATTERY AND
DIFFERENTIAL APTITUDE STRATEGIES

The primary function of the Standard Battery and Differential Aptitude test administration strategies is to efficiently provide reliable and valid estimates of an individual's general ability or scholastic aptitudes. The Broad Cogni-tive Ability and Scholastic Aptitude cluster scores provided by these two strategies possess the necessary technical characteristics to satisfactorily fulfill this function.

When compared to the Extended Battery strategy, the time saved with the Standard Battery and Differential Aptitude strategies is approximately 50%. At a minimum, clinicians only need to administer seven or eight tests when using either of these two brief strategies. However, this savings in time is not without a price. The comprehensive Extended Battery approach to generating strength and weakness hypotheses is not possible with these two time-efficient strategies. This does not negate the usefulness of the strat-egies. Many referral situations may be best addressed by these two shorter assessment options.

Generating strength and weakness hypotheses on the basis of seven or eight cognitive tests is not recommended. With the exception of fluid rea-soning in the case of Differential Aptitude strategy, the Standard Battery and Differential Aptitude administration strategies provide only one indi-vidual test for each *Gf-Gc* ability domain. Recommendations cannot be gen-erated when only using single tests. The number and breadth of tests needed to implement the shared ability interpretive process described for the Ex-tended Battery strategy are not present in these two brief strategies. How-ever, the Standard Battery and Differential Aptitude strategies can serve as starting points for more in-depth assessment and clinical interpretation.

Step 1: Identify Significant Strengths and Weaknesses
Within the WJTCA-R Test Profile

This step is identical to that described for identifying strengths and weak-nesses at the individual test level for the Extended Battery strategy and is illustrated by the completion of the strength and weakness worksheet presented in Figure 6-8. The case study of John that was used to demonstrate the Extended Battery interpretive process is used to demonstrate these procedures. For illustrative purposes it is assumed that only the seven-test Standard Battery (Figure 6-9) or eight-test Differential Aptitude (Figure 6-10) strategies were used to address this referral.

The standard scores for the tests administered for each strategy are recorded in the appropriate columns, and the respective calculations are completed. The only difference from the Extended Battery strategy is the need to multiply both the Analysis-Syntheses and Concept Formation standard scores by 0.5 when using the Differential Aptitude strategy (see Figure 6-10). This step is necessary since two fluid reasoning tests are administered in the Differential Aptitude strategy, in comparison to only one each of the other six *Gf-Gc* abilities. The interpretive process outlined in this chapter is based on the principle that the *Gf-Gc* abilities should serve as the foundation for the identification of strengths and weaknesses. Each *Gf-Gc* ability should be proportionally equal when making the strength and weakness calculations. The net effect of multiplying the two fluid reasoning tests by 0.5 is to make the fluid reasoning abilities proportionally equal to the other *Gf-Gc* abilities in the strength and weakness calculations.

The *S* and *W* test designations are then made in the left-most column of the worksheet. This step is completed in both Figures 6-9 and 6-10. Similar to the Extended Battery Strategy example, borderline *S* and *W* tests are so indicated on the two completed worksheets. If John had been approached with the Standard Battery strategy, the Memory for Sentences test would have been designated as a borderline weakness and the Analysis-Synthesis test a borderline strength (Figure 6-9). These two tests would have also received the same designation in the Differential Aptitude strategy (Figure 6-10), together with the identification of Oral Vocabulary as a weakness and Concept Formation as a strength.

If no additional information beyond a person's performance on the Broad Cognitive Ability or Scholastic Aptitude clusters is needed, no additional interpretive steps are required. The clinician would report and interpret findings based on the respective WJTCA-R cluster scores. In depth discussion of strengths and weaknesses among the individual tests would not be encouraged. Clinicians who want to shed greater light on a person's cognitive strengths and weaknesses would need to move to the next step in the interpretive process.

Step 2: Administer Additional Supplemental Tests
Based on the Identified Strength and Weakness Tests

Before hypotheses can be generated about a person's strengths and weaknesses, additional assessment is required. In the case of the Standard Battery example (Figure 6-9), additional supplementary testing would be necessary

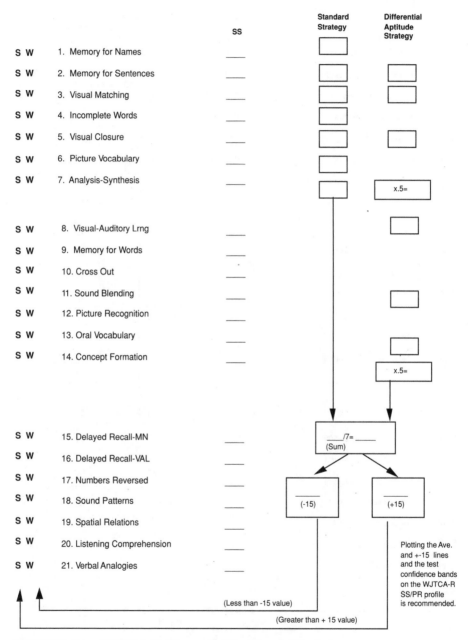

FIGURE 6-8 WJTCA-R Strength/Weakness Worksheet: Standard and Differential Aptitude Strategies

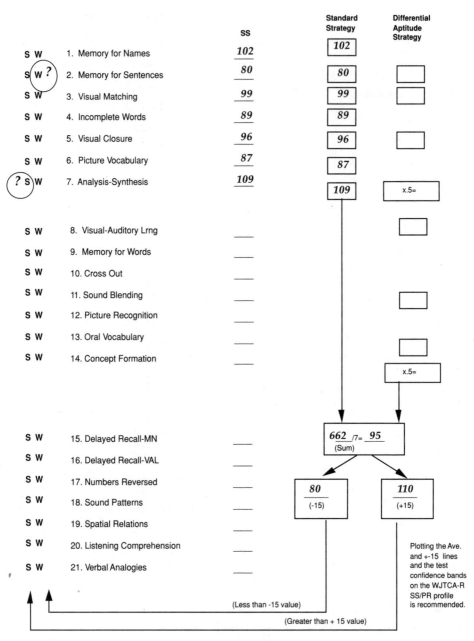

FIGURE 6-9   WJTCA-R Strength/Weakness Worksheet for Standard Strategy for John

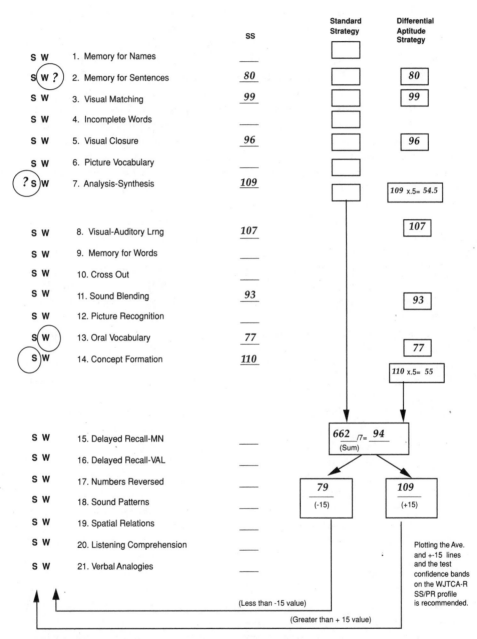

FIGURE 6-10 WJTCA-R Strength/Weakness Worksheet for Differential Aptitude Strategy for John

to verify the short-term memory weakness (i.e., Memory for Sentences) and the fluid reasoning strength (i.e., Analysis-Synthesis). By consulting the WJTCA-R selective testing tables, clinicians should, at a minimum, select the other *Gf-Gc* tests from the first 14 WJTCA-R tests.

In the case of the Standard Battery strategy demonstrated in Figure 6-9, the clinician should administer the Memory for Words test to follow up the Memory for Sentences weakness. The strength suggested by the Analysis-Synthesis test should be followed up by the administration of the Concept Formation test. The decision to administer additional supplementary tests should be based on a review of observed behavior, referral concerns or background information, and/or previous assessment data (see description of this process in the Extended Battery interpretation discussion).

As described for the Extended Battery strategy example, John displayed no unusual test behavior that should be investigated in greater detail. His reported inattentiveness in large group settings, coupled with the reports of a possible mild high frequency hearing loss, would suggest that additional supplemental testing with auditory or listening related tests may be appropriate. Given that a clinician is trying to maximize efficiency of testing time with the Standard Battery strategy, test selection decisions should be based on a number of considerations.

The information summarized in Table 6-2 and the test grouping worksheet (Figure 6-4) should be used to identify additional tests that might be administered. Given the observations regarding John's auditory acuity and listening, the tests contained in the Auditory Attention/Listening test grouping should receive serious consideration. A review of the Auditory Attention/Listening test grouping indicates that the clinician might consider administering either the Sound Blending, Sound Patterns, or Listening Comprehension tests. The Sound Blending test is a better selection than Sound Patterns since more is known about the abilities measured by the Sound Blending test (see Chapter 3). Given that a clinician is trying to maximize efficient testing time and that a weakness has been suggested in short-term auditory memory (i.e., Memory for Sentences weakness), the Listening Comprehension test would be a better choice than Sound Patterns. The Listening Comprehension test is present in both the Auditory Attention/ Listening and Expanded Short-Term Memory groupings.

The Listening Comprehension test is also present in the Expanded Fluid Reasoning grouping, a possible strength for John as indicated by the Analysis-Synthesis test. The administration of the Listening Comprehension test would be a good selection, as it provides additional information related to the strength and weakness areas identified in Step 1. Finally, close inspection of the test grouping worksheet (Figure 6-4) suggests that the Numbers Reversed test might also be administered. This test is present in both the Short-Term Memory and Fluid Reasoning Test groupings.

Clinicians should follow the principle of selectively administering those additional tests that provide maximum information for the maximum number of strength and weakness hypotheses under consideration. Following this principle, a clinician would decide that the additional WJTCA-R tests of Memory for Words, Sound Blending, Concept Formation, Numbers Reversed, and Listening Comprehension should be administered to John. The results from these additional tests would then be recorded on the strength and weakness worksheet (Figure 6-11) and plotted on the WJTCA-R Standard Score/Percentile Rank Profile (Figure 6-12) using the procedures previously described for the Extended Battery strategy.

A review of Figure 6-11 reveals that of those additional tests administered, Memory for Words was identified as a weakness and Concept Formation as a borderline strength. The three other tests were not identified as either strengths or weaknesses. Recording the test results on a WJTCA-R Test Grouping Strength/Weakness Worksheet is not necessary since the use of this worksheet is based on the requirement to administer at least all of the first 14 WJTCA-R tests.

Step 3: Integrate the Strength and Weakness Test Information With Observed Test Behavior and Any Other Relevant Information

This step is identical to Step 3 described previously for the Extended Battery strategy. The primary difference in the case of the Standard Battery and Differential Aptitude strategies is that the test grouping worksheet cannot be formally used. Clinicians will need to rely on a more informal, less structured process for grouping tests and generating hypotheses. The test grouping worksheet can be used informally to help with this step.

Using the Standard Battery strategy with John's referral, the weakness designations of Memory for Sentences and Memory for Words suggest a weakness in short-term memory. Although the Listening Comprehension test is not significantly high or low, a review of John's profile (Figure 6-12) finds this test to be below John's average score and close to being a weakness. Based on the content of the Expanded Short-Term Memory grouping (see Figure 6-4) and knowledge that a relatively stronger Numbers Reversed performance is not necessarily inconsistent with a weakness in short-term memory (see the discussion of the Numbers Reversed test in the Extended Battery strategy example), the clinician could conclude that John has a possible weakness in short-term memory abilities. The information presented in Figures 6-11 and 6-12 also suggests a borderline or mild strength in fluid reasoning abilities. Both the Analysis-Synthesis and Concept Formation tests are identified as borderline strength tests.

Additional Steps

Steps 4 through 6 are identical to those described for the Extended Battery strategy. The only difference is that a clinician will have a smaller amount of

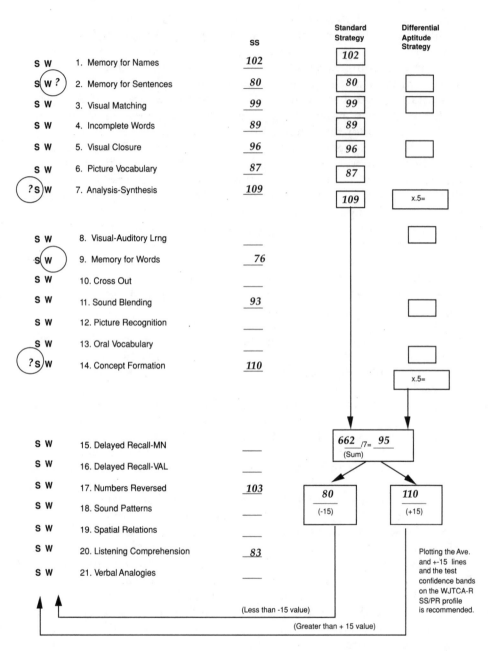

FIGURE 6-11   Completed Strength/Weakness Worksheet for Standard Strategy for John

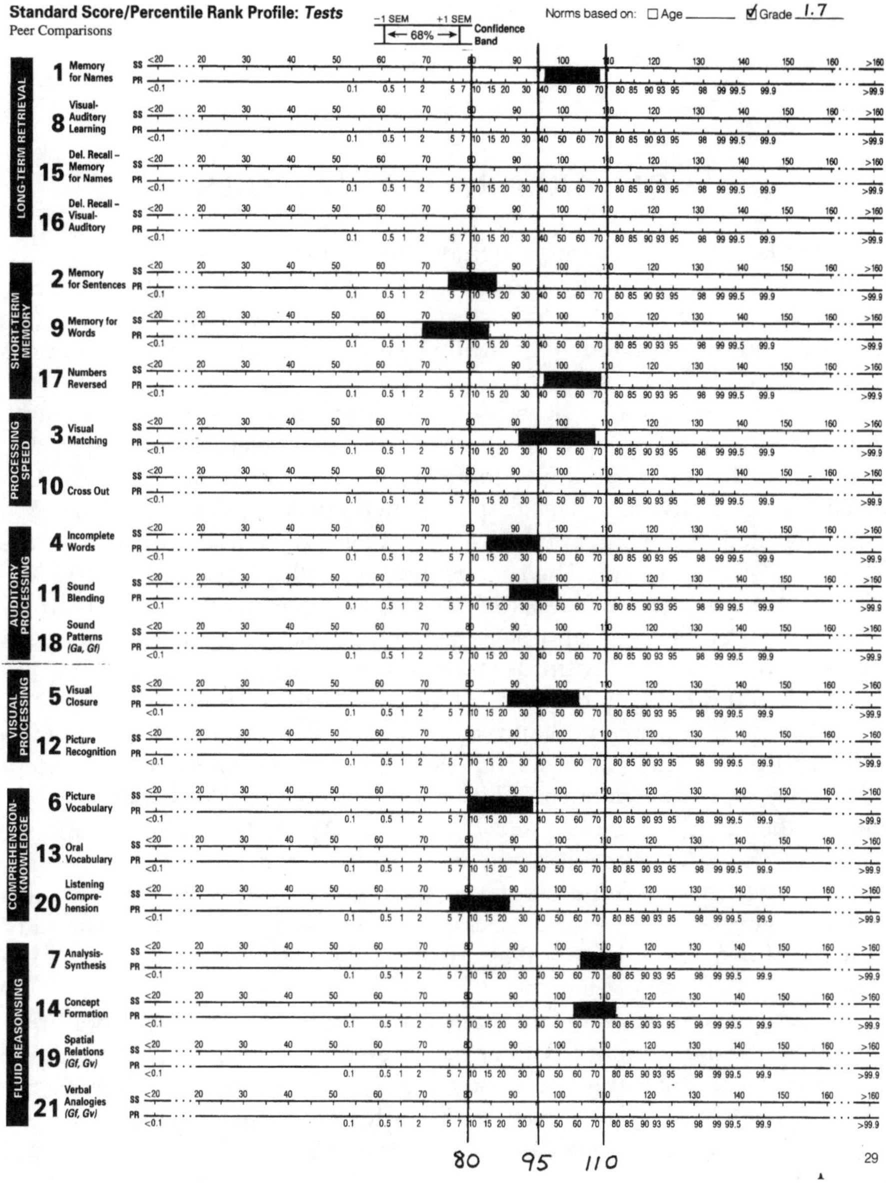

Standard Score/Percentile Rank Profile: *Tests*
Peer Comparisons

Norms based on: ☐ Age _____ ☑ Grade *1.7*

80 95 110

29

FIGURE 6-12 Standard Score/Percentile Rank Profile for Completed Standard Strategy for John

test-based information upon which to draw when generating hypotheses. As a result, these steps must be approached cautiously when using the Standard Battery and Differential Aptitude strategies.

COMPARISON OF STRATEGIES

The Standard Battery example demonstrates that this test administration strategy can result in useful hypotheses about a person's strengths and weaknesses. The Differential Aptitude strategy was not demonstrated, although the logic and the supplementary testing process described for the Standard Battery strategy would simply be applied to a different starting point.

The identification of a possible weakness in short-term memory and a strength in fluid reasoning is similar to the conclusions reached when using the Extended Battery strategy. However, the broader auditory-linguistic/ verbal versus nonverbal/visual-spatial dichotomy in John's abilities that was suggested in the Extended Battery strategy was not identified with the Standard Battery strategy. The number and breadth of tests needed to identify this strength and weakness dichotomy are not available in the Standard Battery strategy. Strength and weakness hypotheses based on the Standard Battery and Differential Aptitude strategies must be offered much more cautiously than those generated by the Extended Battery strategy.

The description of the Standard Battery and Extended Battery strategies with the same case suggests that although similar hypotheses were identified, they were not identical. The validity of the final hypotheses generated by the Standard Battery and Differential Aptitude strategies depends largely on the amount of supplementary testing a clinician pursues and the clinical expertise and logic displayed during the process. In the Standard Battery example, the assessment decisions resulted in the administration of 12 tests. This number is only 2 short of the 14 tests needed to initiate the Extended Battery strategy.

If clinicians anticipate following up strength or weakness identified after Step 1 of the Standard Battery or Differential Aptitude strategies, they should be aware that ultimately they may spend the same amount of time administering tests than if they had started with the Extended Battery strategy. If the generation of clinical hypotheses is a goal, clinicians should seriously consider starting with the Extended Battery administration strategy. Although there will be exceptions, the Standard Battery and Differential Aptitude administration strategies are best suited to cases where clinicians know a priori that all they need is an estimate of a person's aptitudes (i.e., either Broad Cognitive Ability or Scholastic Aptitude cluster scores) and in-depth clinical interpretation of the person's test profile will not be pursued.

EXTENDED STRATEGY EXAMPLE:
SECOND CASE STUDY

A second case study further demonstrates the Extended Battery interpretive strategy. The case is that of a 17-year-old woman named Rima. This case is drawn from Mather and Jaffe's (1992) WJ-R interpretative book. This case was selected for a number of reasons. Rima is an older individual than the other case study presented in this chapter. This case also involves the administration of almost all (i.e., 20) of the 21 WJTCA-R tests, a situation not often encountered in clinical practice. In addition, Rima's case demonstrates the flexible way the interpretive process described in this chapter must be implemented.

Step 1: Identify Significant Strengths and Weaknesses Within the WJTCA-R Test Profile

Using the ±1.50 SD DIFF intra-cognitive discrepancy criterion, Rima demonstrated significant weaknesses on the WJTCA-R Processing Speed (-1.54) and Fluid Reasoning (-1.61) cognitive clusters. No significant positive intra-cognitive discrepancies were identified. The identification of strengths and weaknesses at the individual test level is illustrated in Figure 6-13.

A review of Figure 6-13 indicates that three tests (i.e., Memory for Sentences, Listening Comprehension, and Verbal Analogies) were identified as significant strengths for Rima. One test (i.e., Incomplete Words) was identified as a tentative strength since it was 1 standard score point less than the strength criterion of 118. The Cross Out test was identified as a significant weakness. Four additional tests (i.e., Analysis-Synthesis, Concept Formation, Delayed Recall—Visual-Auditory Learning, and Numbers Reversed) were identified as tentative weaknesses since they were either equal to or 1 standard score point greater than the weakness criterion of 88.

The individual test confidence bands and the average (i.e., 103) and strength (i.e., 118) and weakness (i.e., 88) criteria lines for Rima's WJTCA-R performance are plotted on the Standard Score/Percentile Rank Profile presented in Figure 6-14. The completed profile will be used during the subsequent steps.

Step 2: Identify Strength and Weakness Test Groupings

The strength and weakness test information recorded in Figure 6-13 was used to complete the WJTCA-R Test Grouping Strength/Weakness Worksheet presented in Figure 6-15. In addition, Rima's test profile (Figure 6-14) played a pivotal role in the identification of possible WJTCA-R strength and weakness test groupings.

SS

S W	1. Memory for Names	_108_
(S)W	2. Memory for Sentences	_122_
S W	3. Visual Matching	_90_
(? S)W	4. Incomplete Words	_117_
S W	5. Visual Closure	_114_
S W	6. Picture Vocabulary	_113_
S (W ?) 7. Analysis-Synthesis		_88_

S W	8. Visual-Auditory Lrng	_109_
S W	9. Memory for Words	_93_
S (W)	10. Cross Out	_82_
S W	11. Sound Blending	_107_
S W	12. Picture Recognition	_97_
S W	13. Oral Vocabulary	_108_
S (W ?)	14. Concept Formation	_88_

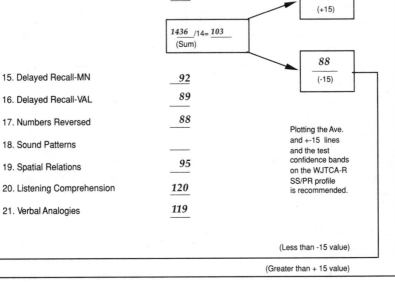

1436 /14= _103_
(Sum)

118
(+15)

88
(-15)

S W	15. Delayed Recall-MN	_92_
S(W ?)	16. Delayed Recall-VAL	_89_
S (W ?)	17. Numbers Reversed	_88_
S W	18. Sound Patterns	___
S W	19. Spatial Relations	_95_
(S) W	20. Listening Comprehension	_120_
(S)W	21. Verbal Analogies	_119_

Plotting the Ave.
and +-15 lines
and the test
confidence bands
on the WJTCA-R
SS/PR profile
is recommended.

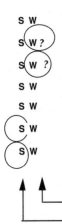

(Less than -15 value)

(Greater than + 15 value)

**FIGURE 6-13   WJTCA-R Strength/Weakness Worksheet for Rima:
Extended Strategy**

Standard Score/Percentile Rank Profile: *Tests*
Peer Comparisons

Norms based on: ☐ Age _____ ☑ Grade **12.0**

88   103   118

29

FIGURE 6-14   Standard Score/Percentile Rank Profile for Rima

The Processing Speed and Expanded Processing Speed groupings were identified as possible weaknesses as a result of the significant –1.54 intra-cognitive discrepancy score for Processing Speed. Although only one (i.e., Cross Out) of the two Processing Speed tests was designated as a weakness test, the –1.54 intra-cognitive discrepancy score indicates that attention should be directed to Rima's test profile. A review of Figure 6-14 reveals that although Rima's Visual Matching test score was not significantly weak, the confidence band for this test is below her average line of 103, and a good portion of the band is below the weakness criterion line (i.e., 88). When combined with the tentative weakness classification (i.e., "W?") for the Numbers Reversed test, the designation of the Expanded Processing Speed grouping as a possible weakness makes sense.

The Fluid Reasoning test grouping is also designated as a possible weakness in Figure 6-15. This designation is due to the significant –1.61 intra-cognitive discrepancy score for the Fluid Reasoning cluster. In addition, of the five tests that were administered in this six-test grouping, three were designated as tentative weaknesses. A review of Rima's test profile (Figure 6-14) finds that the Spatial Relations test, although not designated as a weakness, is consistent with this designation. The confidence band for the Spatial Relations test is below the average line of 103 on the profile. Thus, four of the five administered tests in the Fluid Reasoning grouping are relatively low.

The observation that the remaining test (i.e., Verbal Analogies) in the Fluid Reasoning grouping is designated as a strength does not negate the designation of this grouping as a possible weakness. In large test groupings the rule is that the majority of the administered tests be internally consistent. Four of the five administered Fluid Reasoning grouping tests are consistently in the weakness direction. Furthermore, knowledge of Verbal Analogies' empirical characteristics provides a reasonable explanation for this finding. As summarized in Chapter 3, Verbal Analogies is a factorially complex test of both fluid reasoning and comprehension-knowledge abilities. It is possible that Rima has stronger verbal comprehension and knowledge abilities that may account for her relatively higher Verbal Analogies test score.

The Expanded Fluid Reasoning grouping requires a closer examination in light of the significant –1.61 intra-cognitive discrepancy score for the Fluid Reasoning cluster. A review of Figures 6-14 and 6-15 reveals an apparent verbal/nonverbal dichotomy within the Expanded Fluid Reasoning grouping. Four of the administered tests (i.e., Analysis-Synthesis, Concept Formation, Numbers Reversed, and Spatial Relations) are in the weakness direction. All of these tests require minimal use of language or verbal abilities. In contrast, the remaining three administered tests in this grouping all require verbal or language abilities and are either designated as significant strengths (i.e., Listening Comprehension and Verbal Analogies) or, as reflected in Rima's test profile (Figure 6-14), have a confidence band that is above her average line of 103. The observation that the Expanded Fluid Reasoning grouping is not internally consistent and displays a verbal/nonverbal dichotomy results in this grouping not being designated as a weakness.

The designation of the Comprehension-Knowledge and Expanded Comprehension-Knowledge groupings as possible strengths in Figure 6-15 was not made during this step. This designation will be explained later.

Step 3: Integrate the Strength and Weakness Test Grouping Information With Other Relevant Information

Behavioral Observations

As described by Mather and Jaffe (1992), no significant test behavior was observed that would cast doubts on the validity of Rima's performance on the WJTCA-R tests. Rima was generally cooperative and attentive during the assessment. However, she did display some avoidance behavior when she encountered the WJ-R mathematics tests. No significant test behavior was described that would suggest that any of the variables listed in Table 6-2 should be considered during interpretation.

Referral Concerns, Observations of Others, and Background Information

As presented by Mather and Jaffe (1992), the primary reason Rima was referred for assessment was her long-standing difficulty in mathematics, especially in memorizing mathematics facts and understanding abstract mathematical concepts. Rima indicated that she has always experienced difficulty with mathematics and courses requiring quantitative reasoning (e.g., chemistry). She reports significant difficulty with mathematical logic and problem solving.

Rima's long-standing mathematics problems provide support for the Fluid Reasoning weakness designation on her grouping worksheet (Figure 6-15). As presented in Chapter 4, fluid reasoning abilities are significantly associated with performance in mathematics. Rima's self-report of difficulty in applying logic and problem solving to new mathematical problems is consistent with a weakness in fluid reasoning.

The weakness designation of the Processing Speed and Expanded Processing Speed groupings (Figure 6-15) may also be consistent with Rima's reported difficulties. As described in Chapter 5, rather than reflecting a general speed of information processing ability, the Expanded Processing Speed grouping may reflect a person's fluency and facility in processing visual symbols. Given the visual symbolic nature of mathematics, the Expanded Processing Speed weakness should be retained for further consideration.

This latter conclusion highlights the importance of clinicians not focusing just on the verbal label for the different test groupings. Although the

Expanded Processing Speed label suggests a focus on speed of processing abilities, the discussion of this grouping in Chapter 5 also focused on two additional hypotheses. Clinicians need to be familiar with the *Gf-Gc* and non–*Gf-Gc* related descriptions for each test grouping. Intimate familiarity with the information presented in Chapters 3 through 5 is required for astute clinical interpretation.

Other Assessment Information

Rima's performance on the WJ-R achievement tests provides additional support for the hypothesized weaknesses noted on her grouping worksheet. When compared to others of the same grade, Rima performed above the 90th percentile on the Broad Reading and Broad Written Language clusters. Rima appears to have strong abilities in the language arts domain. She was at the 50th percentile on the Broad Knowledge cluster. In contrast, Rima displayed a relative weakness on the Broad Mathematics cluster (i.e., 23rd percentile). The large difference between her language arts and mathematical skills is consistent with her hypothesized Fluid Reasoning and Expanded Processing Speed weaknesses.

Investigate New Insights

Additional insights regarding Rima's strengths and weaknesses emerge when one goes beyond the simple step-by-step completion of the grouping worksheet. The first insight comes from the designation of the Fluid Reasoning grouping, but not the Expanded Fluid Reasoning grouping, as a weakness. As discussed previously, Rima's performance on the tests in the Expanded Fluid Reasoning grouping was not consistent. Rima's performance on the tests in this grouping suggested that her ability to reason varies as a function of the degree of verbal or language involvement in a task. This observation requires an additional examination of Rima's performance on other verbal or language tests.

Inspection of Rima's test profile (Figure 6-14) and the Expanded Comprehension-Knowledge grouping reveals a possible strength in comprehension-knowledge abilities. Four of the seven tests listed in the Expanded Comprehension-Knowledge grouping are designated as either strengths or tentative strengths for Rima (see Figure 6-15). Rima's test profile (Figure 6-14) reveals that the confidence bands for the other three tests in this grouping (i.e., Visual Closure, Picture Vocabulary, and Oral Vocabulary) are all above her average line of 103. This suggests a possible relative strength in verbal comprehension and knowledge abilities. The possibility of a relative strength in comprehension-knowledge is consistent with Rima's achievement test results, which show her well within or above the average range for her grade on the WJ-R Broad Knowledge, Broad Reading, and Broad Written Language clusters. This hypothesized strength is designated by circling the appropriate *S* on the grouping worksheet (Figure 6-15).

WJTCA-R Test Grouping Strength/Weakness Worksheet
(Developed by Kevin S. McGrew)

Circle possible S or W test groupings →

Label as S or W or + or - →

		Standard Tests 1-7							Supplemental Tests 8-14							Supplemental Tests 15-21						
	Intra-Cog. Disc.	**Test Grouping**	MN	MS	VM	IW	VC	PV	AS	VAL	MW	CO	SB	PR	OV	CF	DRMN	DRVAL	NR	SP	SR	LC	VA
S W	+0.81	Long-Term Retrieval (Glr)	S			S?			W?							W?		W?	W?				S
S W		Exp. Long-Term Retrieval (Glr)																					
S W	+0.15	Short-Term Memory (Gsm)	S															W?			S	
S W		Exp. Short-Term Memory (Gsm)	S															W?				
(S) W	-1.54	Processing Speed (Gs)									W											
(S) W		Exp. Processing Speed (Gs)									W							W?				
S W	+1.10	Auditory Processing (Ga)				S?													X			
S W	+0.31	Visual Processing (Gv)																				
(S) W	+1.07	Comprehension-Knowledge (Gc)	S			S?			W?							W?		W?			S	S
(S) W		Exp. Comp-Knowledge (Gc)	S			S?			W?							W?		W?	X		S	S
(S) W	-1.61	Fluid Reasoning (Gf)																			S	
S W		Exp. Fluid Reasoning (Gf)																				
S W		Aud. Seq. Processing/Memory	S			S?					W											
S W		Visual Perceptual Fluency															W?	X				
S W		Auditory Attention/Listening				S?			W?		W											S
S W		New Learning Efficiency																W?	X			
S W		Broad Synthesis Ability				S?																
S W		Word Finding/Verbal Retrieval				S?																
S W		Nonverbal Ability (nonspeeded)							W?							W?		W?				

Gf-Gc Groupings

FIGURE 6-15 Completed Grouping Worksheet for Rima

189

Given the consistent findings that suggest possible strengths in comprehension-knowledge abilities and language arts achievement, inspection of other abilities often associated with strengths in these areas is suggested. A review of Rima's test profile (Figure 6-14) reveals slight relative strengths (both confidence bands above her average line of 103) on the two auditory processing tests that were administered. Thus, the hypothesis could be advanced that Rima displays relative strengths in the broad area of auditory-linguistic abilities, and not just comprehension-knowledge abilities.

Additional inspection of Rima's test profile (Figure 6-14) reveals a potentially important dichotomy within the four WJTCA-R long-term retrieval *(Glr)* tests. The confidence bands for the two delayed recall tests (Delayed Recall—Memory for Names and Delayed Recall—Visual-Auditory Learning) are significantly below the confidence bands for the Memory for Names and Visual-Auditory Learning tests. As discussed in Chapter 4, the diagnostic and clinical implications of such a discrepancy have yet to be empirically studied.

This discrepancy suggests that Rima may not demonstrate observable difficulty when initially learning associational information, but she may experience significant difficulty in retaining and recalling associational information on a long-term basis. The generation of this hypothesis did not flow directly from the completion of the grouping worksheet. This reinforces the point that the grouping worksheet is provided only as one aid to help clinicians interpret WJTCA-R profiles. *The grouping worksheet cannot think for a clinician.* Clinicians need to pay careful attention to the various nuances present in a person's test profile that are not captured by the grouping worksheet.

Additional Steps

If Steps 1 through 3 do not produce any clear hypotheses, then Steps 4 through 6 need to be considered. In the case of Rima, the additional steps are not necessary. The hypothesized strengths and weaknesses suggested for Rima by the end of Step 3 are supported by non–WJTCA-R information. The hypothesis can be advanced that Rima is a person with strengths in auditory-linguistic abilities. Relative weaknesses are suggested in fluid reasoning ability, ability to fluently process and manipulate visual symbols, and ability to store and retrieve associational information after initial learning. This profile is consistent with her academic strengths in the language arts areas of reading and writing and her weakness in mathematics and quanitative reasoning. The completion of Steps 4 through 6, steps that focus on generating unique child-specific hypothesis, interpreting individual WJTCA-R tests, or administering additional supplemental tests, do not appear warranted.

CONCLUDING COMMENTS

The following comments need to be considered by those seeking to use the interpretive procedures described in this chapter.

First, the interpretive procedures described in this chapter must be used flexibly. The strength and weakness groupings are not to be considered in isolation, but are evaluated simultaneously in a global analysis. The usefulness of this interpretive process rests on the clinician's familiarity with the information presented in the prior chapters and the clinician's skill in pursuing a logical, flexible detective process.

Although the sequential interpretive process can assist clinicians in unlocking WJTCA-R profiles, the process should not be employed in a lock-step "cookbook" fashion. Sequential steps and "rules, no matter what their empirical foundation, cannot replace good judgment and must not supersede clinical, neuropsychological, or psychoeducational insights" (Kaufman, 1990, p. 483). The art of clinical interpretation is a skillful process that cannot be learned by simply reading a book. The process described in this chapter only provides clinicians a framework from which to develop new clinical skills.

Second, the overriding goal of the interpretive process is the generation of hypotheses that will serve as the basis for meaningful intervention recommendations. When presented with the challenge of evaluating an individual, which usually is precipitated by some difficulty in functioning, the universe of potential interventions is large. Thus, it is best to conceptualize assessment (in this case with the WJTCA-R) as the use of standardized data collection procedures that increase the probability of locating the best interventions.

Hypothesis formation is the primary goal. Clinicians are discouraged from making definitive factual statements such as "this individual 'has' a weakness in . . . ." or "this individual 'will' respond best to an approach that . . ." Clinicians must acknowledge that the assessment data are gathered in an artificial and isolated testing environment. Assessment data should not be accorded greater powers than they deserve. Phrasing all WJTCA-R interpretations and subsequent recommendations within the language of hypotheses and probabilities is strongly recommended.

Third, hypothesis generation implies further verification. Hypotheses are meant to be tested to determine their validity and usefulness. Clinicians must encourage those who receive the results of their WJTCA-R interpretations to consider the reported strengths, weaknesses, and recommendations as possibilities needing verification in the individual's natural environment. In the context of psychoeducational assessment, this verification could take the form of supplementary assessment or the implementation of the hypotheses-based recommendations during actual learning, with concurrent monitoring and evaluation of the subject's response (e.g., diagnostic teaching; curriculum-based assessment methods).

Fourth, the individual tests in intelligence batteries represent samples from the large domain of intelligent behavior. The individual tests from the WJTCA-R and other intelligence batteries are not intended to be *the* list of abilities necessary for success. If someone is weak on a test, this does not mean that training should be directed at remediation of the abilities tapped by the test. The goal of assessment is not to generate remedial plans for individual tests. This endorsement of a non–test remediation philosophy is based on a substantial body of literature that has suggested that this practice is not effective or useful (Hammill & Larsen, 1978; Ross, 1976).

Fifth, clinicians need to appreciate that the usefulness of the shared ability approach to interpreting intelligence test profiles has been seriously questioned. Research studies with most intelligence batteries have not supported the diagnostic or treatment relevance of specific test profiles (McDermott et al., 1990). However, Reynolds (1988) argues that the negative research findings are based on studies that only focused on gross group characteristics rather than on multivariate characteristics of individuals. Furthermore, most profile studies have not used assessment instruments that provide for comprehensive coverage of all the broad *Gf-Gc* abilities. The development of tests such as the WJTCA-R, according to modern *Gf-Gc* theory, provides the first opportunity to conduct sound aptitude profile–based diagnostic and intervention research (Ysseldyke, 1990).

Until studies are completed that investigate the usefulness of profile analysis based on modern *Gf-Gc* theory, clinicians need to recognize that direct links between specific WJTCA-R profiles and specific diagnostic classifications or treatment responses have not been empirically demonstrated. I am in agreement with Kamphaus (1993), who stated that *"clinicians need to be aware of the fact that profile analysis depends exclusively on the clinical acumen of the examiner, not on sound research"* (p. 165). All cautions presented in this conclusion section need to be taken seriously.

Finally, the art of intelligent test interpretation requires significant additional knowledge beyond that presented in this text. In order to become the best clinicians they can be, clinicians need to be familiar with many other interpretive issues and concepts. Clinicians serious about developing solid interpretive skills are directed to the works of Kamphaus (1993) and Kaufman (1979, 1990) for discussions of many interpretive issues and concepts.

7

THE WJTCA-R DIFFERENTIAL
APTITUDE CLUSTERS

The previous four chapters dealt extensively with information related to Type II or intra-cognitive interpretation of the WJTCA-R. In contrast, the WJTCA-R differential aptitude clusters (i.e., Scholastic and Oral Language Aptitude clusters) are the cornerstone for Type I or aptitude/achievement discrepancy analysis in the WJ-R pragmatic decision-making model. In many respects the Scholastic Aptitude clusters represented the philosophical heart and soul of the 1977 WJ battery (McGrew, 1986). However, a review of the literature suggests that the true value of the Scholastic Aptitude clusters was not appreciated in the original WJ battery. This chapter puts the WJTCA-R differential aptitude clusters in proper perspective.

TECHNICAL CONSIDERATIONS

Cluster Composition

The WJTCA-R differential aptitude clusters are designed to function as specialized measures of intelligence that make statements about an individual's present level of predicted achievement in reading, mathematics, written language, knowledge, and oral language. The WJTCA-R differential aptitude clusters facilitate the determination of an individual's aptitude/achievement (Type I) discrepancies performance (see Chapter 1 for an overview of this feature in the WJ-R battery).

The Development Process
The five WJTCA-R differential aptitude clusters were developed with the aid of a series of stepwise multiple regression analyses completed across

the entire WJTCA-R age range (McGrew et al., 1991). In simple terms, *multiple regression* is a statistical procedure that identifies the optimal linear combination of variables that best predicts a selected criterion variable. In the case of the WJTCA-R, these statistical procedures identified the specific combinations of four WJTCA-R tests that best predicted performance on the WJ-R reading, mathematics, written language, and knowledge achievement clusters, and the WJTCA-R Oral Language cluster. Each differential aptitude cluster is based on only four tests since no appreciable increase in predictive power was found beyond this number (McGrew et al., 1991). These procedures resulted in four separate Scholastic Aptitude clusters named Reading, Mathematics, Written Language, and Knowledge Aptitude. The fifth differential aptitude cluster is Oral Language Aptitude, a cluster designed to predict performance on the WJTCA-R Oral Language cluster.

Since it is inappropriate to include in predictor measures variables that share content with the criterion (Anastasi, 1982; Woodcock, 1978), certain cognitive tests were eliminated as possible cluster tests prior to the completion of the multiple regression studies (McGrew et al., 1991). For example, although the correlations between the WJTCA-R comprehension-knowledge *(Gc)* tests (i.e., Picture Vocabulary, Oral Vocabulary, Verbal Analogies, and Listening Comprehension) and the Broad Knowledge achievement criterion were quite high, these cognitive tests were not allowed to be included in the stepwise regression analyses because of shared content with the criterion. In the second example, tests with language content were eliminated from the Oral Language regressions. The selective elimination of specific tests from inclusion in certain differential aptitude clusters ensured that the aptitude measures did not share content with the criteria measures.

An additional constraint placed on possible tests to include in the differential aptitude clusters was that they could only be drawn from the first 14 cognitive tests. This constraint made practical sense, as it made it possible for practitioners to obtain all the major cognitive cluster scores (including scores for the differential aptitude clusters) when giving the first 14 tests.

The Quantitative Concepts test is no longer included in any of the differential aptitude clusters. This achievement-oriented test was included in two of the differential aptitude clusters in the original WJTCA. Research and clinical experience (McGrew, 1984, 1986) found that the inclusion of the Quantitative Concepts test in two differential aptitude clusters could result in significantly distorted scores on these measures for individuals with problems in mathematics achievement. The placement of the Quantitative Concepts test in the WJ-R achievement section eliminated this concern for the WJTCA-R.

As described above, the five WJTCA-R differential aptitude clusters were developed empirically. As noted by Hessler (1982) regarding the original WJTCA differential aptitude clusters, "the clusters were not developed to meet some preconceived theoretical or rational concept regarding the nature of the processes that relate closely to academic achievement. Rather, they were developed entirely by using statistical procedures" (p. 75). The final composition and weighting of the four tests in each of the five differential aptitude clusters, as well as similar comparative information for the WJTCA differential aptitude clusters, are presented in Table 7-1.

Composition of Clusters

A review of Table 7-1 indicates that the WJTCA-R differential aptitude clusters differ from the original WJTCA differential aptitude clusters. The WJTCA-R clusters are each based on an *equally* weighted combination of four tests. This differs from the original WJTCA differential aptitude clusters that were *unequally* weighted.

The original WJTCA Scholastic Aptitude clusters were criticized for using differential weights (McGue et al., 1982) and disproportionately weighting the Antonyms-Synonyms test (i.e., Oral Vocabulary in the WJTCA-R) in all four Scholastic Aptitude clusters (McGrew, 1986). As presented in Table 7-1, the Antonyms-Synonyms test was weighted from .29 to .46 across the four WJTCA Scholastic Aptitude clusters. Antonyms-Synonyms accounted for 29% to 46% of the total score for the four WJTCA Scholastic Aptitude clusters. Although these criticisms were found to be inaccurate, and upon careful analyses demonstrated a strength of the WJTCA differential aptitude clusters (McGrew, 1986)—they did create concerns among practitioners. Regardless of the correctness of the original criticisms they no longer exist, as each of the five WJTCA-R differential aptitudes is based on equally weighted combinations of four tests.

The composition of three of the four WJTCA-R Scholastic Aptitude clusters has changed from the original WJTCA clusters (see Table 7-1). The WJTCA-R Reading and Mathematics Aptitude clusters include two tests each that were present in the same WJTCA clusters. The WJTCA-R Reading Aptitude cluster still comprises Oral Vocabulary and Sound Blending, but now also includes Visual Matching and Memory for Sentences and not Visual-Auditory Learning and Verbal Analogies. The WJTCA-R Written Language Aptitude cluster retained the Oral Vocabulary and Visual Matching tests and replaced Quantitative Concepts and Numbers Reversed with Sound Blending and Visual-Auditory Learning. The Knowledge Aptitude cluster changed the most, with the only common test being Memory for Sentences. Finally, although the test weightings are different, the composition of the WJTCA-R Mathematics Aptitude cluster is identical to the original WJTCA Mathematics Aptitude cluster.

Seven of the eight tests used to derive the Scholastic Aptitude clusters are present in both the WJTCA and the WJTCA-R clusters. The inclusion of the Visual Closure test in the WJTCA-R Knowledge Aptitude cluster represents the only "new" test that contributes to the four Scholastic Aptitude clusters. Despite the addition of nine new tests in the WJTCA-R, seven of the eight most important tests for predicting academic success were present

TABLE 7-1 Test Composition and Weighting Comparisons of WJTCA and WJTCA-R Differential Aptitude Clusters

| | | Scholastic Aptitudes | | | | | | | | | |
| | | Reading | | Mathematics | | Written Language | | Knowledge | | Oral Language Aptitude | |
Tests	Gf-Gc Factor	WJTCA	WJTCA-R	WJTCA	WJTCA-R	WJTCA	WJTCA-R	WJTCA	WJTCA-R	WJTCA	WJTCA-R
Oral Vocabulary	(Gc)	.42	.25	.39	.25	.29	.25	.46	—	—	—
Visual Matching	(Gs)	—	.25	.26	.25	.15	.25	—	—	—	—
Sound Blending	(Ga)	.17	.25	—	—	—	.25	—	.25	—	.25
Concept Formation	(Gf)	—	—	.08	.25	—	—	—	.25	—	.25
Memory for Sentences	(Gsm)	—	.25	—	—	—	—	.10	.25	—	—
Analysis-Synthesis	(Gf)	—	—	.27	.25	—	—	—	—	—	—
Visual-Auditory Learning	(Glr)	.23	—	—	—	—	.25	—	—	—	—
Numbers Reversed	(Gsm)	—	—	—	—	—	—	—	—	—	.25
Visual Closure	(Gv)	—	—	—	—	.08	—	—	.25	—	—
Picture Recognition	(Gv)	—	—	—	—	—	—	—	—	—	.25
Sound Patterns	(Ga)	—	—	—	—	—	—	—	—	—	.25
Verbal Analogies	(Gf/Gc)	.18	—	—	—	—	—	.16	—	—	—
Quantitative Concepts	(Gq)	—	—	—	—	.47	—	.28	—	—	—

Note: Boxes indicate common tests in respective clusters across WJTCA and WJTCA-R. Test names are from WJTCA-R. Three of the tests have different names in WJTCA (Oral Vocabulary = Antonyms–Synonyms; Sound Blending = Blending; Verbal Analogies = Analogies).

in the original WJTCA. This validates the composition of the original WJTCA that consisted of tests that were most closely associated with school success (McGrew, 1986).

The changed composition of three of the four Scholastic Aptitude clusters is most likely due to the removal of the Quantitative Concepts test from the pool of possible predictor tests in certain of the multiple regression analyses and to improvements made in other tests. Given the presence of the Visual Matching test in the WJTCA-R Reading, Mathematics, and Written Language Aptitude clusters, it appears that increasing this test from a two-minute to a three-minute measure significantly increased its reliable variance. The Visual Matching test has become a more powerful predictor of academic achievement.

Although the specific tests that compose three of the four WJTCA-R Scholastic Aptitude clusters may differ from the WJTCA, this should not be a major concern. The primary purpose of these clusters is to provide predicted levels of achievement. The only concern should be how well the revised differential aptitude clusters predict achievement. Information reviewed later in this chapter finds the predictive validity of the WJTCA-R clusters to be just as strong as the original WJTCA clusters.

Cluster Overlap

Information presented in Table 7-1 reveals that the four WJTCA-R Scholastic Aptitude clusters are not composed of tests unique to each cluster. The Oral Vocabulary and Visual Matching tests are present in all but the Knowledge Aptitude cluster. The Sound Blending test is in all but the Mathematics Aptitude cluster. The Concept Formation and Memory for Sentences tests are both in two Scholastic Aptitude clusters. This overlap is statistically evident in the high degree of average intercorrelation among the Scholastic Aptitude clusters (McGrew et al., 1991). The median intercorrelations among the four WJTCA-R Scholastic Aptitude clusters are presented in Table 7-2.

With the exception of the median Reading and Written Language Aptitude cluster correlation of .94, the typical intercorrelations between the WJTCA-R Scholastic Aptitude clusters range from .81 to .87. (The high .94 average Reading and Written Language Aptitude correlation is significant and will be discussed in greater detail later in this chapter.) These values are similar to those reported for the WJTCA and are bound to raise concerns similar to those voiced by McGue et al. (1982) regarding the original WJTCA Scholastic Aptitude clusters. McGue et al. interpreted the intercorrelations in the .80s as evidence that the Scholastic Aptitude clusters were not measuring what they were intended to measure—that they were not specialized intelligence measures in four separate curriculum areas. McGue et al. viewed the test overlap and resulting high intercorrelation as evidence that the four clusters may only be measuring a "general propensity toward achievement" (p.283). It was their interpretation that these specialized ability measures should demonstrate a lower degree of interdependence.

TABLE 7-2   Median Correlations Between WJTCA-R Scholastic Aptitude Clusters

	Reading	Mathematics	Written Language	Knowledge
Reading	—			
Mathematics	.81	—		
Written Language	.94	.85	—	
Knowledge	.87	.81	.82	—

Median values across seven age groups presented in *WJ-R Technical Manual* (McGrew et al., 1991).

Although it makes intuitive sense that the specialized Scholastic Aptitude clusters should be more independent, it is an assumption that is inconsistent with the known relationship between aptitude measures. As noted by Jensen (1984); "Some 80 years ago, Spearman (1904) discovered that all cognitive tests, however diverse, provided they possess at least some minimum degree of complexity, are positively intercorrelated to varying degrees in the general population" (p. 381). This high degree of intercorrelation has historically been interpreted as an indication of a general ability factor (i.e., *g*) that exerts a substantial influence in almost all mental tasks. Since the WJTCA-R Scholastic Aptitude clusters are actually four miniature ability tests, a high degree of intercorrelation is expected. The observed interdependence between the four Scholastic Aptitude clusters in one sense validates their function, as this finding is consistent with a long research history with aptitude tests. However, the question raised by McGue et al. (1982) is *how much* intercorrelation is appropriate when attempting to develop differential aptitude measures.

According to McGue et al. (1982), median intercorrelations in the .80s are too high. However, by squaring the .81 to .87 median correlations reported in Table 7-2, one concludes that there is approximately 65% to 75% shared variance between all the Scholastic Aptitude clusters (except Reading and Written Language). Whether this degree of shared variance is too high is a relative question that may be best answered by examining other instruments. Table 7-3 compares the test overlap in the WJTCA-R Scholastic Aptitude clusters and in the Wechsler Full Scale when both are used as predictors of achievement in four curriculum areas. The Wechsler Full Scale is used only for discussion purposes; any other broad-based ability measure (i.e., DAS, K-ABC, SB-IV) would reveal the same findings.

In the field of psychoeducational assessment, when predictions are made concerning an individual's expected achievement in different curriculum domains, the established practice has been to use the same broad-based full-scale score across academic areas. This results in the *same* aptitude

TABLE 7-3 Weighted Contribution and Overlap of WJTCA-R and WISC-III Tests Used as Achievement Predictors

WJTCA-R Tests	Knowledge	Reading	Written Language	Mathematics
Oral Vocabulary		.25	.25	.25
Visual Matching		.25	.25	.25
Sound Blending	.25	.25	.25	
Concept Formation	.25			.25
Memory for Sentences	.25	.25		
Analysis-Synthesis				
Visual-Auditory Learning			.25	.25
Visual Closure	.25			

WISC-III Tests	Knowledge	Reading	Written Language	Mathematics
Information	.10	.10	.10	.10
Similarities	.10	.10	.10	.10
Arithmetic	.10	.10	.10	.10
Vocabulary	.10	.10	.10	.10
Comprehension	.10	.10	.10	.10
Picture Completion	.10	.10	.10	.10
Picture Arrangement	.10	.10	.10	.10
Block Design	.10	.10	.10	.10
Object Assembly	.10	.10	.10	.10
Coding	.10	.10	.10	.10

Boxes indicate shared content or overlap of aptitude predictors across four achievement domains.

measure (e.g., Wechsler Full Scale) predicting achievement in *all* curriculum domains. In Table 7-3 this is demonstrated by the box around the ten individual Wechsler tests that are used to predict achievement by curriculum area.

The fact that the identical 10 tests are used to provide expectancy information in any academic area reveals 100% shared variance. Statistically this would mean that the intercorrelation among the Wechsler aptitude measures across curriculum areas is always a perfect 1.0. In contrast, in Table 7-3 it can be seen that the overlap across the four WJTCA-R Aptitude clusters is less. With the exception of Reading and Written Language Aptitude, the 100% shared variance in the case of the Wechsler scales is substantially higher than the 65% to 75% noted for the WJTCA-R Scholastic Aptitude clusters. If the WJTCA-R Scholastic Aptitude clusters are to be faulted for test overlap, then other measures in the field (viz., Wechsler scales, SB-IV, K-ABC, DAS) suffer from this same flaw to an even greater degree. If one uses the same broad-based ability measure to predict achievement across curriculum areas, one is then making the assumption that "cognitive ability is a single unitary trait with the same predictive relationship to various psychoeducational capabilities" (Woodcock, 1984a, p. 359). Such an assumption flies in the face of the common sense observation that individuals do not possess the same identical aptitudes in every area.

Readers should reflect upon their own educational experiences and determine if they achieved uniformly in all subjects. Most people do not generally achieve at the same identical level in all areas, a finding inconsistent with expectancy information based on broad-based ability measures with 100% test overlap across curriculum areas. The WJTCA-R Scholastic Aptitude clusters provide the ability to reflect this intra-individual variability by providing differential predictors across academic domains. The 65% to 75% shared variance across the Scholastic Aptitude clusters reflects the real and long-acknowledged influence of a general ability (i.e., *g*). In addition, there is still approximately 25% to 35% residual variance within each Scholastic Aptitude cluster that reflects the combination of unique abilities and error variance. In contrast, other intelligence tests (i.e., Wechsler scales, SB-IV, K-ABC, DAS) do not acknowledge any intra-individual aptitude variability when their respective broad-based scores are used to predict achievement in all academic domains.

The .94 Reading and Written Language correlation reported in Table 7-2, a correlation that indicates nearly 90% common variance, suggests that these two clusters may overlap too much. A review of Table 7-3 finds that both of these clusters contain the Oral Vocabulary, Visual Matching, and Sound Blending tests. These two clusters are nearly identical, with the exception being the Memory for Sentences and Visual-Auditory Learning tests. A review of Table 7-1 indicates that this high degree of overlap is much greater than was present for these two clusters in the original WJTCA. Additional discussion about this issue is presented later in this chapter when the differential predictive validity of these two clusters is reviewed.

Reliability

The reliability of the differential aptitude clusters was calculated in a manner similar to that described for the Cognitive factor clusters in Chapter 4. Table 7-4 summarizes the reliability figures reported in the WJ-R technical manual (McGrew et al., 1991).

Since the differential aptitude clusters play a pivotal role in Type I or aptitude-achievement discrepancy determination, which is frequently the discrepancy used to determine eligibility for certain special education programs (e.g., learning disabilities), the reliability standard against which they should be compared is the stringent .90 or above (Salvia & Ysseldyke, 1991). As presented in Table 7-4, the average or median reliability for all the differential aptitude clusters satisfies this criterion. The WJTCA-R differential aptitude clusters possess adequate reliability for making critical educational decisions, such as those in a Type I or aptitude-achievement discrepancy analysis.

Validity

Correlations With Other Intelligence Tests

Since the WJTCA-R differential aptitude clusters are intended to serve as the aptitude component in Type I discrepancy determination, the relationship between these clusters and other established aptitude measures used for similar purposes is important. A summary of the available research is presented in Table 7-5.

As presented in Table 7-5, the median correlations between the WJTCA-R Scholastic Aptitude clusters and the respective full scale scores from the Wechslers, K-ABC, and the SB-IV range from .59 to .68. However, as reported by McGrew et al. (1991), the correlations for the McCullogh-Wiebe samples included in Table 7-5 suffered from significant range restriction that most likely underestimates of the true population correlations.

TABLE 7-4   Reliability of the WJTCA-R Differential Aptitude Clusters From Age 5 to 80+

Cluster	Range	Median
Reading Aptitude	.88–.99	.94
Mathematics Aptitude	.92–.98	.95
Written Language Aptitude	.88–.98	.94
Knowledge Aptitude	.90–.97	.94
Oral Language Aptitude	.92–.97	.95

Reliability coefficients as reported in the *WJ-R Technical Manual* (McGrew et al., 1991)

TABLE 7-5 Concurrent Validity of WJTCA-R Scholastic Aptitude Clusters With Full-Scale Scores From Wechslers, SB-IV, and K-ABC

Scholastic Aptitude Cluster	Scarr (1991) Grade 3	McCullough-Wiebe (1991) Grades 3–4			McCullough-Wiebe (1991) Grades 10–11		Median Correlation
	WISC-R	WISC-R	SB-IV	K-ABC	WAIS-R	SB-IV	
Reading	.74(92)	.62(72)	.61(70)	.46(70)	.66(50)	.74(51)	.64
Mathematics	.62(93)	.80(72)	.79(70)	.61(70)	.67(50)	.70(51)	.68
Written Language	.67(92)	.60(72)	.58(70)	.48(70)	.62(50)	.68(51)	.61
Knowledge	.71(92)	.58(72)	.60(70)	.54(70)	.55(50)	.68(51)	.59

Values in parentheses indicate sample size for correlation. Correlations are unpublished data from Scarr (1991) and McCullough-Wiebe (1991) studies reported in WJ-R Technical Manual (McGrew et al., 1991).

Visual inspection of Table 7-5 suggests that the WJTCA-R Scholastic Aptitude clusters are more strongly correlated with the Wechslers and the SB-IV than with the K-ABC. Taken as a whole, the median concurrent validity coefficients reported in Table 7-5 are all significant and generally in the range typically found between major intelligence tests. These results indicate that the WJTCA-R Scholastic Aptitude clusters have adequate concurrent validity when defined by other intelligence tests.

Correlations With Achievement Tests

Since the expressed purpose of the WJTCA-R differential aptitude clusters is the prediction of current levels of achievement, their correlation with achievement tests is the most important validity evidence.

McGrew et al. (1991) presented achievement correlation comparisons in three different samples between the WJTCA-R Scholastic Aptitude clusters and the full-scale composites of the Wechslers, SB-IV, and K-ABC. The achievement criteria were drawn from the WJ-R achievement tests, the Peabody Individual Achievement Test (PIAT) (Dunn & Markwardt, 1970), the Peabody Individual Achievement Test—Revised (PIAT-R) (Markwardt, 1989), the achievement tests from the K-ABC (Kaufman & Kaufman, 1983), the Kaufman Tests of Educational Achievement (K-TEA) (Kaufman & Kaufman, 1985), the Wide Range Achievement Test—Revised (WRAT-R) (Jastak & Wilkinson, 1984), and the Basic Achievement Skills Individual Screener (BASIS) (Psychological Corporation, 1983). The aptitude-achievement correlations are summarized in Table 7-6.

A review of comparisons between the WJTCA-R Scholastic Aptitude clusters and full-scale scores from other intelligence tests finds the WJTCA-R Scholastic Aptitude clusters to be better predictors of school achievement than the Wechslers, the SB-IV, and the K-ABC. When comparisons are made across reading, mathematics, written language, and knowledge, the difference is large for the K-ABC comparison (.63 vs .39) and only slight for the Wechslers (.63 vs .58) and SB-IV (.61 vs .57).

However, both the Wechslers and the SB-IV suffer from predictor contamination in their mathematics correlations (McGrew et al., 1991). The Wechslers include the Arithmetic test, while the SB-IV includes the Quantitative, Number Series, and Equation Building tests. The inclusion of these quantitative tests in these two intelligence batteries spuriously inflates the Wechsler and SB-IV mathematics validity coefficients. Similar problems are present in the Wechsler and SB-IV correlations with measures of knowledge, given that both intelligence batteries have significant knowledge *(Gc)* components.

When the mathematics and knowledge correlations are removed from consideration (second column in Table 7-6), the WJTCA-R Scholastic Apti-

TABLE 7-6 Predictive Validity Comparisons Between WJTCA-R Scholastic Aptitude Clusters and Wechslers, SB-IV, and K-ABC

	Achievement Criteria	
Comparison	Reading, Math, Written Language & Knowledge	Reading & Written Language
WJTCA-R Scholastic Aptitude Cluster	.61 (51)	.61 (30)
Wechsler Full Scale	.58 (51)	.54 (30)
WJTCA-R Scholastic Aptitude Cluster	.61 (47)	.61 (27)
SB-IV Composite	.57 (47)	.52 (27)
WJTCA-R Scholastic Aptitude Cluster	.63 (27)	—
K-ABC Mental Processing Composite	.39 (27)	—

Correlations are median values for samples reported in *WJ-R Technical Manual* (McGrew et al., 1991). Values in parentheses indicate the number of pairs of correlations used in each comparison.

tude clusters are found to be noticeably stronger in their prediction of reading and written language achievement than either the Wechslers or the SB-IV. The superior prediction of achievement across three samples and a variety of achievement tests suggests that the WJTCA-R Scholastic Aptitude clusters "are the best predictors of achievement currently available in the field of psychoeducational assessment" (McGrew et al., 1991, p. 151). This conclusion is similar to that reached for the WJTCA Scholastic Aptitude clusters (McGrew, 1986).

It is important to note that the WJTCA-R Scholastic Aptitude clusters are not superior predictors of achievement because of excessive achievement-like content. This was a frequently stated criticism of the original WJTCA test that was later found to be inaccurate (McGrew, 1986; Woodcock, 1990). The original WJTCA's superior prediction of achievement was often attributed to the false belief that it contained too many achievement-like tests (i.e., measures of *Gc* and *Gq*). This is also not true of the WJTCA-R Scholastic Aptitude clusters.

A review of Table 7-1 finds that the Reading, Mathematics, and Written Language aptitude clusters each contain only one test (i.e., Oral Vocabulary) that is a measure of crystallized intelligence *(Gc)*. This test accounts for only 25% of the total cluster scores. Conversely, empirical analysis of the two intelligence tests (i.e., Wechslers and SB-IV) that were closest to the Scholastic Aptitude clusters in the prediction of school achievement finds these tests to contain approximately 50% to 60 % of these types of measures (Woodcock, 1990). *Despite containing only approximately one-half the achievement-like content found in the Wechslers and the SB-IV, the WJTCA-R Scholastic Aptitude clusters still predict achievement better than other intelligence tests.*

THE ADVANTAGES OF THE WJTCA-R APTITUDE CLUSTERS IN APTITUDE-ACHIEVEMENT COMPARISONS

When used in combination with the WJ-R achievement tests, the WJTCA-R differential aptitude clusters provide the most technically sophisticated method available for measuring aptitude-achievement discrepancies. This advantage is based on the WJ-R's technical and conceptual approach to the aptitude/achievement measurement issues of: (a) differential versus broad-based aptitude scores, (b) conormed aptitude and achievement tests, (c) regression to the mean, and (d) discrepancy norms.

Differential Versus Broad-Based Aptitude

The Differential versus Broad Distinction
Historically, the field of psychoeducational assessment has relied heavily on intelligence tests for making diagnostic, selection, and classification decisions. Given the historical prominence of the Stanford-Binet and Wechsler intelligence tests, as well as the prominence of the general intelligence construct in the diagnosis of many exceptionalities (e.g., mental retardation, giftedness, learning disabilities), the established practice has been to develop estimates of a person's predicted achievement from a single broad-based full scale intelligence score (McGrew, 1986). The major competing approach has emphasized the measurement of specific or differentiated abilities that may demonstrate higher validity coefficients for specific subject matter areas (McNemar, 1964; Pellegrino & Varnhagan, 1985). McGrew et al. (1991) provide a good analogy from the field of athletics that highlights the major difference between these two approaches to measuring aptitude for school achievement.

When developing a test to predict athletic performance, the first question that should be asked is "athletic ability for which sport?" If the answer is tennis, the aptitude test should include the specific skills and abilities most associated with success when playing tennis. If the answer is playing offensive line in football, the test to predict success as an offensive lineman would contain a number of specific abilities that differ from those included in the tennis aptitude test. If the goal is to predict average athletic performance across a variety of sports, including tennis and football, then a test would need to include a broad sampling of a variety of different abilities.

An athletic ability battery that measures a broad variety of abilities that are summed to produce a single score would most likely be a more accurate predictor of success, on the average, across a variety of sports than the specialized tennis or offensive lineman aptitude tests. However, the specialized tennis and offensive lineman tests would most likely demonstrate superior prediction of their respective criterion sports than the broad-based athletic index.

Broad-based intelligence test scores (e.g., WJTCA-R Broad Cognitive Ability; Wechsler Full Scale) are analogous to the single broad athletic ability index. The differential aptitude tests (i.e., WJTCA-R differential aptitude clusters) are analogous to the specialized tennis and offensive lineman aptitude tests. Although the notion of specialized aptitude tests makes intuitive sense and is consistent with clinical experience, it has been infrequently used in the development of psychoeducational assessment instruments. However, this approach to prediction has been common in other psychological applications such as in industrial and military selection. For example, the same combinations of predictors are not used to select trainees for pilot or electronic technician training programs. The concept of differential prediction has been successfully implemented outside of psychoeducational settings.

The preference for using broad-based intelligence scores to predict achievement across such different areas as reading and mathematics is related to the historical precedent set by educators' use of early intelligence tests (i.e., Stanford-Binet and Wechslers) and the failure to find empirical support for the differential prediction of school success (Carroll, 1978; McNemar, 1964; Pellegrino & Varnhagan, 1985). Therefore, why should one use the WJTCA-R differential aptitude clusters rather than the Broad Cognitive Ability clusters when making aptitude-achievement comparisons? The answer is simple. The WJTCA-R differential aptitude clusters demonstrate adequate differential validity to support their use.

Differential Prediction Research
If the WJTCA-R differential aptitude clusters are to be used as specialized predictors of achievement in different curriculum areas, they need to demonstrate differential prediction of school achievement. With the exception of Written Language Aptitude, reviews of the original WJTCA research found support for their differential prediction of school achievement (McGrew, 1986). Using the WJTCA-R norm data, McGrew and Murphy (1993) presented information on the differential predictive validity of the four WJTCA-R Scholastic Aptitude clusters across 17 norm subsamples from age 6 to age 70.

McGrew and Murphy (1993) presented the results of research that investigated the relationship between the WJTCA-R Scholastic Aptitude clusters and achievement. The correlations between each of the four Scholastic Aptitude clusters and the WJ-R tests of reading, mathematics, and written language achievement at each of the seventeen age groups were plotted.

Smoothed curves were fit to the correlations to provide the best estimate of the population correlations. An example of this approach can be found by reviewing Figure 4-1 and the related text in Chapter 4. The results of the McGrew and Murphy (1993) study are presented in Figures 7-1 to 7-3.

Figure 7-1 demonstrates that the Math Aptitude cluster (MAPT) is a stronger predictor of mathematics achievement (WJ-R Broad Mathematics cluster) than the Reading (RAPT), Written Language (WAPT), and Knowledge (KAPT) Aptitude clusters. The superior prediction of mathematics achievement for the Mathematics Aptitude cluster is consistent across all ages.

The differential prediction of reading achievement (WJ-R Broad Reading cluster) is presented in Figure 7-2. Although not as dramatic as found in the prediction of mathematics (Figure 7-1), the smoothed correlation curve for the Reading Aptitude cluster is the highest of the four, particularly before approximately age 45. The Reading Aptitude cluster is consistently a stronger predictor of reading achievement than the Mathematics and Knowledge Aptitude clusters across all ages. In contrast, the differences between Reading and Written Language are not as great, particularly during adulthood. As noted earlier in this chapter, this finding is most likely due to the high degree of shared content between these two differential aptitude clusters (i.e., three of their four respective tests are identical). This may be due to the reading and written language criteria sharing a common underlying language use factor.

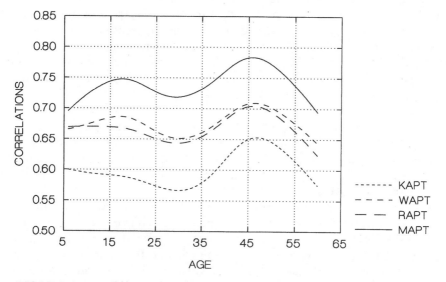

FIGURE 7-1 Differential Prediction of Math

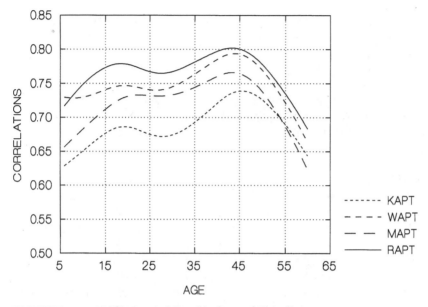

FIGURE 7-2 Differential Prediction of Reading

Similar to the findings with the original WJTCA, the results presented in Figure 7-3 are not as consistently supportive of the superior prediction of written language achievement by the Written Language Aptitude cluster. The Written Language Aptitude cluster predicts written language achievement better than the Mathematics and Knowledge Aptitude clusters. The smoothed correlation curves for Written Language and Reading Aptitude are very close across all ages, although, on the average, the Written Language Aptitude cluster correlations are higher. However, the differences are not great and may not be significant. The relatively close levels of prediction of written language achievement by the Reading and Written Language Aptitude clusters are most likely due to their high degree of test overlap and a possible common underlying language dimension in the achievement criteria.

Differential versus Broad Cognitive Ability Prediction Research

McGrew and Murphy (1993) also presented comparisons between the relative predictive validity of each Scholastic Aptitude cluster and two of the Broad Cognitive Ability clusters (Standard and Extended). These results are presented in Figures 7-4 to 7-6.

A review of Figure 7-4 indicates that the Mathematics Aptitude cluster is consistently a superior predictor of mathematics achievement when compared to the Broad Cognitive Ability Standard (BCASTD) and Extended (BCAEXT) scales. Since WJ-R aptitude-achievement discrepancy norms are only available for the Scholastic Aptitude clusters and the Broad Cognitive Ability Standard cluster, the comparison of the smoothed correlations for

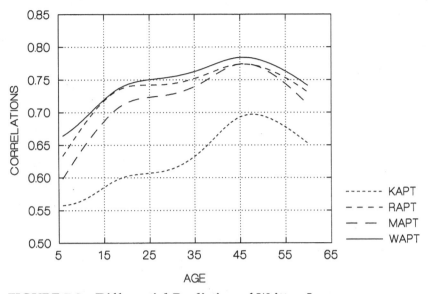

FIGURE 7-3   Differential Prediction of Written Language

these two clusters is most important. A clear and consistent difference between these two clusters is apparent in Figure 7-4. Although discrepancy norms are not provided for the Broad Cognitive Ability Extended scale, the information presented in Figure 7-4 suggests that this 14-test broad cluster is a better predictor of mathematics achievement than the seven test Broad Cognitive Ability Standard scale.

A review of Figure 7-5 indicates that the Reading Aptitude cluster is consistently a better predictor of reading achievement when compared to the Broad Cognitive Ability Standard cluster, except after approximately age 55. Although discrepancy norms are not available for the Broad Cognitive Ability Extended cluster, this cluster appears very similar in predictive power to that demonstrated by Reading Aptitude. The Reading Aptitude cluster may be a slightly stronger predictor when compared to the Broad Cognitive Ability Extended scale during the school years, after which the Broad Cognitive Ability Extended cluster is slightly stronger up until approximately age 55.

A review of Figure 7-6 finds the Written Language Aptitude cluster to be a consistently stronger predictor of written language achievement than the Broad Cognitive Ability Standard cluster. Although the differences are slight and may not be practically significant, the Written Language Aptitude cluster is a slightly better predictor of written language achievement than the Broad Cognitive Ability Extended cluster, particularly during the school years.

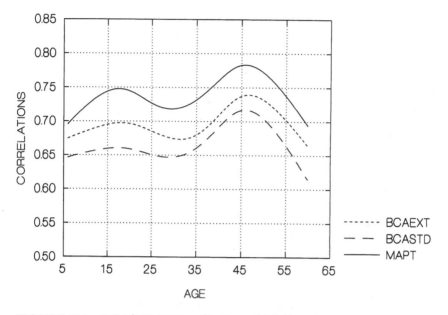

FIGURE 7-4   BCA/MAPT Prediction of Math

Summary Comments

The WJTCA-R differential aptitude clusters are designed to provide differential estimates of predicted school achievement to be used in the calculation of aptitude-achievement discrepancies. In general, a review of the available research supports the differential predictive validity of the Scholastic Aptitude clusters. The Scholastic Aptitude clusters clearly demonstrate differential prediction of reading and mathematics achievement. Similar to the original WJTCA, evidence for differential prediction of written language is not as convincing. The Written Language and Reading Aptitude clusters appear to be equally strong predictors of written language achievement. The significant test overlap between these two clusters most likely accounts for this finding, which together with their similar success in predicting reading and written language achievement due to possible criterion overlap, suggests that a single "language arts" or "reading/written language" aptitude cluster would be a good idea.

The research reviewed supports the superior prediction of achievement by the Scholastic Aptitude clusters when compared to the Broad Cognitive Ability Standard cluster, the only other option within the WJ-R battery for calculating aptitude-achievement discrepancies. The Broad Cognitive Ability Extended cluster is a stronger predictor of achievement than the Broad Cognitive Ability Standard scale, although no aptitude discrepancy norms are provided for this broad cluster. However, even this 14-test broad cluster could not predict mathematics achievement better than the four-test

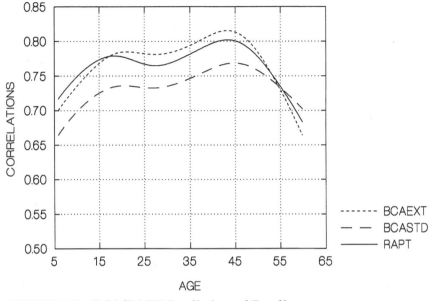

FIGURE 7-5 BCA/RAPT Prediction of Reading

Mathematics Aptitude cluster, and it was generally no better in the prediction of reading and written language than the 4-test Reading and Written Language Aptitude clusters. The differential predictive validity evidence, when combined with the superior prediction of achievement when compared to other intelligence batteries (i.e., Wechslers, K-ABC, SB-IV) (McGrew et al., 1991), indicates that the WJTCA-R Scholastic Aptitude clusters are the best available measures to use when calculating aptitude/achievement discrepancies.

Conormed Aptitude and Achievement Tests

The original WJ was the first major psychoeducational assessment battery to address the now widely accepted recommendation that aptitude-achievement discrepancy scores be calculated from measures normed on the same sample (Cone & Wilson, 1981; Reynolds, 1985; Reynolds et al., 1984–1985; Salvia & Ysseldyke, 1981; Wilson & Cone, 1984). The use of conormed tests removes the possibility that aptitude and achievement discrepancy scores may contain error due to differences in the test norming samples.

The norm samples of tests may differ in a number of ways that may introduce error into the calculation of aptitude-achievement discrepancy scores. For example, if an intelligence test is standardized on a sample that overrepresents individuals in the lower end of the socioeconomic status (SES) distribution, the known relationship between SES and intelligence would

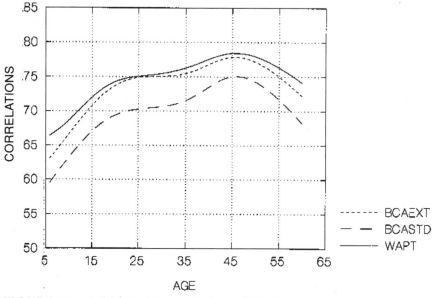

FIGURE 7-6   BCA/WAPT Prediction of Written Language

predict that the test norms may be too "easy" when applied to the general population. An individual with a true intelligence test standard score of 100 (if it was possible to determine the person's true score), when assessed with this poorly normed intelligence test, may receive a score of 105. This test overestimates the person's true ability by 5 standard score points.

Assume the same person is administered an achievement test that was normed on a sample biased in the direction of individuals from high SES communities. Assuming that the person's true achievement standard score is also 100, the use of this achievement test with its "hard" norms would most likely result in an underestimate of the person's achievement. Let's assume the person's resulting achievement score was 95, or 5 points lower than the person's true ability. By using intelligence and achievement tests with different norms that are both biased in different directions, this person demonstrates (before correcting for regression effects) a 10-point (105 − 95 = 10) standard score difference, when in actuality their true difference is zero.

A similar problem occurs when scores are compared from intelligence and achievement tests that were standardized at markedly different times. It has been estimated that norms on intelligence tests become "softer" by approximately 1/3 of a standard score point each year (Flynn, 1984; Kamphaus, 1993). Aptitude-achievement discrepancy scores based on tests that differ by 10 years may be inaccurate by approximately 3 points. This phenomenon is the primary reason that standardized intelligence and achievement tests are recommended to be renormed after approximately ten years (Kamphaus, 1993).

When the aptitude and achievement test scores that are compared are derived from tests that are normed on the same sample of individuals, no significant norming differences can influence the discrepancy score. In the absence of conormed tests, clinicians need to carefully compare the standardization samples of tests and determine if the samples are generally similar. This is largely a judgment call that requires clinicians to devote significant time to studying the norming procedures used for each test. The most efficient and optimal solution is to use aptitude and achievement tests from within the same conormed battery. Aptitude-achievement discrepancy scores derived by using the WJTCA-R Scholastic Aptitude clusters (or the Broad Cognitive Ability Standard cluster) together with the WJ-R achievement tests exemplify this optimal solution.

Regression to the Mean

"Mother nature abhors extremes." This statement provides an intuitive understanding of the phenomenon of regression to the mean, a confounding influence present when comparisons are made between two imperfectly correlated test scores (Kamphaus, 1993; Reynolds, 1990). Regression to the mean is the tendency of extreme scores on one test to be less extreme on a second related test. If a person is administered two tests that are related but not perfectly correlated (e.g., intelligence and achievement tests), and the person scores above or below the average score on one test (e.g., intelligence test), on the average the person will most likely score above or below the average on the second test, *but not as far above or below as on the first test.* The second score "moves" or "regresses" to the mean or average score. The amount of regression is dependent on the degree of correlation between the two tests. The greatest regression effect occurs if two tests have a zero correlation. The regression to the mean phenomenon has been understood for many years (Horn, 1941; Garrett and Woodworth, 1958), but only recently has been applied to psychoeducational assessment practices.

Since intelligence and achievement tests are imperfectly correlated, the regression to the mean phenomenon occurs. The practical implication is that clinicians cannot assume a one-to-one correspondence between a person's measured intelligence and achievement, particularly as a person's abilities diverge from the average. A person found to score well above average on an intelligence test (e.g., standard score of 130) should not be predicted to demonstrate achievement on a correlated achievement test at the same level of 130. The person's predicted achievement score would most likely be lower than 130, with the degree of regression away from 130 and toward the mean being a function of the strength of the correlation between the intelligence and achievement tests. The movement or regression of scores below the average occurs in the opposite direction, with regression bringing the scores back to a higher level closer to the mean.

Recognition of the regression to the mean phenomenon dictates that procedures be used to account for its influence on aptitude-achievement discrepancy scores (Cone & Wilson, 1981; McLeod, 1979; Reynolds, 1985; Reynolds et al., 1984-1985; Salvia & Ysseldyke, 1981; Wilson & Cone, 1984). In order to account for regression effects in aptitude/achievement comparisons, one needs knowledge of the correlation between the intelligence and achievement tests used. The correlation can be used in a regression formula to estimate the persons's predicted (often called expected) achievement score that includes the effect of regression.

The problem in accurately calculating regression-based predicted achievement scores is that intelligence and achievement correlations often vary as a function of the selected sample, age, and area of achievement. This poses significant problems when practitioners want to make aptitude-achievement comparisons with intelligence and achievement tests for which little correlational information is available. For example, since the Wechsler intelligence scales are not conormed with the WJ-R achievement tests, an estimate of the correlation between the Wechslers and the various WJ-R achievement clusters must be abstracted from available research reports. For this example, practitioners can turn to the respective Wechsler intelligence test manuals, the WJ-R technical manual, and available journal articles to locate as many correlations as possible. A problem immediately arises since correlations are typically only reported for a handful of special validity studies at select age or grade levels. Correlational information is often missing for many age or grade levels.

Practitioners or others charged with developing special tables or software used to estimate the effect of regression typically must make a significant leap of faith and assume that the available, yet often limited number of correlations are similar for other ages or grades. An approach for estimating correlations in the absence of real data has been presented, although the accuracy of the proposed equation "is far from the degree desired" (Reynolds, 1990, p. 581).

The optimal solution can be found when intelligence and achievement tests are conormed. In this situation it is possible to calculate correlations between the intelligence and respective conormed achievement tests at most age or grade levels for which norm data are available. Since these correlations include sampling error and often change as a function of age, an even more optimal estimate of the intelligence and achievement test correlations can be obtained by using curve fitting procedures that produce a smoothed estimate of all correlations as a function of age or grade. The smoothed curves presented in Figures 7-2 to 7-6 are examples of this approach. The smoothed correlations can then be used in the development of special tables, equations, or software to provide a regression-adjusted estimate of a person's predicted achievement level.

This latter approach was used in the development of the WJ-R aptitude-achievement discrepancy norms (McGrew et al., 1991). Practitioners who use the discrepancy scores obtained from administering the WJ-R differential aptitude clusters (or Broad Cognitive Ability Standard cluster) together with the WJ-R achievement clusters are using the most accurate and sophisticated procedures for adjusting for regression to the mean. The resulting predicted achievement scores are calculated with the aid of correlational information at each age or grade level that is based on actual norm data. The predicted achievement test scores take into account differences in the aptitude and achievement correlations that vary by achievement area and by age or grade. As evidenced by the changing nature of the smoothed correlation curves displayed in Figures 7-2 to 7-6, other procedures that require the estimating of correlations from limited data, or the assumption that the limited correlations available are similar across ages or grades, are bound to contain more error.

Actual versus Pseudo Discrepancy Norms

There is one final advantage in using the WJTCA-R Scholastic Aptitude clusters (or the Broad Cognitive Ability Standard cluster) together with the WJ-R achievement clusters in the calculation of aptitude/achievement discrepancies. This advantage is that a person's WJ-R based aptitude-achievement discrepancy score can be compared against *actual or real discrepancy norms* (McGrew et al., 1991).

With knowledge of the correlations between the respective WJ-R aptitude and achievement clusters across all ages or grades (described in prior section), and with knowledge of all norming subjects' respective aptitude cluster scores, McGrew et al. (1991) calculated a predicted or expected achievement score for subjects in the WJ-R norming sample. This predicted score was based on the correlations between the respective aptitude and achievement clusters in the WJ-R norm data and thus, reflected the regression to the mean phenomenon. These predicted scores represent the average achievement score observed for all persons of the same age (or grade if grade norms are used) with the same level of aptitude in the WJ-R norm sample.

For each norming subject, the person's actual achievement was then subtracted from the regression-based predicted achievement score, producing the person's regression-adjusted aptitude-achievement discrepancy score. With norming subjects having actual aptitude/achievement discrepancy scores available for analysis, it was then possible to subject these scores to the same norm-generation procedures used to develop norms for the other WJ-R scores (McGrew et al., 1991). The final results are tables of actual discrepancy norms that allow practitioners to compare a person's aptitude-achievement discrepancy against *actual distributions of discrepancy scores based on real data*. These norms provide the ability to describe a person's aptitude-achievement discrepancies in terms of percentile ranks and standard error of estimate units (i.e., the WJ-R Standard Deviation Difference score) derived from actual data.

The alternative to actual discrepancy norms is to use "pseudo discrepancy norms." The development of pseudo discrepancy norms involves estimating a person's predicted or expected achievement based on the estimated correlation between an intelligence and achievement test, subtracting the person's actual achievement, and then evaluating the frequency of occurrence of the discrepancy as determined by using a statistical formula and knowledge about the theoretical characteristics of the normal curve. Although this approach is required in situations when intelligence and achievement tests are not conormed, it is not the same as using actual discrepancy norms. In this approach no actual discrepancy scores are available in a representative sampling of individuals that allows for the precise calculation of actual discrepancy norms that will vary as a function of age or grade and curriculum area. Regression-adjusted pseudo discrepancy norms must be used when intelligence and achievement tests are not conormed, or when such tests are conormed and actual discrepancy norms are not provided. A more accurate and technically superior approach is to develop and use actual discrepancy norms. The WJ-R aptitude-achievement discrepancy scores use this technically superior approach.

A Hierarchy of Discrepancy Procedures

A variety of approaches are used in practice to calculate and evaluate aptitude-achievement discrepancies. The approaches differ in how they address the issues of using differential versus broad-based predictor measures, conorming of aptitude and achievement tests, regression to the mean, and actual versus pseudo discrepancy norms. Two of these issues (viz., conorming and regression to the mean) have been recognized and mentioned frequently in the aptitude/achievement discrepancy literature. The technical issues involved in differential versus broad-based aptitude predictors and actual versus pseudo-discrepancy norms have received little attention in the literature, largely because most intelligence tests do not provide a differential aptitude predictor option and have not developed actual discrepancy norms. The lack of attention to these latter two issues does not negate their importance in aptitude-achievement discrepancy procedures. Rather, it reflects the lack of attention to these important issues in the development of most intelligence tests and psychoeducational batteries.

A hierarchy of discrepancy procedures for evaluating the technical validity of the aptitude-achievement discrepancy score options is presented in Table 7-7. This table presents the 10 levels of technical validity that are possible when using different procedures to calculate and evaluate aptitude-achievement discrepancies. The different levels of technical adequacy reflect the possible levels of sophistication based on the different approaches to the issues of differential versus broad-based predictors, conorming of aptitude and achievement tests, regression to the mean, and actual versus pseudo discrepancy norms. The information presented in Table 7-7 can be used to evaluate any aptitude-achievement discrepancy procedure according to levels of technical validity.

The discrepancy procedure options available in the Absolute Score Difference section of Table 7-7 should not be used, as they are all technically invalid. Although the Level 7 to Level 10 procedures vary as a function of whether they use differential (Level 7 and Level 9) versus broad aptitude (Level 8 and Level 10) predictors, and whether conormed (Level 7 and Level 8) versus separately normed (Level 9 and Level 10) tests are used, none addresses regression to the mean.

An example of Level 10 would be the simple subtraction of a person's Wide Range Achievement Test—Revised (WRAT-R) reading test standard score from the person's Wechsler Full Scale or WJTCA-R Broad Cognitive Ability cluster standard score. Such a procedure does not take advantage of differential aptitude predictors and uses aptitude and achievement tests that are not conormed. In addition, the simple subtraction of aptitude and achievement scores fails to adjust for regression to the mean. Although the substitution of the WJTCA-R Reading Aptitude cluster for the broad-based aptitude scores would improve the procedure to Level 7, this alternative

TABLE 7-7 Hierarchy of Discrepancy Procedures by Technical Validity

---

Discrepancy Norms (all measures must be co-normed)

Level 1—a differentiated scholastic aptitude measure and a measure of achievement

Level 2—a broad (general) ability measure and a measure of achievement

Pseudo Discrepancy Norms (based on a correction for regression)

Level 3—a differentiated scholastic aptitude measure and a measure of achievement that are conormed

Level 4—a broad (general) ability measure and a measure of achievement that are conormed

Level 5—a differentiated scholastic aptitude measure and a measure of achievement that are *not* conormed

Level 6—a broad (general) ability measure and a measure of achievement that are *not* conormed

Absolute Score Difference (technically invalid)

Level 7—an absolute score difference between a differentiated scholastic aptitude measure and a measure of achievement that are conormed

Level 8—an absolute score difference between a broad (general) ability measure and a measure of achievement that are conormed

Level 9—an absolute score difference between a differentiated scholastic aptitude measure and a measure of achievement that are *not* conormed

Level 10—an absolute score difference between a broad (general) ability measure and a measure of achievement that are *not* conormed

---

does not address the important issues of conormed tests, regression to the mean, and using actual discrepancy norms. *Under no circumstances should any aptitude discrepancy procedure be used that is at Level 7 or lower.*

The four levels of procedures listed in the Pseudo Discrepancy Norms section of Table 7-7 (Level 3 to Level 6) include those most commonly used in the field of psychoeducational assessment. All of the procedures in Level 3 to Level 6 address the regression to the mean phenomenon by using a formula to correct for regression. Levels 3 and 4 differ from Levels 5 and 6 by the use of conormed aptitude and achievement tests in the former. The four levels also differ by whether they use differential (Level 3 and Level 5) or broad-based (Level 4 and 6) aptitude predictors.

Within the four levels of Pseudo Discrepancy Norms procedures, the lowest level (i.e., Level 6) is probably the most frequent type of discrepancy procedure used in psychoeducational assessment practice. An example would be taking a person's broad aptitude score (e.g., Wechsler Full Scale, SB-IV Composite) and using a correction-for-regression procedure to obtain an estimate of predicted achievement. The person is also administered an achievement test that is not conormed with the intelligence test (e.g., WJ-R achievement; WRAT-R), and the resulting achievement standard scores are subtracted from the regression-adjusted predicted achievement score. Since the intelligence and achievement tests are not conormed, the person's discrepancy cannot be compared against actual discrepancy norms, but must be evaluated against pseudo discrepancy norms.

A review of Table 7-7 indicates that the commonly used Level 6 practice is far from being the best approach in terms of technical validity. Level 6 procedures can be improved on by using conormed aptitude and achievement tests (i.e., Levels 1–4). A significant and important improvement in technical validity can also be achieved by using procedures that provide actual and not pseudo discrepancy norms (Levels 1-2).

The top two levels in the Discrepancy Norms category reflect aptitude-achievement discrepancy procedures that use the most technically sound approaches for addressing the issues of test norming differences (i.e., tests are conormed), regression to the mean (i.e., correlation-based regression adjustments are used that accurately reflect the changing relationship between aptitude and achievement as a function of achievement area and age or grade), and evaluating the significance of the discrepancy (i.e., actual discrepancy norms).

The WJ-R battery is the only psychoeducational assessment battery that provides aptitude-achievement discrepancy procedures at Levels 1 and 2. Within the WJTCA-R, the highest level of technical validity (Level 1) is achieved by using the differential aptitude clusters instead of the Broad Cognitive Ability cluster (Level 2). The aptitude-achievement discrepancy options provided by the WJTCA-R (together with the WJ-R achievement tests) are the most technically valid procedures available in the field of psychoeducational assessment.

THE CLINICAL UTILITY OF THE
DIFFERENTIAL APTITUDE CLUSTERS

The information presented to this point regarding the WJTCA-R differential aptitude clusters has focused on technical considerations. This information finds the WJTCA-R differential aptitude clusters to be reliable and valid measures for calculating and evaluating aptitude-achievement comparisons. In addition, research supports using the Scholastic Aptitude clusters instead of broad-based aptitude scores (e.g., WJTCA-R Broad Cognitive Ability cluster; Wechsler Full Scale).

Additional support for using the Scholastic Aptitude clusters over the broad-based aptitude clusters comes in the form of "clinical utility" (Woodcock, 1984a). *Clinical utility* refers to the observation that the WJTCA-R Scholastic Aptitude clusters more accurately distinguish between Type I (i.e., aptitude-achievement) and Type II (i.e., intra-cognitive) discrepancies than do broad-based aptitude scores. Broad-based aptitude measures often confound these types of discrepancies, a situation that can result in inappropriate diagnostic conclusions and interventions. The clouding of Type I and II discrepancies is the result of broad-based ability measures including tests that have little actual relationship to the area of concern. This point is best demonstrated by an example.

Clinical Validity Example
The information presented in Table 7-8 demonstrates the impact of a specific cognitive weakness in comprehension-knowledge *(Gc)* abilities on differential (i.e., WJTCA-R Reading and Mathematics Aptitude) and broad-based (i.e., WJTCA-R Broad Cognitive Ability cluster) aptitude measures.

In this example it is assumed that a subject was referred for problems in reading. Those WJTCA-R tests that may be impacted the most by a cognitive deficit in comprehension-knowledge abilities are indicated by minus signs in Table 7-8. According to the Expanded Comprehension-Knowledge grouping presented in Chapter 5, this cognitive weakness may impact performance on the WJTCA-R Memory for Sentences, Picture Vocabulary, and Oral Vocabulary tests, and possibly the Incomplete Words and Visual Closure tests.

A review of the Percent of Tests Affected by Weakness section of Table 7-8 reveals that the impact of a weak performance on the comprehension-knowledge tests is greatest for the WJTCA-R Reading Aptitude cluster. Fifty percent of the Reading Aptitude clusters' tests are impacted. In contrast, only 25% of the tests in the Mathematics Aptitude cluster are affected by this specific cognitive weakness. This person's Reading Aptitude cluster score will most likely be significantly lower than the Mathematics Aptitude cluster score.

TABLE 7-8   Relative Effect of Broad Comprehension-Knowledge *(Gc)* Weakness on Broad-based and Specific Aptitude Measures

WJTCA-R Tests	Broad Cognitive Ability (Extended)	Reading Aptitude	Mathematics Aptitude
Memory for Names	0		
Memory for Sentences	−	−	
Visual Matching	0	0	0
Incomplete Words	−		
Visual Closure	−		
Picture Vocabulary	−		
Analysis-Synthesis	0		0
Visual-Auditory Learning	0		
Memory for Words	0		
Cross Out	0		
Sound Blending	0	0	
Picture Recognition	0		
Oral Vocabulary	−	−	−
Concept Formation	0		0
Percent of tests affected by weakness	35.7	50.0	25.0

Minus sign indicates tests within each aptitude measure affected by specific cognitive weakness.

Is this differential impact appropriate? Yes. The research summarized in Chapter 4 indicates that although comprehension-knowledge *(Gc)* abilities are strongly related to both reading and mathematics achievement, other abilities are more important in each respective area. In the case of Mathematics, fluid reasoning abilities *(Gf)* were found to be highly related to mathematics achievement and relatively less related to reading. In contrast, auditory processing *(Ga)* abilities were related to certain aspects of reading, but not mathematics.

The Reading and Mathematics Aptitude clusters are composed of those tests most strongly related to their respective achievement domains. Comprehension-knowledge abilities are proportionally more important in reading, and thus a weakness in this area has a greater impact on the Reading Aptitude cluster. Assuming that this person's other cognitive abilities are not widely different, this person would display a profile suggestive of higher Mathematics than Reading Aptitude. Such an observed difference would accurately reflect real differences in this person's ability to achieve in these two different achievement areas due to a comprehension-knowledge weakness.

The sensitivity of the WJTCA-R Scholastic Aptitude clusters to different patterns of cognitive abilities that demonstrate differential achievement relationships highlights the clinical utility of these clusters. Simply put, the WJTCA-R differential aptitude clusters are sensitive to, and thus more accurately reflect, the real world phenomena of intra-individual or within-person differences in abilities.

As presented in Table 7-8, approximately 36% of the tests included in the Broad Cognitive Ability cluster would be impacted by this person's comprehension-knowledge weakness. When compared to the Reading Aptitude cluster, the Broad Cognitive Ability cluster would be less impacted by this person's specific cognitive weakness (i.e., 36% versus 50% of the tests impacted). As a result, the Reading Aptitude cluster would most likely be the lower aptitude estimate. This would result in this person's aptitude-achievement discrepancy being smaller when calculated with the Reading Aptitude and not the Broad Cognitive Ability cluster score. When operating under an aptitude-achievement learning disability criterion, this person would stand a lessor chance of being identified as needing special education services when using the relatively lower WJTCA-R Reading Aptitude cluster score.

This example highlights a common complaint and misunderstanding regarding the WJTCA-R Scholastic Aptitude clusters. Clinicians are often concerned that a person with a specific cognitive disability (e.g., comprehension-knowledge deficit) will obtain a lower score on certain Scholastic Aptitude clusters that contain many of the tests related to the person's disability. This translates into the person not qualifying for specific services that require evidence of a large aptitude/achievement discrepancy (e.g., learning disability services). Clinicians often complain that a person's specific cognitive disability is unduly impacting his or her aptitude-achievement discrepancy score. Although reflecting real concerns based on the reality of many existing practices, the focus of this concern is typically misdirected.

These concerns arise because specific program eligibility procedures have been developed as a result of administrative regulations and guidelines that are often incongruous with sound psychological practice. Most practitioners would agree that a main purpose of any aptitude measure, whether it be a WJTCA-R Scholastic Aptitude cluster or another ability test, is to provide the best predictor of a person's *current* achievement. If the person does have a specific cognitive weakness in comprehension-knowledge abilities, because of the importance of these abilities to reading achievement (see Chapter 4), this person's current reading expectancy should also be low. The relatively lower Reading Aptitude cluster, which is due to half of the cluster's content being based on comprehension-knowledge tests, provides clinicians with precisely what they need to know—this person's reading expectancy is lower due to a specific comprehension-knowledge weakness.

As a result, this individual may not demonstrate a large enough reading aptitude-achievement discrepancy to qualify for learning disability services under many existing criteria. Although this person does demonstrate unique learning problems that may dictate the need for intervention, decisions in the field of special education are frequently dictated by strict aptitude-achievement discrepancy criteria. If this person is indeed learning-disabled, in systems that rely only on an aptitude-achievement criterion the individual may not be eligible for service. This scenario demonstrates the problem with decision making that only acknowledges Type I and not Type II discrepancies.

The individual in this example has an intra-cognitive or Type II discrepancy in comprehension-knowledge abilities. Because of the nature of this intra-cognitive deficit and its relationship to reading achievement, this individual should have a lower reading expectancy. Such lowered expectancies would be accurately communicated by the Reading Aptitude cluster but would not be accurately reflected by the Broad Cognitive Ability cluster, which is less influenced by the weakness. The Broad Cognitive Ability cluster would not be as accurate in conveying current reading expectancies since it includes tests of additional abilities that have little relationship to reading achievement.

By using the lower Reading Aptitude score, a clinician would conclude that this person's problem is not of the aptitude-achievement discrepancy variety warranting remedial academic services, but an intra-cognitive discrepancy possibly warranting language training. The problem this may create for some practitioners is that Type II discrepancies are not often recognized as a legitimate basis for recommending special services.

Frequently, eligibility for services is dictated solely by Type I or aptitude-achievement discrepancy procedures (Mather, 1993). In such rigid systems the person in this example would probably not receive any services due to the lack of an aptitude-achievement discrepancy. This point can be a major concern to practitioners, who may confuse the problem of inflexible and rigid criteria with a problem with the WJTCA-R Scholastic Aptitude clusters. The problem in this example is not the WJTCA-R Reading Aptitude cluster because it produces a lower score, but with administrative or legal systems that force all decisions into a Type I or aptitude-achievement discrepancy model. *The problem is not with the instrument* (which is based on sound psychological principles and research) *but with how practitioners are forced to use an instrument.* This point is similar to Kamphaus' (1993) discussion of how composite full scale intelligence test scores often cloud accurate diagnosis when practitioners are forced to use them within inflexible regulatory frameworks that do not allow the use of well-grounded professional judgment.

The pressures surrounding regulation-driven professional practice can result in practitioners preferring broad-based aptitude measures that provide higher aptitude results (since they contain abilities unrelated to the area of concern) in order to "get the kid qualified." Although the motives may be admirable, even this process can do more harm than good. In the example, using the broad-based scores as the aptitude estimate, or, even more inappropriately, using only the WISC-III Performance Scale under the rationalization that it is not affected by the individual's comprehension-knowledge problem may result in a large enough Type I discrepancy that qualifies the person for services. However, these broad-based aptitude estimates suggest a "gap" between ability and achievement that warrants remedial services. In reality this person may be doing the best he or she currently can based on those abilities most directly related to reading. Remedial reading services may be vended, while in reality this individual needs more help in the development of basic comprehension-knowledge abilities. Thus, programming efforts may be misdirected and inappropriately high expectations formed.

Summary Comments

The purpose of the WJTCA-R differential aptitude clusters is to provide predictions of *current* levels of achievement. If a person obtains low scores on individual tests that measure cognitive abilities related to a specific achievement area and these tests are included in the aptitude cluster, then the person's current achievement expectancies should also be lowered. This expectancy information will be more accurately communicated by the narrower WJTCA-R differential aptitude clusters than by any broad-based scores from the WJTCA-R or other tests. The inability to provide the most appropriate services for an individual because of systems that only acknowledge Type I discrepancies reflects a problem with the systems and not the measurement instrument. After all, if you give a monkey a Stradivarius violin and you get bad music, you don't blame the violin.

The clinical utility example demonstrates the advantage of using aptitude measures comprising tests most directly related to the curriculum area of concern. It is because of their differential content that the WJTCA-R differential aptitude clusters provide the best curriculum-specific expectancy information available in the field of psychoeducational assessment. In contrast, broad-based measures contain tests that introduce extraneous "noise" into expectancy formulation (i.e., some of the abilities measured by certain tests demonstrate little relationship to the academic area of concern). The use of broad-based measures can result in the masking of Type I discrepancies or may suggest Type I discrepancies where none really exist. Broad-based aptitude measures may frequently confound Type I and Type II discrepancies.

CAVEATS REGARDING THE INTERPRETATION OF APTITUDE-ACHIEVEMENT DISCREPANCY SCORES

The WJTCA-R differential aptitude clusters, when combined with the WJ-R achievement tests, provide clinicians with the most psychometrically sound aptitude-achievement discrepancy scores available in the field of psycho-educational assessment. However, aptitude-achievement scores, no matter how technically sound, are frequently misused, misunderstood, and misinterpreted.

Technically sound aptitude-achievement discrepancy scores are not inherently "bad." There is a large body of psychoeducational and special education literature that criticizes the *use* of aptitude-achievement discrepancy scores in the identification of individuals with learning disabilities. These criticisms focus on such issues as the reliability of discrepancy scores, reliance on aptitude-achievement discrepancy scores to identify individuals as having a learning disability, and the use of technically unsound aptitude-achievement discrepancy procedures (Reynolds, 1990; Telzrow, 1990). Most of these criticisms are well founded. However, most are directed at the *improper* use and interpretation of aptitude-achievement discrepancy scores.

Negative aptitude-achievement discrepancies only identify a pool of individuals who are not achieving at predicted achievement levels due to a myriad of reasons (Reynolds, 1990; Telzrow, 1990). Some individuals may not be achieving at predicted levels due to environmental factors (e.g., poor or inconsistent instruction, history of poor school attendence). For others, a negative aptitude-achievement discrepancy may be due to factors inherent in the individual (e.g., attentional deficit disorder, emotional problems, a specific intra-cognitive deficit). It is incorrect to assume that all significant negative aptitude-achievement discrepancies are indicators of a deficit or learning disability within the inidividual. The clinicial interpretation process presented in Chapter 6 should be used to help determine whether a negative aptitude-achievement discrepancy is the outcome of a specific intra-cognitive deficit within the individual.

The finding of positive aptitude-achievement discrepancies is often misunderstood by practitioners. After all, "how can a person be achieving above their aptitude?" The answer is simple when one examines the correlations between most aptitude and achievement tests. The typical correlations between frequently used aptitude and achievement measures range from .60 to .70. Correlations of this magnitude indicate that the aptitude measures account for approximately 40% to 50% of the achievement test variance (estimate based on the squared validity correlations). This means that 50% to 60% of the achievement variance is accounted for by other variables (e.g., measurement error, quality of instruction, motivation, task persistence).

Aptitude, as measured by the WJTCA-R and other intelligence batteries, is only part of the achievement equation. Whether interpreting significant positive or negative aptitude-achievement discrepancies, clinicians need to recognize that at least half of the equation in predicting achievement is accounted for by variables not included in the calculation of aptitude-achievement discrepancy scores. The complexity of human behavior cannot be captured by any single number.

CONCLUDING COMMENTS

The WJTCA-R provides five differential aptitude clusters for predicting estimated achievement levels in the areas of reading, mathematics, written language, knowledge, and oral language. Research indicates that the differential aptitude clusters possess adequate reliability and validity characteristics for making important decisions about individuals. These five aptitude clusters, and the four Scholastic Aptitude clusters in particular, are the primary WJTCA-R scores that should be used for calculating and evaluating Type I or aptitude-achievement discrepancies.

The procedures used to develop the WJTCA-R differential aptitude clusters are similar to those used in the development of the original WJTCA Scholastic Aptitude clusters. However, a number of changes have eliminated prior concerns about unequal test weighting and achievement-like content. Due to the use of stepwise multiple regression procedures and tests that measure seven *Gf-Gc* abilities, the resulting Scholastic Aptitude clusters are found to be superior predictors of achievement when compared to the other intelligence batteries (i.e., Wechslers, SB-IV, K-ABC). The superior predictive validity of the WJTCA-R Scholastic Aptitude clusters is not due to the clusters being excessively contaminated with achievement-like content. Rather, the Scholastic Aptitude clusters are superior predictors of achievement because they contain tests of important school-related abilities that are missing from other intelligence batteries.

The WJTCA-R Scholastic Aptitude clusters demonstrate adequate differential predictive validity and are superior predictors of achievement when compared to the WJTCA-R Broad Cognitive Ability Standard scale. Although the Broad Cognitive Ability Extended scale may predict achievement as well as the four Scholastic Aptitude clusters, aptitude-achievement discrepancy norms are not provided for this cluster. In addition, the Scholastic Aptitude clusters provide the benefits of economy of testing time and clinical utility. Current research suggests that the WJTCA-R Scholastic Aptitude clusters are the best available measures within the field of psychoeducational assessment, as well as within the WJTCA-R, to be used for making aptitude-achievement comparisons.

When the WJTCA-R Scholastic Aptitude clusters are used in combination with the WJ-R achievement tests, the resulting aptitude-achievement comparisons are based on the best available procedures in the field of psychoeducational assessment. These aptitude-achievement procedures are at the highest levels of technical validity in terms of addressing the issues of regression to the mean, conorming of tests, actual versus pseudo discrepancy norms, and differential versus broad-based aptitude predictors of achievement. Clinicians must recognize that aptitude-achievement procedures commonly used with other intelligence tests are not as technically sound as those available when using the WJTCA-R Scholastic Aptitude clusters. This conclusion is often overlooked by practitioners who have developed their professional knowledge and skills with other intelligence batteries that have not incorporated recent advances in the development of technically sound aptitude-achievement comparison procedures. The WJTCA-R differential aptitude clusters are on the cutting edge of technical sophistication when calculating and evaluating aptitude-achievement comparisons.

8

THE WJTCA-R BROAD COGNITIVE ABILITY CLUSTERS

The three WJTCA-R Broad Cognitive Ability clusters (i.e., Early Development, Standard, and Extended) are the broadest of the WJTCA-R interpretive options. They are the clusters that should be used if the goal is to predict quality of performance, *on the average*, across a variety of tasks. The three broad clusters should perform this function well given the diverse sampling of *Gf-Gc* abilities included in these measures.

Unlike other intelligence batteries that provide a broad-based full scale score (e.g., Wechsler Full Scale; K-ABC Mental Processing Composite; SB-IV Composite), the WJTCA-R Broad Cognitive Ability clusters are not considered to be the primary aptitude measures to use in aptitude-achievement discrepancy analysis (i.e., Type I discrepancies). Although aptitude-achievement discrepancy norms are provided for the Broad Cognitive Ability Standard cluster, for the reasons presented in Chapter 7, the WJTCA-R differential aptitude clusters are recommended for this purpose. The Broad Cognitive Ability clusters serve an important function in the assessment and identification of exceptionalities whose definitions or program criteria require an estimate of general or broad intellectual ability (e.g., giftedness; mental retardation).

TECHNICAL CONSIDERATIONS

Cluster Composition

The composition of the three Broad Cognitive Ability clusters is presented in Table 8-1. With the exception of the Early Development scale, each cluster

TABLE 8-1 Composition of the Three WJTCA-R Broad Cognitive Ability Clusters

| Test | Gf-Gc Factor | Broad Cognitive Ability Cluster | | |
		Early Development	Standard	Extended
Memory for Names	(Glr)	X	X	X
Memory for Sentences	(Gsm)	X	X	X
Visual Matching	(Gs)		X	X
Incomplete Words	(Ga)	X	X	X
Visual Closure	(Gv)	X	X	X
Picture Vocabulary	(Gc)	X	X	X
Analysis-Synthesis	(Gf)		X	X
Visual-Auditory Learning	(Glr)			X
Memory for Words	(Gsm)			X
Cross Out	(Gs)			X
Sound Blending	(Ga)			X
Picture Recognition	(Gv)			X
Oral Vocabulary	(Gc)			X
Concept Formation	(Gf)			X

includes at least one test from each of the seven *Gf-Gc* factors measured by the WJTCA-R. The Standard and Extended clusters are composed of one and two tests respectively from each of the *Gf-Gc* factors. The three Broad Cognitive Ability clusters intercorrelate at high levels, with the median correlations between the clusters in the mid .90s (McGrew et al., 1991).

Missing from the Early Development cluster are measures of processing speed *(Gs)* and fluid reasoning *(Gf)*. The Early Development cluster is analogous to the 1977 WJTCA Preschool cognitive cluster. The Early Development cluster consists of those tests within the developmental range of preschoolers. Although this cluster is labeled Early Development, norms are provided for all ages covered by the WJTCA-R. These norms allow the Early Development cluster to serve as a short-form measure of broad cognitive ability for individuals above the preschool level.

Although both the WJTCA and WJTCA-R provide three forms of broad cognitive clusters, the options are different. First, both batteries provide a broad cognitive scale for preschoolers, although the name has been changed from Preschool to Early Development. Second, the WJTCA provides a two-test Brief cluster, an option not available in the WJTCA-R. Third, the WJTCA provides a single broad-score option comprising 12 tests. The WJTCA-R provides the 7- and 14-test Standard and Extended options. Finally, the WJTCA broad clusters comprise differentially weighted combinations of tests derived from the results of principal components analysis (Woodcock, 1978). All three WJTCA-R Broad Cognitive Ability clusters are based on equally weighted combinations of tests.

Reliability

The reliability of the Broad Cognitive Ability clusters was calculated in a manner similar to that described for the Cognitive factor clusters in Chapter 4. Table 8-2 summarizes the reliabilities reported in the WJ-R technical manual (McGrew et al., 1991).

Since the Broad Cognitive Ability clusters will frequently play a pivotal role in the identification and classification of individuals for special programs, the reliability standard of .90 or above is used to evaluate their reliability (Salvia & Ysseldyke, 1991). As summarized in Table 8-2, the median reliabilities for all three Broad Cognitive Ability clusters satisfy this criterion. The WJTCA-R Broad Cognitive Ability clusters possess adequate reliability for making critical educational decisions.

Validity

Correlations With Other Intelligence Tests

McGrew et al. (1991) report concurrent correlations between the WJTCA-R Broad Cognitive Ability clusters and the respective full-scale scores from the McCarthy Scales of Children's Abilities (MSCA) (McCarthy, 1972), K-ABC, WISC-R, WAIS-R, and SB-IV in four samples ranging from preschool to 11th grade. The results from these concurrent validity studies are summarized in Table 8-3.

TABLE 8-2 Reliability of the WJTCA-R Broad Cognitive Ability Clusters from Age 2 to 80+

Cluster	Range	Median
Early Development	.90–.98	.93
Standard	.92–.98	.95
Extended	.95–.99	.97

Reliability coefficients as reported in the *WJ-R Technical Manual* (McGrew et al., 1991)

TABLE 8-3   Concurrent Validity of WJTCA-R Broad Cognitive Ability Clusters With Full Scales from Wechslers, SB-IV, K-ABC, and MSCA

		Broad Cognitive Ability Cluster		
Measure	Sample	Early Development	Standard	Extended
MSCA	Preschool	.71	—	—
K-ABC	Preschool	.74	—	—
K-ABC	Gr. 3–4	.47	.61	.66
WISC-R	Gr. 3	.73	.73	.75
WISC-R	Gr. 3–4	.49	.67	.67
WAIS-R	Gr. 10–11	.54	.70	.65
SB-IV	Preschool	.77	—	—
SB-IV	Gr. 3–4	.50	.70	.72
SB-IV	Gr. 10–11	.55	.65	.72

Correlations as reported in *WJ-R Technical Manual* (McGrew et al., 1991).

The correlations between the WJTCA-R Standard and Extended Broad Cognitive Ability clusters and the full-scale scores from other intelligence batteries range from .61 to .75. The concurrent validity correlations for the Early Development scale are more variable, with values consistently in the .70s in the preschool sample and values ranging from .47 to .73 (most between .47 to .55) in the school-age samples. These findings suggest that the Early Development Broad Cognitive Ability Cluster has good concurrent validity at the preschool level and weaker concurrent validity during the school years. These findings argue for making cautious statements about a person's general intellectual ability during the school years when only using the briefer Early Development cluster. The Standard and Extended Broad Cognitive Ability clusters are the recommended measures above the preschool age range.

The correlations reported for the Grade 3–4 and Grade 10–11 samples in Table 8-3 may be spuriously low due to significant sample restriction (McGrew et al., 1991). The concurrent validity correlations reported for the Standard and Extended clusters are all significant and generally in the range typically found between major intelligence batteries. The correlations presented in Table 8-3 indicate that the WJTCA-R Broad Cognitive Ability clusters have adequate concurrent validity when defined by other intelligence tests.

Correlations With Achievement Tests

As discussed in Chapter 7, the WJTCA-R Scholastic Aptitude clusters are the intended WJTCA-R clusters for making statements about a person's predicted achievement levels. However, some clinicians may prefer or may be required by legal or administrative constraints to use the Broad Cognitive Ability clusters for predicting achievement. Comparisons of the correlations between the Broad Cognitive Ability and Scholastic Aptitude clusters and the WJ-R achievement clusters were presented earlier in Chapter 7 (see Figures 7-4 to 7-6 and related discussion). A review of these correlations indicated that the WJTCA-R Scholastic Aptitude clusters are stronger predictors of school achievement than the Broad Cognitive Ability Standard cluster. The Broad Cognitive Ability Extended cluster predicts achievement as well as the Scholastic Aptitude clusters, although this equal level of prediction requires the administration of more tests (i.e., 14 tests for the Extended cluster versus 4 tests for each Scholastic Aptitude cluster).

The WJTCA-R Standard and Extended Broad Cognitive Ability clusters predict academic achievement at a level similar to other major intelligence batteries. Predictive validity comparisons between these two WJTCA-R Broad Cognitive Ability clusters and the respective full-scale scores from the Wechslers, SB-IV, and K-ABC are summarized in Table 8-4. The achievement criteria summarized in Table 8-4 were the same as those presented for the Scholastic Aptitude clusters (see Chapter 7) and include achievement tests drawn from the WJ-R, the PIAT, PIAT-R, K-ABC, K-TEA, WRAT-R, and BASIS.

The average correlations between the WJTCA-R Standard and Extended Broad Cognitive Ability clusters and achievement criteria in reading, mathematics, written language, and knowledge range from .56 to .60. Very similar average values are noted for the Wechsler Full Scale (.59) and SB-IV Composite (.59). The WJTCA-R Standard and Extended Broad Cognitive Ability clusters and the Wechsler and SB-IV respective full-scale composite scores correlate at similar levels with academic achievement. The K-ABC Mental Processing Composite is much weaker in its relationship to academic achievement (average correlation of .39).

The first column of average correlations reported in Table 8-4 includes a number of correlations that are spuriously inflated due to predictor-criterion contamination (see Chapter 7). Both the Wechslers and the SB-IV contain tests measuring quantitative abilities, content that spuriously inflates their correlations with the mathematics achievement tests. Similarly, the WJTCA-R Broad Cognitive Ability clusters, the Wechslers, and the SB-IV all contain comprehension-knowledge or crystallized intelligence *(Gc)* measures, content that spuriously inflates their correlations with the various knowledge tests summarized in Table 8-4. It is important to compare the intelligence tests based only on the correlations not spuriously inflated by shared predictor-criterion content.

The second column in Table 8-4 presents comparisons between the four

TABLE 8-4 Predictive Validity Comparisons Between WJTCA-R Broad Cognitive Ability Clusters and Wechslers, SB-IV, and K-ABC

	Achievement Criteria	
Comparison	Reading, Math, Written Language, & Knowledge	Reading & Written Language
WJTCA-R Standard Cluster	.57 (57)	.55 (30)
WJTCA-R Extended Cluster	.57 (57)	.57 (30)
Wechsler Full Scale	.59 (57)	.53 (30)
WJTCA-R Standard Cluster	.57 (49)	.53 (27)
WJTCA-R Extended Cluster	.56 (49)	.56 (27)
SB-IV Composite	.59 (49)	.52 (27)
WJTCA-R Standard Cluster	.60 (28)	.58 (15)
WJTCA-R Extended Cluster	.60 (28)	.57 (15)
K-ABC Mental Processing Composite	.39 (28)	.38 (15)

Correlations are median values for samples reported in *WJ-R Technical Manual* (McGrew et al., 1991). Value in parentheses indicates the number of pairs used in each comparison.

intelligence batteries that are based only on the reading and written language correlations. The findings are similar to those observed when the contaminated correlations were included. The WJTCA-R Standard and Extended Broad Cognitive Ability clusters correlate with academic achievement as well as the Wechsler and SB-IV composite scales. All of these intelligence batteries are superior to the K-ABC composite in their correlations with achievement. These findings support the validity of using the WJTCA-R Broad Cognitive Ability clusters for making important psychoeducational decisions.

The WJTCA-R Broad Cognitive Ability clusters are just as strongly related to academic achievement as the Wechslers and SB-IV, and this is *not* due to the WJTCA-R being excessively saturated with achievement content. This was an early major criticism of the original WJTCA that was later demonstrated to be inaccurate (McGrew, 1986; Woodcock, 1990). The original WJTCA's superior prediction of achievement was often attributed to the erroneous belief that it contained too many achievement-type tests (i.e., measures of *Gc* and *Gq*). This is not true of the WJTCA-R, nor was it true of the 1977 WJTCA.

A review of Table 8-1 finds that the WJTCA-R Standard and Extended Broad Cognitive Ability clusters each contain only 1 of 7 (14.3%) or 2 of 14

(14.3 %) tests that are often labeled "achievement" (i.e., measures of *Gc* or *Gq*). Joint factor analysis of the WJTCA-R with the Wechslers and SB-IV found that these other two intelligence batteries each contain approximately 50% to 60% of these types of achievement measures (Woodcock, 1990). *Despite containing only approximately one-fourth the achievement content found in the Wechslers and the SB-IV, the WJTCA-R Broad Cognitive Ability clusters still correlate as well with academic achievement as these other two major intelligence batteries.* This is possible because the WJTCA-R battery includes tests of important cognitive abilities (i.e., auditory processing, processing speed, fluid reasoning, long-term retrieval) that are associated with academic achievement (see Chapter 4). Many of these important abilities are not included or are greatly underrepresented in the Wechslers and SB-IV.

THE POTENTIAL MEAN SCORE DISCREPANCY ISSUE

The technical features of the WJTCA-R Broad Cognitive Ability clusters indicate that these broad measures of intellectual ability should be accorded the same respect and stature as the broad-based scores from other intelligence batteries. The Standard and Extended scales are composed of tests from each of seven of the *Gf-Gc* cognitive factors that make up the most comprehensive theory of intellectual abilities available today (see Chapter 2). These broad clusters possess excellent reliability for making important educational and clinical decisions regarding individuals. These clusters also demonstrate adequate concurrent validity with other major intelligence batteries. Finally, the Broad Cognitive Ability clusters predict achievement as well as, or better than, the other major intelligence batteries, and do so with less crystallized or achievement content.

Despite these positive technical features, history suggests that acceptance of the WJTCA-R may be affected by the degree to which the Broad Cognitive Ability cluster scores correspond to those provided by other intelligence batteries. Comparisons to the Wechsler scales will be particularly important. Historically, the finding of different scores between new and established intelligence tests has "created a moderate level of consernation [sic] among both researchers and practitioners" (Cummings & Moscato, 1984a, p. 47). The finding that the original WJTCA did not always provide similar scores to the Wechsler scales and typically provided lower average scores in research studies played a significant role in generating a flurry of critical literature that resulted in many psychoeducational professionals (psychologists in particular) not giving the test serious consideration (McGrew, 1986; McGrew, 1987).

Although psychoeducational professionals are now more comfortable with new intelligence tests not producing identical scores to the Wechsler scales (due in large part to the publication of other new or revised tests that have not always produced the same scores—i.e., K-ABC; SB-IV; DAS), this issue is still a perplexing one for many clinicians (Kamphaus, 1993). The Wechsler scales are still the default standard against which all new intelligence tests are compared for many assessment professionals (McGrew, 1986). It is important to address the'potential issues and concerns that may arise when the WJTCA-R produces different scores than the Wechslers and other intelligence tests. *Different scores are inevitable and need to be understood.*

The following material reviews possible reasons for differences between the WJTCA-R Broad Cognitive Ability cluster scores and full scale scores from other intelligence batteries. In my original WJTCA text (McGrew, 1986), four categories of hypotheses were advanced to explain WJTCA/WISC-R mean score differences. It is important to review these hypotheses since they are bound to resurface as clinicians and researchers again face the same issue with the WJTCA-R. The four categories of hypothesis are: (1) procedural issues, (2) norm development procedures, (3) research methodology, and (4) content differences. Discussion of other reasons for differing scores between intelligence tests can be found in Kamphaus (1993).

Procedural Issues

Scoring Errors

Reeve, Hill, and Zakreski (1979) suggested that one possible reason for WJTCA/WISC-R differences was the increased probability of scoring errors with the WJTCA. Although the scoring of the WJTCA, and now the WJTCA-R, is not excessively complex for each single score, the scoring task can become quite arduous and complex when multiple cluster and individual test scores are calculated by hand (McGrew et al., 1993). Reeve et al.'s hypothesis may possess face validity for explaining why WJTCA-R scores may vary markedly from other intelligence tests.

It is unlikely that consistent mean score discrepancies that are reported in future research studies will be the result of consistent WJTCA-R scoring errors by a number of independent researchers. Scoring errors would most likely be both positive and negative and would cancel out across studies. Although systematic scoring errors across a number of studies is not a viable hypothesis to explain any consistent mean score discrepancy research findings that may emerge, this hypothesis occasionally may be relevant for *individual* cases.

Clinical experience with a variety of tests indicates that clinicians frequently make scoring errors. In some cases scoring errors can produce results that are significantly different from the correct score. Fortunately, computer scoring software for the WJTCA-R (Riverside, 1989) is available to ensure accurate and consistent scoring of WJTCA-R protocols. With the increased availability of microcomputers in most work environments, it is strongly recommended that such software be used to minimize scoring problems.

In the absence of computer scored results, significant differences between an individual's WJTCA-R Broad Cognitive Ability cluster score and full scale score from another instrument (e.g., Wechsler Full Scale) should be checked immediately for possible scoring errors. On occasion score differences between instruments are reduced or eliminated when scoring errors are corrected. Although the scoring error hypothesis may apply to select individual cases in clinical practice, the validity of this hypothesis for explaining any consistent mean score differences across independent research samples is highly questionable.

Grade Versus Age Norms

The other procedural issue is the possibility of obtaining different scores if grade norms are used in the calculation of the WJTCA-R scores. Unique to the WJTCA-R is the option of comparing an individual's performance against others of the same grade placement or the same chronological age. Most other intelligence batteries provide only the age norm option. A review of the prior WJTCA/WISC-R comparison research (McGrew, 1986) indicates that most researchers are cognizant of this possible problem and will correctly compare WJTCA-R age-based scores with the age-based scores from other intelligence batteries. However, at the *individual* case level, grade versus age-based full-scale scores may occasionally account for discrepancies between the WJTCA-R and other intelligence batteries.

If grade norms are used in the computation of the WJTCA-R scores and the Broad Cognitive Ability score is found to vary significantly from another test score based on age norms (e.g., Wechsler Full Scale), clinicians should entertain the possibility that this difference, or a portion of it, may be a function of different normative comparison groups. This would most likely occur for individuals who are either the youngest or oldest members of their school grade (especially those who are older due to grade retention or younger due to early school entrance).

If a discrepancy is observed between an individual's Broad Cognitive Ability cluster score and a full scale score from another intelligence battery, the WJTCA-R results should be examined to determine if they were computed with grade norms. If they were, the WJTCA-R scores should be recomputed with age norms to ensure a correct comparison with other age-based norm scores. On occasion the recomputation of the WJTCA-R Broad Cognitive Ability score with age norms reveals that some of the discrepancy, and on occasion all of it, is a function of the difference between age- or grade-based normative scores.

Norm Development Differences

The hypotheses in the norm development category reflect issues that are transparent to the clinician. These hypotheses deal with differences between test standardization procedures and thus are not hypotheses that a clinician can verify for individual cases. Three different norming related hypotheses were advanced regarding the WJTCA norms that may resurface as new comparative WJTCA-R research is reported.

Error in the Norms

In trying to explain mean score differences between the original WJTCA and the WISC-R, Reeve et al. (1979) advanced the hypothesis that the difference may reflect a systematic error in the development of the WJTCA norms. The advancement of this hypothesis was a serious charge, especially since Reeve et al. had *no empirical evidence* to substantiate this possibility. As noted by Woodcock (1984b), "this hypothesis has no empirical basis other than the observation of a difference" (p. 348). Thompson and Brassard (1984) also discounted this hypothesis based on the reported pattern of WJTCA-R/WISC-R mean score differences observed across all types of research samples. This hypothesis did not warrant serious consideration in the case of the WJTCA and should not resurface if WJTCA-R score differences are reported in future research studies.

Norm Sample Selection

Cummings and Moscato (1984a, 1984b) suggested that a portion of the mean score difference between the original WJTCA and the Wechsler scales might be due to different techniques for controlling for socioeconomic status (SES) in the respective norm samples. The WJTCA-R has different approaches to SES control from most other intelligence batteries.

This hypothesis suggests that a differential rate of return of permission forms for involvement in the norming of the WJTCA (and now the WJTCA-R) may result in the underrepresentation of low SES subjects in the WJTCA-R norm sample. In order to understand the basis for this hypothesis and to evaluate its utility, a brief description of the sampling differences between the WJTCA-R and most other intelligence batteries is necessary.

In the case of most other intelligence batteries, subjects are selected to meet certain SES requirements based on parental answers to SES questions on a form sent home to elicit permission to use their children in the norming project. Based on his experience with these procedures, Cummings (1985) noted that lower SES families tend to return a lower percentage of permission forms.

The WJTCA-R norming procedures control for SES variables at the *community* and not the *individual* level. The WJTCA-R norming plan controlled for SES by selecting communities based on 13 SES characteristics and then randomly selecting subjects within targeted communities. The parent permission letters that were sent home elicited only permission to participate in the norming; no SES data about the families were requested. The WJTCA-R norming procedure is based on Woodcock's involvement in the norming of other tests, particularly the Woodcock Reading Mastery Test (Woodcock, 1973). The Woodcock Reading Mastery Test manual reports the results of multiple regression analysis of 11 community SES indexes with the average reading score for each community. Strong relationships are reported between the community SES indexes and reading achievement, with multiple correlations ranging from a low of .52 at grade 1, to an ever increasing value of .89 at grade 12. As a result of this research, Woodcock (1984b) suggests:

> Community SES characteristics may be the most significant, but least controlled, variable in the sampling plan for many tests . . . it makes a difference whether the child of a blue-collar worker comes from a community predominantly composed of blue-collar and service workers or from a community predominantly composed of professional and managerial-level employees. (p. 349)

Cummings and Moscato's (1984b) hypothesis is based on the assumption that in the absence of individual SES data it is impossible to know to what extent a differential rate of return (as a function of SES) may have affected the composition of the WJTCA (and now WJTCA-R) norming sample. Although the individual data are not reported that would allow an examination of the return rate, McGrew et al. (1991) report that the WJTCA-R norming teams were cognizant of this possible sampling bias and were persistent in obtaining as many permission returns as possible. Nonresponse was followed up after two days by a second request. Frequently these second requests were also supplemented by a personal telephone call from the school encouraging the parent to allow the child to participate.

In conclusion, there is a difference between the norming strategies used to control for SES variables in the WJTCA-R and most other instruments. Although individual level SES data are not available for investigating the viability of this hypothesis, Woodcock (1973, 1984b) offers interesting food for thought regarding the control of SES variables. The strong relationship reported between community SES and reading achievement suggests that controlling for community SES may be an extremely critical norming procedure often ignored in the development of most tests (McGrew et al., 1991). If the community SES variables are as important as Woodcock's (1973) data suggest, then concerns should be raised regarding the norming characteristics of other intelligence batteries that control only for individual SES. Research investigating the impact of these different norming procedures is needed.

Recency of Norms

Another plausible reason for the score differences that may be found between the WJTCA-R and certain other intelligence tests is the recency of the respective test norms (Kamphaus, 1993). Research has consistently found that a test with older norms, on the average, will produce higher scores than more recently normed tests. The norms for the older test are considered "softer" as the population becomes "smarter" with the passage of time. Empirical studies (Flynn, 1984; Kamphaus, 1993) have suggested that the norms for intelligence tests standardized in the United States become more difficult by approximately 3 standard score points every 10 years.

This finding is frequently attributed to the increased acculturation of society with the passage of time that results in individuals being administered the "older" test appearing brighter, when in actuality their performance is simply being compared against a less advanced norm group. For example, when the WISC was renormed, there were numerous research reports, as well as informal clinical observations, that the WISC-R provided lower results. Kaufman (1979) noted that discrepancies of 5–7 points were typical across the age range of the WISC and WISC-R. Fortunately, Kaufman succinctly put this issue into proper perspective when he concluded:

> Examiners who have much experience with the WISC . . have to accept the fact that the WISC norms are now out of date; . . . the WISC norms give better "news" in the form of higher scores, but the WISC-R norms provide a more meaningful reference group for children and adolescents of today. (p. 128)

A portion of any observed difference between the full-scale scores from the WJTCA-R and certain other intelligence test batteries may be related to differences in the recency of the tests' norms. The extent to which this factor explains score differences between the WJTCA-R and other intelligence tests is much less prominent than with the original WJTCA. The WJTCA-R's publication date differs by less than plus or minus five years for the WPSSI-R, WISC-III, SB-IV, and DAS. WJTCA-R Broad Cognitive Ability scores that differ noticeably from the full-scale scores of these respective batteries are most likely not due to major differences in the age of the respective test norms.

Using the 3 points-per-decade rule of thumb (Flynn, 1984; Kamphaus, 1993), lower WJTCA-R scores in the range of 2 to 3 standard score points might be anticipated when compared to the K-ABC or WAIS-R. WJTCA-R scores that are 5 to 6 points lower could easily be expected when they are compared to the MSCA, an instrument published in 1972 and not yet revised. Such research findings should raise concerns about the older intelligence batteries since older norms may no longer provide an appropriate reference point for individuals in today's society (Kaufman, 1979).

Research Methodology

In a response to the original WJTCA/WISC-R mean score discrepancy controversy, a controversy focused on explaining why the WJTCA produced lower scores than the WISC-R (McGrew, 1986), Woodcock (1984b) suggested that these discrepancies were largely due to significant methodological biases in most of the reported research studies. Although no WJTCA-R mean score comparative research has yet been published, such research will most likely surface and generate a new round of concerns about the WJTCA-R's comparability to other intelligence batteries.

It is important for researchers and clinicians alike to become fully informed of the methodological issues that will most likely surface regarding these studies. An understanding of these issues will help researchers and practitioners objectively evaluate future WJTCA-R comparative research and, for that matter, any study that compares mean scores on different intelligence batteries. The three "biases" that are important to understand are: selection, score, and interpretation bias (Woodcock, 1984b).

Selection Bias

One flaw present in many studies that reported lower WJTCA scores when compared to the WISC-R was that the WJTCA scores were compared to WISC-R scores that had been used in the prior selection or subclassification of the research samples. Most of this comparison research was conducted with samples of students with learning disabilities (LD). The subjects with LD were originally identified on the basis of relatively high WISC-R scores coupled with low achievement. Woodcock (1984b) noted that this sample preselection bias was present in many of the WJTCA/WISC-R comparative studies. This form of bias can often cause marked skewing of statistics (Gullikson, 1950; Lord & Novick, 1968). Given that the Wechsler scales are still the predominantly used intelligence batteries for identifying individuals for special programs, future WJTCA-R comparison research could suffer from this same preselection bias.

If past research studies are a guide, many future research studies will use samples of individuals identified for inclusion in the sample based on their performance on a different intelligence battery (e.g., Wechsler). In the case of samples of individuals with LD, they will have had to demonstrate average or above intellectual ability. Past practice suggests that the Wechsler scales will be used during this process.

This prior subject selection on the basis of relatively high Wechsler scores results in the elimination of relatively lower Wechsler scores. Individuals with lower Wechsler and higher WJTCA-R scores might have been included in the sample if the WJTCA-R had been used in the prior selection. The prior sample selection on the basis of the other test (e.g., Wechsler) results in the absence of individuals with higher WJTCA-R and lower Wechsler scores. The result is a biased estimate of the two tests' means. In the case of LD samples, the intelligence test used to preselect the sample (e.g., Wechsler) will be biased in the higher direction. The instrument not used for sample preselection (e.g., WJTCA-R) will be biased in the lower direction.

Borrowing from the methodology of personnel selection, Woodcock

(1984b) suggests that the most appropriate approach for evaluating intelligence batteries used for selecting individuals is to compare the different batteries in referral samples, not preselected samples. Additional discussion of this methodological bias can be found in Kamphuas (1993) and Woodcock (1984a). Researchers and clinicians need to be cognizant that studies that compare the WJTCA-R scores with scores from other intelligence batteries that were used to preselect the sample will contain this bias and, thus, should be viewed very cautiously.

Score Bias

Most of the research studies that compared scores from the original WJTCA with other intelligence batteries used preselected samples (e.g., students in programs for persons with LD). Failure to readminister the intelligence test (e.g., WISC-R) used to preselect the sample prior to statistical comparison with the WJTCA is a methodological bias (Woodcock, 1984b).

In samples of individuals selected based on average or above intelligence test scores (e.g., LD), any scores that were used in the prior selection of the subjects should not be used in the data analysis. The "scores that survived the selection procedures were based on the most fortuitous score combination of true ability and positive error" (Woodcock, 1984b, p. 343). The impact of this *score bias* is higher mean scores for the intelligence test used to preselect the sample. Any new studies that compare scores from the WJTCA-R and other intelligence batteries, where the other intelligence battery is used to preselect the sample, will suffer from this source of bias. To eliminate this bias in new studies, investigators should readminister the intelligence battery that was used to preselect the sample. These second scores should be used for statistical comparisons with the WJTCA-R.

Interpretation Bias

The final bias regarding the original mean score discrepancy controversy was a lack of objectivity in the evaluation and reporting of the WJTCA/WISC-R comparison research results (Woodcock, 1984b). Woodcock noted that the interpretation of research findings can be affected by certain beliefs and assumptions held by a researcher. Woodcock observed that most researchers who reported the original WJTCA/WISC-R discrepancy focused exclusively on "attempts only to explain why the WJTCA scores are 'too low'—the assumption being that the other set of scores is 'just right' " (p. 343).

An objective implementation of the scientific method would suggest other possibilities, among them the possibility that the WISC-R scores were "too high." When evaluating the original WJTCA mean score discrepancy controversy, most researchers and practitioners considered the WISC-R the default standard against which all other ability tests should be measured. Given the rich tradition of the Wechsler tests, it is very likely that similar assumptions and beliefs will be present when new WJTCA-R comparison research is reported.

When the new round of WJTCA-R comparison research is reported, it is important for researchers and practitioners to remember that the 12 Wechsler subtests are not divinely ordained. Although the Wechsler tests have a rich clinical and research history, we have learned much about intelligence since the publication of the original Wechsler scales in 1939. Much of what we have learned suggests that the venerable Wechsler verbal and nonverbal model may not be the best standard against which all new tests should be judged.

The significant research on human abilities during the past two decades reveals that progress has been made. The *Gf-Gc* model "summarizes much of what is known about the organization of human abilities, and it is, in the main, consistent with the abilities Carroll... has thus far identified in his massive review and reanalysis of 60 years of factor-analytic studies of human abilities" (Lohman, 1989, p. 340). As presented in Chapter 2, the structure and content of the WJTCA-R are consistent with this knowledge base. When new research studies report that the WJTCA-R produces scores that differ from other intelligence tests, researchers and practitioners must not immediately assume that such findings reflect negatively on the WJTCA-R. Given that the WJTCA-R is the only intelligence battery to comprehensively measure most of the *Gf-Gc* abilities identified by Carroll (1993), scores that differ from those provided by the WJTCA-R should raise equal concerns about the other intelligence batteries.

Content Differences

Hypotheses focused on content differences were the most controversial and prominent in the WJTCA mean score difference literature. A number of content difference hypotheses were advanced, such as differences in *g*, verbal, or achievement content (McGrew, 1986). Content differences will most likely be the primary reason for explaining differences between the WJTCA-R and other intelligence batteries.

A review of Tables 4-7 to 4-14 (Chapter 4) reveals significant content differences between the WJTCA-R and the other intelligence batteries. These empirically documented differences are summarized in Table 8-5. The information summarized in Table 8-5 is based on joint confirmatory factor analyies studies of the WJTCA-R with the other intelligence batteries (Woodcock, 1990).

The information presented in Table 8-5 indicates that the WJTCA-R content covers seven of the *Gf-Gc* factors. Missing from the WJTCA-R are measures of quantitative ability *(Gq)*. Quantitative abilities are measured in the WJ-R achievement section. The other intelligence batteries listed in Table 8-5 include tests that measure from four (Wechslers) to five (K-ABC, SB-IV) of the eight *Gf-Gc* factors. The content differences presented in Table 8-5 indicate that the full-scale scores from the different intelligence batteries are based on different mixes of *Gf-Gc* abilities. Full-scale score differences should be expected.

TABLE 8-5 Factorial Composition of the Broad Measure of Intelligence Provided by Six Cognitive Batteries

Factor	WJ-R BCA Sum	WJ-R BCA %	K-ABC MPC Sum	K-ABC MPC %	SB-IV CSAS Sum	SB-IV CSAS %	WISC-R FSIQ Sum	WISC-R FSIQ %	WAIS-R FSIQ Sum	WAIS-R FSIQ %	WJ (1977) BCA Sum	WJ (1977) BCA %
Long-Term Retrieval (Glr)	2	14	0.0	0	0.0	0	0	0	0	0	1.0	8
Short-Term Memory (Gsm)	2	14	2.5	31	3.0	20	0	0	1	9	1.5	12
Processing Speed (Gs)	2	14	0.5	6	0.0	0	1	10	1	9	2.0	17
Auditory Processing (Ga)	2	14	0.0	0	0.0	0	0	0	0	0	1.0	8
Visual Processing (Gv)	2	14	3.5	44	3.5	23	3	30	3	27	0.0	0
Comprehension-Knowledge (Gc)	2	14	0.0	0	4.5	30	5	50	5	45	2.5	21
Fluid Reasoning (Gf)	2	14	1.0	12	1.0	7	0	0	0	0	3.0	25
Quantitative Ability (Gq)	0	0	0.5	6	3.0	20	1	10	1	9	1.0	8
Total Battery	14	100	8	100	15	100	10	100	11	100	12	100
Applicable Age Range	(5 to 90+)		(6 to 12-5)*		(12 to 13)**		(6 to 16-6)		(16 to 74)		(5 to 80+)	
Achievement (Gc and Gq)	2	14	0.5	6	7.5	50	6	60	6	55	3.5	29

*Fewer tests and a different factorial mix will be observed below age 6.
**Fewer tests and different factorial mixes will be observed below age 12 and above age 13.

Reprinted from "Theoretical Foundations of the WJ-R Measures of Cognitive Ability," by R. W. Woodcock, 1990, *Journal of Psychoeducational Assessment, 8*, p. 250. Copyright 1990 by the Psychoeducational Corporation. Reprinted by permission.

The information summarized in Table 8-5 can be used to explain differences between full-scale scores on the WJTCA-R and other intelligence batteries. For example, if an individual is administered both the WJTCA-R and the K-ABC and significant full scale score differences are found, the individual tests of each battery should be carefully inspected. Generally, similar levels of performance might be expected on the WJTCA-R and K-ABC tests that measure the same *Gf-Gc* abilities (see Table 8-5). The most likely explanation of the full scale score difference may lie in those WJTCA-R tests that measure *Gf-Gc* abilities not measured by the K-ABC (i.e., long-term retrieval, auditory processing, and comprehension-knowledge). The information presented in Table 8-5 may help practitioners better understand full-scale score differences between the WJTCA-R and the other intelligence batteries.

Given the prominence that the achievement content hypothesis played in generating significant misconceptions about the original WJTCA (McGrew, 1986), a misconception this author hears being generalized to the WJTCA-R, it is important to examine the achievement-related content of the major intelligence batteries. As summarized in Table 8-5, when achievement-related content is defined as tests measuring quantitative *(Gq)* and comprehension-knowledge *(Gc)* abilities (i.e., crystallized intelligence), the original WJTCA contained 29% of such content. The SB-IV and Wechsler scales consist of 50% to 60% achievement content. The achievement content criticism of the original WJTCA was inaccurate (McGrew, 1986).

More importantly, the WJTCA-R consists of tests that only reflect 14% achievement content. *The WJTCA-R has approximately three to four times less achievement content than the SB-IV and Wechsler scales.* The only intelligence battery included in Table 8-5 that has a lower degree of this type of content is the K-ABC (i.e., 6%).

THE TOTAL DOES NOT EQUAL
THE AVERAGE OF THE PARTS

Things Don't Add Up

Traditionally, most intelligence batteries (e.g., Wechslers, K-ABC) report subtest scores in a standard score metric with a mean of 10 and a standard deviation of 3. The SB-IV is idiosyncratic (Kamphaus, 1993), as individual test scores are reported on a standard score scale with a mean of 50 and a standard deviation of 8. The WJTCA-R is different from all the major intelligence batteries by providing individual test scores based on the same metric used to report full-scale or composite scores (i.e., mean = 100; SD = 15). There has been an unintended outcome of using the same scale for the individual WJTCA-R tests and the composite cluster scores. Clinicians are becoming confused by a statistical phenomenon that has always been present in the interpretation of intelligence test scores but which up until now has been hidden.

The issue is that a composite standard score (e.g., Broad Cognitive Ability cluster; Wechsler Full Scale) is not the simple average of the individual standard scores that are comprised in the composite. For example, a student tested at grade 6.5 obtained standard scores (mean = 100; SD= 15) that ranged from 73 to 88 on the seven WJTCA-R Standard tests. Although the average of the seven standard scores was 81, the Broad Cognitive Ability cluster standard score was 67. This reflects a 14-point standard score difference between the average and the obtained composite cluster standard score. Why? Is there something wrong with the WJTCA-R norm tables? It has been this author's observation that this phenomenon has generated questions among a number of practitioners. However, this observation is not unique to the WJTCA-R.

A hypothetical WISC-R case study is presented in Table 8-6. This example assumes that an individual obtained scaled scores of 4 (2 standard deviations below the mean) on all 10 individual WISC-R tests. When this performance is converted to the standard score scale with a mean of 100 and standard deviation of 15, the individual test scores are 70. The average of these standard scores is 70. However, the obtained WISC-R Full Scale score is 59, a score that is 11 points lower than the average of the subtest standard scores.

An Explanation

The phenomenon of a total score not equaling the average of the individual tests is not unique to the WJTCA-R. This apparent aberration will be observed for most all tests that provide composite scores. However, this discrepant finding is typically masked in all other intelligence batteries by the use of different standard score metrics for reporting the individual and composite scores. Why does this occur?

This phenomenon is most noticeable the farther away from the mean a person consistently scores on tests that make up a composite. To be significantly below or above the mean on a number of different tests is a less frequent or rarer occurrence than being low or high on just one or two of a number of tests. The composite score will reflect this "rareness" by being lower (in the case of consistently low performance on a number of tests) or higher (in the case of consistently high performance on a number of tests) than the average, as the purpose of the standard score (or percentile rank) is to "indicate the likelihood in a population of obtaining a particular score or combination of scores" (McGrew et al., 1991, p. 42).

This phenomenon is a function of the intercorrelations and number of tests comprised in the composite score (Paik & Nebenzahl, 1987). The lower the intercorrelations between the tests that make up a composite score, the more extreme this average/obtained score discrepancy will be (McGrew et al., 1991). This phenomenon is particularly noticeable for the WJTCA-R

TABLE 8-6   The Total Does Not Equal the Average of the Parts: WISC-R Example

Subtest	Scaled Score (Mean = 10, SD = 3)	Standard Score (Mean = 100, SD = 15)
Information	4 (– SD)	70 (– 2 SD)
Similarities	4 "	70 "
Arithmetic	4 "	70 "
Vocabulary	4 "	70 "
Comprehension	4 "	70 "
Picture Completion	4 "	70 "
Picture Arrangement	4 "	70 "
Block Design	4 "	70 "
Object Assembly	4 "	70 "
Coding	4 "	70 "
Average Standard Score = 70		
Full Scale Standard Score = 59		
Difference = 11		

Standard or Extended Broad Cognitive Ability clusters since these composites are made up of 7 to 14 tests that have been designed to be measures of distinct abilities (i.e., low intercorrelations). The reader should consult Paik and Nebenzahl (1987) for a detailed treatment of the statistical basis of this phenomenon.

Although the example presented in Table 8-6 indicates that the same phenomenon occurs for the WISC-R, the magnitude of the observed score difference will be less with intelligence batteries that are more homogeneous. As presented in Table 8-5 and Chapter 4, most other intelligence batteries measure a smaller range of *Gf-Gc* abilities and, thus, typically show higher degrees of intercorrelations among the individual tests. As a result, this phenomenon will occur in other intelligence batteries, but it will be less dramatic. The only situation where a composite intelligence test score will equal the average of the individual tests for all individuals is when all the individual tests are perfectly correlated. Such a situation would defeat the purpose of having intelligence batteries that contain individual tests that measure different abilities.

Researchers and clinicians need to be aware that this score discrepancy phenomenon will be seen frequently in the WJTCA-R, particularly for the Broad Cognitive Ability cluster standard scores. Clinicians should be reassured that there is nothing "wrong" with the WJTCA-R norm tables or scores. The same phenomenon occurs with all intelligence test batteries, although it is usually masked by different individual test and composite score metrics.

Consistent with material presented in Chapter 2, this observation adds additional weight to the argument that single full-scale general intelligence test scores are problematic. Emphasis on the multiple intelligences of individuals is a more sound theoretical practice.

CONCLUDING COMMENTS

Although research suggests that more emphasis should be placed on the interpretation of multiple intelligences (Carroll, 1993) (see Chapter 2), clinicians are often required to use full-scale or broad-based intelligence test scores. The WJTCA-R provides three Broad Cognitive Ability cluster score options to fulfill this need.

The Early Development Broad Cognitive Ability cluster is a 5-test composite relevant to the assessment of individuals at the preschool level. Although norms are provided for the Early Development Broad Cognitive Ability cluster above the preschool age range, the 7-test Standard and 14-test Extended Broad Cognitive Ability clusters should be used at these ages. The Standard and Extended Broad Cognitive Ability clusters contain an equal mix of tests from seven of the *Gf-Gc* abilities. All three clusters are composed of equally weighted tests.

The three WJTCA-R Broad Cognitive Ability clusters demonstrate adequate reliability for making important decisions about individuals. The concurrent validity of the clusters has been demonstrated by moderate to strong correlations with other intelligence batteries. The Standard and Extended Broad Cognitive Ability clusters correlate with achievement tests at levels similar to that observed for other intelligence batteries. The Standard and Extended Broad Cognitive Ability clusters correlate with achievement as well as other intelligence batteries. More importantly, these two broad clusters have less achievement content (i.e., *Gc* and *Gq*) than most intelligence batteries.

Although theoretical and empirical evidence (see Chapter 2) suggests that broad-based full scale intelligence test scores should play a less prominent role in the interpretation of intelligence tests, history suggests that the comparability of the WJTCA-R broad-based composite scores with full scale scores from other intelligence batteries will receive significant attention. Drawing on the earlier WJTCA research literature, it is anticipated that a number of procedural, norm development, research methodology, and content difference hypotheses will be advanced to explain score differences between the WJTCA-R Broad Cognitive Ability clusters and other full scale intelligence test scores. An objective consideration of all hypotheses indicates that discrepant scores from other intelligence batteries should be expected, do not reflect poorly on the WJTCA-R, and, in fact, highlight significant strengths of the WJTCA-R.

Finally, the reporting of individual WJTCA-R test scores on the same scale (mean = 100; SD = 15) as the composite clusters has revealed a statistical phenomenon that has been present with all intelligence batteries. Composite scores such as the WJTCA-R Broad Cognitive Ability clusters or the Wechsler Full Scale scores will not always approximate the average of the individual test scores comprised in the composite. There are real statistical reasons for the observed phenomenon of the total scores not equaling the average of the individual tests. Nothing is wrong with a test's norms when the average of the individual tests comprised in a composite does not equal the obtained composite score.

SUMMARY COMMENTS

The practice of individual intelligence testing has a long and rich tradition. Unfortunately, the inertia of this tradition has until recently resulted in little significant progress in the development and use of assessment technology based on the best available knowledge from cognitive science.

Few would argue that the Wechsler intelligence batteries have dominated the field of individual intelligence testing. Many in the field of psychlogical and psychoeducational assessment continue to ignore the fact that even the most recent Wechsler revision (i.e., WISC-III) "represents the status quo, and only the smallest step in the evolution of intelligence. Despite more than 50 years of advancement of theories of intelligence, the Wechsler philosophy of intelligence . . . , written in 1939, remains the guiding principle of the WISC-III" (Shaw, Swerdlik, & Laurent, 1993, p. 151). During the same year that saw the birth of the Wechsler batteries (1939), the following significant social and historical events occurred:

Gone With the Wind and *The Wizard of Oz* opened.
Some of the top box-office stars are Mickey Rooney, Spencer Tracy, Clark Gable, Shirley Temple, and Bette Davis.

Some of the top musical performers are Benny Goodman, Tommy Dorsey, and Bing Crosby.

The Grapes of Wrath is a best seller.

The first helicopter is constructed by Igor Sikorsky.

Hahn and Strassman discover nuclear fission by bombarding uranium with neutrons.

Lou Gehrig retires, and Ted Williams makes his baseball debut.

Al Capone is released from prison.

Franklin D. Roosevelt is president of the United States.

FM radio transmission and reception are developed by Edwin Armstrong.

Germany invades Poland and Britain and France declare war on Germany.

We've come a long way since 1939. Despite rapid changes in all of society and technology since 1939, the practice of individual intelligence testing, most typically embodied in the use of the Wechsler batteries, has evolved very little. Research in cognitive science, particularly that focusing on the factor analysis of a wide variety of cognitive variables, has advanced our conceptualization of intelligence during the past 50 years. As described in this book, the WJTCA-R represents the new breed of intelligence tests that bridges the significant gap between cognitive science and intelligence testing technology.

The WJTCA-R is the first individually administered intelligence battery to incorporate a number of innovations in intelligence testing. Foremost is the organization of the WJTCA-R according to modern *Gf-Gc* theory, the most comprehensive empirically based theoretical conceptualization of intelligence available today (see Chapter 2). Additional WJTCA-R innovations described in this text (see Chapter 7) are: (a) the use of differential aptitude clusters for making statements about a person's predicted achievement, (b) the use of aptitude-achievement discrepancy norms that implicitly account for regression to the mean, and (c) the use of norm-based intra-cognitive discrepancy scores. Practitioners who use the WJTCA-R will be using an intelligence battery that incorporates the most recent advances available regarding the structure of cognitive abilities and the development of technically sound aptitude-achievement and intra-cognitive discrepancy scores.

Practitioners will find the WJTCA-R to be the richest individually administered intelligence battery available for clinical interpretation. The ability to use 21 individual tests that can be organized within the comprehensive *Gf-Gc* model (see Chapters 3 and 4) or alternative frameworks (see Chapter 5) provides clinicians with a large "tool box" for use in clinical interpretation. The marriage of the breadth of the WJTCA-R with the classic shared-ability approach to clinical interpretation of intelligence tests (see Chapter 6) gives clinicians a unique opportunity to expand their repertoire of clinical skills.

The WJTCA-R provides practitioners and the field of psychological and psychoeducational assessment the opportunity to begin to push the "edge of the envelope" of intelligence testing research, theory, and practice. I hope this book contributes to these developments.

REFERENCES

American Psychological Association. (1985). *Standards for educational and psychological testing.* Washington, DC: Author.

Anastasi, A. *Psychological testing.* (1982). New York: McMillan.

Bracken, B. A., & Fagan, T. K. (Eds.). (1990). Intelligence: Theories and practice [Special Issue]. *Journal of Psychoeducational Assessment, 8.*

Brandys, C. F., & Rourke, B. P. (1991). Differential memory abilities in reading- and arithmetic-disabled children. In B. P. Rourke (Ed.), *Neuropsychological validation of learning disability subtypes* (pp. 73–96). New York: Guilford Press.

Bruininks, R. H., Woodcock, R. W., Weatherman, R. F., & Hill, B. K. (1984). *Scales of Independent Behavior.* Chicago: Riverside.

Bruininks, R. H., Woodcock, R. W., Weatherman, R. F:, & Hill, B. K. (in press). *Scales of Independent Behavior-Revised.* Chicago: Riverside.

Bruininks, R. H, Hill, B. K., Weatherman, R. F., & Woodcock, R. W. (1985). *Inventory of Client and Agency Planning.* Chicago: Riverside.

Carroll, J. B. (1978). On the theory-practice interface in the measurement of intellectual abilities. In P. Suppes (Ed.), *Impact of research on education* (pp. 1–105). Washington, DC: National Academy of Education.

Carroll, J. B. (1983). Studying individual differences in cognitive abilities: Through and beyond factor analysis. In R. F. Dillon & R. R. Schmeck (Eds.), *Individual differences in cognition* (Vol. 1, pp. 1–33). New York: Academic Press.

Carroll, J. B. (1985). *Domains of cognitive ability.* Paper presented at the meeting of the American Association for the Advancement of Science, Los Angeles.

Carroll, J. B. (1986a). *Dimensions and structures of cognitive abilities: Reanalyses of data sets reported in the literature.* Paper presented at the 21st International Congress of Applied Psychology, Jerusalem, Israel.

Carroll, J. B. (1986b). Psychometric approaches to cognitive abilities. In S. E. Newstead, S. H. Irvine, & P. L. Dann (Eds.); *Human assessment: Cognition and motivation* (pp. 3–15). Dordrecht, Netherlands: Nijhoff.

Carroll, J. B. (1987). New perspectives in the analysis of abilities. In R. R. Ronning, J. A. Glover, J. C. Conoley, & J. C. Witt (Eds.), *The influence of cognitive psychology on testing* (pp. 267–284). Hillsdale, NJ: Erlbaum.

Carroll, J. B. (1989). Factor analysis since Spearman: Where do we stand? What do we know? In R. Kanfer, P. L. Ackerman, & R. Cudeck (Eds.), *Abilities, motivation, and methodology* (pp. 43–67). Hillsdale, NJ: Erlbaum.

Carroll, J. B. (1993). *Human cognitive abilities: A survey of factor-analytic studies.* New York: Cambridge University Press.

Cattell, R. B. (1941). Some theoretical issues in adult intelligence testing. *Psychological Bulletin, 38,* 592.

Cattell, R. B. (1943). The measurement of adult intelligence. *Psychological Bulletin, 40,* 153–193.

Cattell, R. B. (1971). *Abilities: Their structure, growth and action.* Boston: Houghton-Mifflin.

Cohen, J. (1959). The factorial structure of the WISC at ages 7-7, 10-6, and 13-6. *Journal of Consulting Psychology, 23,* 285–299.

Cole, D. (1987). Utility of confirmatory factor analysis in test validation research. *Journal of Consulting and Clinical Psychology, 55,* 584–594.

Coles, G. (1978). The learning disabilities test battery: Empirical and social issues. *Harvard Educational Review, 48,* 313–340.

Cone, T., & Wilson, L. (1981). Quantifying a severe discrepancy: A critical analysis. *Learning Disability Quarterly, 4,* 359–371.

Cooney, J. B., & Swanson, H. L. (1990). Individual ifferences in memory for mathematical story problems: Memory span and problem perception. *Journal of Educational Psychology, 82,* 570–577.

Crocker, L., & Algina, J. (1986). *Introduction to classical and modern test theory.* New York: Holt, Rinehart, & Winston.

Cummings, J. (1985). Review of the Woodcock-Johnson Psycho-Educational Battery. In J.F. Mitchell (Ed.), *The ninth mental measurements yearbook* (pp. 1759–1762). Lincoln, NE: Buros Institute of Mental Measurements, University of Nebraska Press.

Cummings, J., & Moscato, E. (1984a). Reply to Thompson and Brassard. *School Psychology Review, 13,* 45–58.

Cummings, J., & Moscato, E. (1984b). Research on the Woodcock-Johnson Psycho-Educational Battery: Implications for practice and future investigation. *School Psychology Review, 13,* 33–40.

Daniels, M., & Elliott, C. (1993). [LISREL confirmatory factor analysis of the WJ-R, DAS, and DTLA-3: Reanalysis of R. McGhee data]. Unpublished raw data.

DeLuca, J. W., Rourke, B. P., & Del Dotto, J. E. (1991). Subtypes of arithmetic-disabled children: Cognitive and personality dimensions. In B. P. Rourke (Ed.), *Neuropsychological validation of learning disability subtypes* (pp. 180–219). New York: Guilford Press.

Dunn, L. M., & Markwardt, F. C. (1970). Peabody Individual Achievement Test. Circle Pines, MN: American Guidance Service.

Elliott, C. D. (1990). The nature and structure of children's abilities: Evidence from the Differential Ability Scales. *Journal of Psychoeducational Assessment, 8,* 376–390.

Fiedorowicz, C., & Trites, R. L. (1991). From theory to practice with subtypes of reading disabilities. In B. P. Rourke (Ed.), *Neuropsychological validation of learning disability subtypes* (pp. 243–266). New York: Guilford Press.

Flynn, J. R. (1984). The mean IQ of Americans: Massive gains 1932 to 1978. *Psychological Bulletin, 95,* 29–51.

French, J. L., & Hale, R. L. (1990). A history of the development of psychological and educational testing. In C. R. Reynolds & R. W. Kamphaus (Eds.), *Handbook of psychological and educational assessment of children: Intelligence and achievement* (pp. 3–28). New York: Guilford Press.

Gagné, E. D. (1985). *The cognitive psychology of school learning.* Boston, MA: Little & Brown.

Gardner, H. (1983). *Frames of mind: The theory of multiple intelligences.* New York: Basic Books.

Garrett, H. E., & Woodworth, R. S. (1958). *Statistics in psychology and education.* New York: Longmans, Green & Company.

Goldman, R., Fristoe, M., & Woodcock, R. (1974). *Goldman-Fristoe-Woodcock Auditory Skills Battery.* Circle Pines, MN: American Guidance Service.

Goodall, C. (1990). A survey of smoothing techniques. In J. Fox & J. Scott Long (Eds.). *Modern methods of data analysis* (pp. 126–176). Newbury Park, CA: Sage Press.

Gullikson, H. (1950). *Theory of mental tests.* New York: Wiley & Sons.

Gustafsson, J.-E. (1984). A unifying model for the structure of intellectual abilities. *Intelligence, 8,* 179–203.

Gustafsson, J.-E. (1988). Hierarchical models of individual differences in cognitive abilities. In R. J. Sternberg (Ed.), *Advances in the psychology of human intelligence* (Vol. 4, pp. 35–71). Hillsdale, NJ: Erlbaum.

Hammill, D., & Bryant, B. (1991). *Detroit Tests of Learning Aptitude—3.* Austin, TX: PRO-ED.

Hammill, D., & Larsen, S. (1978). The effectiveness of psycholinguistic training: A reaffirmation of position. *Exceptional Children, 44,* 402–414.

Hessler, G. L. (1982). *Use and interpretation of the Woodcock-Johnson Psycho-Educational Battery.* Chicago: Riverside.

Hessler, G. L. (1993). *Use and interpretation of the Woodcock-Johnson Psycho-Educational Battery—Revised.* Chicago: Riverside.

Horn, A. M. (1941). *Uneven distribution of the effects of specific factors* (Southern California Education Monographs No. 12). Los Angeles, CA: University of Southern California.

Horn, J. L. (1985). Remodeling old models of intelligence. In B. B. Wolman (Ed.), *Handbook of intelligence* (pp. 267–300). New York: Wiley.

Horn, J. L. (1988). Thinking about human abilities. In J. R. Nesselroade & R. B. Cattell (Eds.), *Handbook of multivariate psychology* (2nd ed., pp. 645–685). New York: Academic Press.

Horn, J. L. (1991). Measurement of intellectual capabilities: A review of theory. In K. S. McGrew, J. K. Werder, & R. W. Woodcock, *WJ-R technical manual,* Chicago: Riverside.

Ittenbach, R., Spiegel, A., McGrew, K., & Bruininks, R. (1992). A confirmatory factor analysis of early childhood ability measures within a model of personal competence. *Journal of School Psychology, 30,* 307–323.

Jastak, S. R., & Wilkinson, G. S. (1984). *Wide Range Achievement Test—Revised.* Wilmington, DE: Jastak Associates, Inc.

Jensen, A. (1984). The black-white difference on the K-ABC: Implications for future tests. *Journal of Special Education, 18,* 377–408.

Jensen, A. R. (1992). Understanding *g* in terms of information processing. *Educational Psychology Review, 4,* 271–308.

Kail, R. (1991). Development of processing speed in childhood and adolescence. In H. W. Reese (Ed.), *Advances in child development and behavior* (Vol. 23, pp. 151–185). San Diego, CA: Academic Press.

Kamphaus, R. W. (1990). K-ABC theory in historical and current contexts. *Journal of Psychoeducational Assessment, 8,* 356–368.

Kamphaus, R. W. (1993). *Clinical assessment of children's intelligence.* Needham Heights, MA: Allyn and Bacon.

Kamphaus, R. W., & Reynolds, C. R. (1984). Development and structure of the Kaufman Assessment Battery for Children. *Journal of Special Education, 18,* 213–228.

Kaufman, A. S. (1979). *Intelligent testing with the WISC-R.* New York: Wiley.

Kaufman, A. S. (1984). K-ABC and controversy. *Journal of Special Education, 18,* 409–444.

Kaufman, A. S. (1985). Review of the Woodcock-Johnson Psycho-Educational Battery. In J. F. Mitchell (Ed.), *The ninth mental measurements yearbook* (pp. 1762–1765). Lincoln, NE: Buros Institute of Mental Measurements, University of Nebraska Press.

Kaufman, A. S. (1990). *Assessing adolescent and adult intelligence.* Needham Heights, MA: Allyn and Bacon.

Kaufman, A. S., & Kaufman, N. L. (1983). *The Kaufman Assessment Battery for Children.* Circle Pines, Mn: American Guidance Service.

Kaufman, A. S., & Kaufman, N. L. (1985). Kaufman Tests of Educational Achievement. Circle Pines, MN: American Guidance Service.

Kaufman, A. S., & O'Neal, M. (1988). Factor structure of the Woodcock-Johnson cognitive subtests from preschool to adulthood. *Journal of Psychoeducational Assessment, 6,* 35–48.

Keith, T. Z. (1985). Questioning the K-ABC: What *does* it measure? *School Psychology Review, 14,* 9-20.

Keith, T. Z. (1987). Assessment research: An assessment and recommended interventions. *School Psychology Review, 16,* 176–289.

Keith, T. Z. (1990). Confirmatory and hierarchical confirmatory analysis of the Differential Ability Scales. *Journal of Psychoeducational Assessment, 8,* 391–405.

Keith, T. Z, & Dunbar, S. B. (1984). Hierarchical factor analysis of the K-ABC: Testing alternative models. *Journal of Special Education, 18,* 367–375.

LaBarge, D., & Samuels, S. J. (1974). Toward a theory of automatic information processing. *Cognitive Psychology, 6,* 293–323.

Lohman, D. F. (1989). Human intelligence: An introduction to advances in theory and research. *Review of Educational Research, 59,* 333—373.

Lord, F., & Novick, M. (1968). *Statistical theories of mental test scores.* Reading, MA: Addison Wesley Publishing.

Markwardt, F. C. (1989). Peabody Individual Achievement Test—Revised. Circle Pines, MN: American Guidance Service.

Matarazzo, J. D. (1990). Psychological assessment versus psychological testing: Validation from Binet to the school, clinic, and courtroom. *American Psychologist, 45,* 999–1017.

Mather, N. (1991). *An instructional guide to the Woodcock-Johnson Psycho-Educational Battery—Revised.* Brandon, VT: Clinical Psychology Publishing Company.

Mather, N. (1993). Critical issues in the diagnosis of learning disabilities addressed by the Woodcock-Johnson Psychoeducational Battery—Revised. *Journal of Psychoeducational Assessment, Monograph Series: WJ-R Monograph,* 103–122.

Mather, N., & Jaffe, L. (1992). *Woodcock-Johnson Psycho-Educational Battery—Revised: Recommendations and reports.* Brandon, VT: Clinical Psychology Publishing Company.

McCarthy, D. A. (1972). *McCarthy Scales of Children's Abilities.* San Antonio, TX: Psychological Corporation.

McDermott, P. A., Fantuzzo, J. W., & Glutting, J. J. (1990). Just say no to subtest analysis: A critique on Wechsler theory and practice. *Journal of Psychoeducational Assessment, 8,* 290–302.

McGhee, R. L. (1993). Fluid and crystallized intelligence: A factor analytic study of second order abilities from three cognitive batteries. *Journal of Psychoeducational Assessment, Monograph Series: WJ-R monograph*, 20–38.

McGrew, K. S. (1984). An analysis of the influence of the Quantitative Concepts subtest in the Woodcock-Johnson Scholastic Aptitude clusters. *Journal of Psychoeducational Assessment, 2*, 325–332.

McGrew, K. S. (1986). *Clinical interpretation of the Woodcock-Johnson Tests of Cognitive Ability.* New York: Grune & Stratton.

McGrew, K. S. (1987). Exploratory factor analysis of the Woodcock-Johnson Tests of Cognitive Ability. *Journal of Psychoeducational Assessment, 5*, 200–216.

McGrew, K. S. (1993a). *The relationship between the WJ-R Gf-Gc cognitive clusters and mathematics achievement across the life-span.* Manuscript in preparation.

McGrew, K. S. (1993b). [Supplementary factor and cluster analysis of the WJTCA-R norm data]. Unpublished raw data.

McGrew, K. S. (1993c). The relationship between the WJ-R *Gf-Gc* cognitive clusters and reading achievement across the life-span. *Journal of Psychoeducational Assessment, Monograph Series: WJ-R Monograph*, 39–53.

McGrew, K. S., & Bruininks, R. H. (1990). Defining adaptive and maladaptive behavior within a model of personal competence. *School Psychology Review, 19*, 53–73.

McGrew, K. S., Bruininks, R. H., & Johnson, D. (1993). *Factor analysis of personal competence measures for young adults with mild to severe disabilities.* Manuscript submitted for publication.

McGrew, K. S., & Knopik, S. N. (1993). *The relationship between the WJ-R Gf-Gc cognitive clusters and writing achievement across the life-span.* Manuscript submitted for publication.

McGrew, K. S., & Murphy, S. R. (1993). *Uniqueness and general factor characteristics of the Woodcock-Johnson Tests of Cognitive Ability-Revised.* Manuscript submitted for publication.

McGrew, K. S., Murphy, S. R., & Knutson, D. J. (1993). *The development and investigation of a brief graphic scoring system for obtaining derived scores for the WJ-R and other tests.* Manuscript submitted for publication.

McGrew, K. S., Werder, J. K., & Woodcock, R. W. (1991). *WJ-R technical manual.* Chicago: Riverside.

McGue, M., Shinn, M., & Ysseldyke, J. (1979). *Validity of the Woodcock-Johnson Psycho-Educational Battery with learning disabled students* (Research Report No. 15). Minneapolis: University of Minnesota, Institute for Research on Learning Disabilities.

McGue, M., Shinn, M., & Ysseldyke, J. (1982). Use of the cluster scores on the Woodcock-Johnson Psycho-Educational Battery with learning disabled students. *Learning Disability Quarterly, 5*, 274–287.

McLeod, J. (1979). Educational underachievement: Toward a defensible psychometric definition. *Journal of Learning Disabilities, 12*, 42–50.

McNemar, Q. (1964). Lost: Our intelligence? Why? *American Psychologist, 19*, 871–882.

Mishra, S., Ferguson, B., & King, P. (1985). Research with the Wechsler Digit Span subtest: Implications for assessment. *School Psychology Review, 14*, 37–47.

Mosier, C. I. (1943). On the reliability of a weighted composite. *Psychometrika, 8*, 161–168.

Naglieri, J. A., & Das, J. P. (1990). Planning, attention, simultaneous, and successive

(PASS) cognitive processes as a model for intelligence. *Journal of Psychoeducational Assessment, 8,* 303–337.

Naglieri, J. A., Kamphaus, R. W., & Kaufman, A. S. (1983). The Luria-Das simultaneous-successive model applied to the WISC-R. *Journal of Psychoeducational Assessment, 1,* 25–34.

Nolting, P. D. (1991). *Math and the learning disabled student: A practical guide for accommodations.* Pompano Beach, FL: Academic Success Press.

Paik, M., & Nebenzahl, E. (1987). The overall percentile rank versus the individual percentile ranks. *The American Statistician, 41,* 136–138.

Pellegrino, J., & Varnhagen, C. (1985). Abilities and aptitudes. In T. Husen & T. Postlethwaite (Eds.), *The international encyclopedia of education* (Vol. 1, pp. 1–8). New York: Pergamon.

Psychological Corporation (1983). *Basic Achievement Skills Individual Screener.* San Antonio, TX: Author.

Reeve, R., Hall, R., & Zakreski, R. (1979). The Woodcock-Johnson Tests of Cognitive Ability: Concurrent validity with the WISC-R. *Learning Disability Quarterly, 2,* 63–69.

Reschly, D. J. (1990). Found: Our intelligences: What do they mean? *Journal of Psychoeducational Assessment, 8,* 259–267.

Reynolds, C. R. (1985). Measuring the aptitude-achievement discrepancy in learning disability diagnosis. *Remedial and Special Education, 6,* 37–55.

Reynolds, C. R. (1988). Putting the individual into aptitude-treatment interaction. *Exceptional Children, 54,* 324–331.

Reynolds, C. R. (1990). Conceptual and technical problems in learning disability diagnosis. In C. R. Reynolds & R. W. Kamphaus (Eds.), *Handbook of psychological and educational assessment of children: Intelligence and achievement* (pp. 571–592). New York: Guilford Press.

Reynolds, C. R., Berk, R. A., Boodoo, G. M., Cox, J., Gutkin, T. B., Mann, L., Page, E. B., & Wilson, V. C. (1984–1985). *Critical measurement issues in learning disabilities.* Report of the Work Group on Measurement Issues in the Assessment of Learning Disabilities. Washington, DC: U.S. Department of Education, Program in Special Education.

Reynolds, C. R., & Kaufman, A. S. (1990). Assessment of children's intelligence with the Wechsler Intelligence Scale for Children—Revised (WISC-R). In C. R. Reynolds & R. W. Kamphaus (Eds.), *Handbook of psychological and educational assessment of children: Intelligence and achievement* (pp. 571–592). New York: Guilford Press.

Riverside (1989). *Compuscore for the WJ-R.* Chicago: Author.

Ross, A. (1976). *Psychological aspects of learning disabilities and reading disorders.* New York: McGraw-Hill.

Rosso, M., & Phelps, L. (1988). Factor analysis of the Woodcock-Johnson with conduct disordered adolescents. *Psychology in the Schools, 25,* 105–110.

Rourke, B. P. (1978). Reading, spelling, arithmetic disabilities: A neuropsychologic perspective. In H. R. Myklebust (Ed.), *Progress in learning disabilities* (Vol. 4, pp. 97–120). New York: Grune & Stratton.

Rourke, B. P. (1981). Neuropsychological assessment of children with learning disabilities. In S. B. Filskov & T. J. Boll (Eds.), *Handbook of clinical neuropsychology* (pp. 453–478). New York: Wiley-Interscience.

Rourke, B. P., Fisk, J. L., & Strang, J. D. (1986). *Neuropsychological assessment of children*. New York: Guilford Press.

Salvia, J., & Ysseldyke, J. (1981). *Assessment in special and remedial education*. Boston: Houghton-Mifflin.

Salvia, J., & Ysseldyke, J. (1991). *Assessment in special and remedial education* (5th ed). Boston: Houghton-Mifflin.

Sattler, J. (1988). *Assessment of children's intelligence and special abilities* (3rd ed.). San Diego, CA: Author.

Shaw, S. R., Swerdlik, M. E., & Laurent, J. WISC-III test review. *Journal of Psychoeducational Assessment Monograph Series: WISC-III Monograph*, pp. 151–159.

Silverstein, A. B. Variance components in the subtests of the WISC-R. *Psychological Reports, 39*, 1109–1110.

Snow, R. E. (1986). Individual differences and the design of educational programs. *American Psychologist, 41*, 1029–1039.

Snow, R. E., & Swanson, J. (1992). Instructional psychology: Aptitude, adaptation, and assessment. *Annual Review of Psychology, 43*, 583–626.

Spearman, C. (1904). "General intelligence," objectively determined and measured. *American Journal of Psychology, 15*, 201–293.

Spearman, C. E. (1927). *The abilities of man*. London: Macmillan.

Stone, B. J. (1992). Joint confirmatory factor analyses of the DAS and WISC-R. *Journal of School Psychology, 30*, 185–195.

Telzrow, C. F. (1990). Best practices in reducing error in identifying specific learning disabilities. In A. Thomas & J. Grimes (Eds.), *Best practices in school psychology-II* (pp. 607–620). Washington, DC: National Association of School Psychologists.

Thompson, P., & Brassard, M. (1984). Cummings and Moscato soft on Woodcock-Johnson. *School Psychology Review, 13*, 41–44.

Thorndike, R. L. (1982). *Applied Psychometrics*. Boston: Houghton Mifflin.

Thorndike, R. L., Hagen, E. P., & Sattler, J. M. (1986). *Stanford-Binet Intelligence Scale—Fourth Edition*. Chicago: Riverside.

Wagner, R. K. (1986). Phonological processing abilities and reading: Implications for disabled readers. *Journal of Learning Disabilities, 19*, 623–630.

Wechsler, D. (1939). *The measurement of adult intelligence*. Baltimore, MD: Williams & Wilkins.

Wechsler, D. (1974). *Wechsler Intelligence Scale for Children—Revised*. San Antonio, TX: Psychological Corporation.

Wechsler, D. (1981). *Wechsler Adult Intelligence Scale—Revised*. San Antonio, TX: Psychological Corporation.

Wechsler, D. (1989). *Wechsler Preschool and Primary Scale of Intelligence—Revised*. San Antonio, TX: Psychological Corporation.

Wechsler, D. (1991). *Wechsler Intelligence Scale for Children—Third Edition*. San Antonio, TX: Psychological Corporation.

Wilkinson, L. (1990). *SYGRAPH: The system for graphics*. Evanston, IL: SYSTAT, Inc.

Wilson, L. R. & Cone, T. (1984). The regression equation method of determining academic discrepancy. *Journal of School Psychology, 22*, 95–110.

Woodcock, R. W. (1973). *Woodcock Reading Mastery Tests*. Circle Pines, MN: American Guidance Service.

Woodcock, R. W. (1978). *Development and standardization of the Woodcock-Johnson Psycho-Educational Battery*. Chicago: Riverside.

Woodcock, R. W. (1982). *Batería Woodcock psico-educativa en Español.* Chicago: Riverside.

Woodcock, R. W. (1984a). A response to some questions raised about the Wood-cock-Johnson: Efficacy of the aptitude clusters. *School Psychology Review, 13,* 355–362.

Woodcock, R. W. (1984b). A response to some questions raised about the Wood-cock-Johnson: The mean score discrepancy issue. *School Psychology Review, 13,* 342-354.

Woodcock, R. W. (1984c). *Some background regarding the design of the Woodcock-Johnson.* Unpublished manuscript.

Woodcock, R. W. (1985). Oral Language and Broad Reasoning Clusters for the Wood-cock-Johnson Psycho-Educational Battery (Assessment Service Bulletin, No. 2). Chicago: Riverside.

Woodcock, R. W., & Mather, N. (1989). *WJ-R Tests of Cognitive Ability—Standard and Supplemental Batteries: Examiner's Manual.* Chicago: Riverside.

Woodcock, R. W. (1990). Theoretical foundations of the WJ-R measures of cognitive ability. *Journal of Psychoeducational Assessment, 8,* 231–258.

Woodcock, R. W. (1993). An information processing view of *Gf-Gc* theory. *Journal of Psychoeducational Assessment, Monograph Series: WJ-R Monograph,* 80–102.

Woodcock, R. W., & Johnson, M. B. (1977). Woodcock-Johnson Psycho-Educational Battery. Chicago: Riverside.

Woodcock, R. W., & Johnson, M. B. (1989). *Woodcock-Johnson Psycho-Educational Battery—Revised.* Chicago: Riverside.

Woodcock, R. W., & Mather, N. (1989). WJ-R Tests of Cognitive Ability—Standard and Supplemental Batteries: Examiner's Manual. In R. W. Woodcock & M. B. Johnson, *Woodcock-Johnson Psycho-Educational Battery—Revised.* Chicago: Riverside.

Woodcock, R. W., & Muñoz-Sandoval, A. F. (in preparation). *Batería Woodcock-Muñoz psico-educativa en Español.* Chicago: Riverside.

Wright, B. D., & Stone, M. H. (1979). *Best test design.* Chicago: MESA Press.

Ysseldyke, J. E. (1990). Goodness of fit of the Woodcock-Johnson Psycho-Educational Battery—Revised to the Horn-Cattell *Gf-Gc* theory. *Journal of Psychological Assessment, 8,* 268–275.

Zachary, R. A. (1990). Wechsler's intelligence scales: Theoretical and practical considerations. *Journal of Psychoeducational Assessment, 8,* 276–289.

AUTHOR INDEX

SUBJECT INDEX